*EDUCATION AND
THE CULT OF EFFICIENCY*

RAYMOND E. CALLAHAN

EDUCATION AND THE CULT OF EFFICIENCY

A STUDY OF THE SOCIAL FORCES
THAT HAVE SHAPED THE ADMINISTRATION
OF THE PUBLIC SCHOOLS

THE UNIVERSITY OF CHICAGO PRESS

CHICAGO AND LONDON

ISBN: 0-226-09150-3 (paperbound)

Library of Congress Catalog Card Number: 62-17961

THE UNIVERSITY OF CHICAGO PRESS, CHICAGO 60637
The University of Chicago Press, Ltd., London
© *1962 by The University of Chicago. All rights reserved. Published 1962*
Paperback edition 1964
Printed in the United States of America

03 02 01 00 99 98 97 96 95 94   12 13 14 15

♾ The paper used in this publication meets the minimum requirements of the American National Standard for Information Sciences—Permanence of Paper for Printed Library Materials, ANSI Z39.48-1984.

To George S. Counts

PREFACE

When I began this study some five years ago, my intent was to explore the origin and development of the adoption of business values and practices in educational administration. My investigation revealed that this adoption had started about 1900 and had reached the point, by 1930, that, among other things, school administrators perceived themselves as business managers, or, as they would say, "school executives" rather than as scholars and educational philosophers. The question which now became significant was *why* had school administrators adopted business values and practices and assumed the posture of the business executive? Education is not a business. The school is not a factory. Of course, by 1910 the scale of operations in both business and education (in the large cities) had produced large organizations, and so it was reasonable and even legitimate to expect the borrowing of ideas and techniques from one set of institutions to another. But the evidence indicated that the extent of the borrowing had been too great for such an explanation to be adequate.

I had felt that the adoption of business values and practices might be explained simply by the process of cultural diffusion in which the flow of ideas and values is generally from high status or power groups in a culture to those with less status and power. By 1905, as James Bryce pointed out, business was king in American society, and certainly between 1910 and 1929 (if not down to the present time) the business and industrial group has had top status and power in America. On the other hand, it does not take profound knowledge of American education to know that educators are, and have been, a relatively low-status, low-power group. So I was not really surprised to find business ideas and practices being used in education.

What was unexpected was the extent, not only of the power of the business-industrial groups, but of the strength of the business ideology in the American culture on the one hand and the extreme weakness and vulnerability of schoolmen, especially school administrators, on the other. I had expected more professional autonomy and I was completely unprepared for the extent and degree of capitulation by administrators to whatever demands were made upon them. I was surprised and then dismayed to learn how many decisions they made or were forced to make, not on educational grounds, but as a means of appeasing their critics in order to maintain their positions in the school.

I am now convinced that very much of what has happened in American education since 1900 can be explained on the basis of the extreme vulnerability of our schoolmen to public criticism and pressure and that this vulnerability is built into our pattern of local support and control. This has been true in the past and, unless changes are made, will continue to be true in the future. Thus it was predictable in 1957 that school administrators would respond quickly to the criticism which followed the launching of the first Russian satellite and would begin to place great emphasis upon science and mathematics. It was also predictable that they would welcome and quickly adopt James B. Conant's recommendations for change in the high schools, for, with his great stature in the country, his suggestions were made to order for defense. Any superintendent who could say that he was adopting Conant's recommendations, or better yet, that his school system had already been following them for years, was almost impregnable.

The point is not whether more or less science and mathematics should be taught in the schools, or whether Conant's suggestions would improve the schools; the point is that when the schools are being criticized, vulnerable school administrators have to respond. The quickness of the response and the nature of the response depend upon the nature and strength of the criticism. Since 1900 this pattern of criticism and response has produced some desirable and some undesirable educational changes, but the real point is that this is an inadequate and inappropriate basis for establishing sound educational policy. It is as far as one can imagine from anything that might be called educational statesmanship. Evidence presented in this study shows that such a method of operation does not necessarily result in "meeting the needs of the community" and it often results in an abdication of responsibility for educational leadership.

As I have pondered the findings of this study and considered their implications for the administration of our schools it seems to me that two major interdependent efforts are needed. One is to change the nature and improve the quality of our graduate work in educational administration; the other is to seek ways and means of reducing the extreme vulnerability of our superintendents in the local school districts. I think the evidence presented in this study indicates that it is time we began to take a hard and realistic look at our patterns of local support and control. These arrangements are supposed to protect us from the tyranny of an all-powerful central government and to provide the opportunity for local initiative and experimentation. Whether either of these ideas is or ever has been valid is at least a legitimate subject for inquiry. It is certain, however, that much of the vulnerability of administrators is due to our traditional means of financing the schools largely through local property taxes and that some basic changes are needed. So long as schoolmen have a knife poised at their financial jugular vein each year, professional autonomy is impossible. And the problem of getting sufficient professional autonomy for schoolmen cannot be separated from the problem of getting schoolmen who are of a caliber and so trained and educated that the lay public will respect them and be willing to grant them this autonomy. To this end schools and colleges of education will have to raise their standards of admission and improve the quality of their programs of graduate studies for school administrators. To grant autonomy to poorly educated schoolmen would be dangerous; to produce highly qualified individuals and then place them in a weak, insecure, vulnerable position is senseless. The American people probably will not consent to the first possibility; they should not tolerate the latter.

I want to thank the many persons who have helped me to bring this book into existence. My major intellectual debt is to George S. Counts, Dietrich Gerhard, and Laurence Iannaccone. George Counts taught me to see the interrelationship between school and society, and his book *The American Road to Culture* (1930) provided important insights into the problem. Dietrich Gerhard started the whole thing by persistently raising questions about the origins of the business influence on American education which I could not answer. I hope this book answers most of his questions. Laurence Iannaccone helped me to see more clearly the implications of my data and especially the significance of what we have been calling the "vulnerability thesis". I now consider this to be the most important outcome of the research.

I am very appreciative of the encouragement and support I have received at Washington University from Robert Schaefer, Thomas Hall, and Lewis Hahn, and from my colleagues in the Graduate Institute of Education. I have of course learned a great deal from my graduate students and I profited especially from my long discussions with Warren Button.

In collecting the data for the book I received able and enthusiastic assistance from Myron Taylor and Dale Doepke as well as from Margaret Wright, Marilyn Vittert, and Marilyn Moldafsky. For the clerical work in connection with the manuscript I am most grateful to Beverly Van Nest for her excellent work and her steady optimism. My thanks also to Marilyn Aach, Jeanine Baab, Jacqueline Ayres, and Carol Huegsen. I am indebted to Joan Hesse and Gail Dimont for their editorial help in the final stage.

My wife, Helen Davidson Callahan, has worked closely with me on the book since the beginning. I deeply appreciate her talent and her dedication to my work.

CONTENTS

1

THE PRELUDE 1900-1910

At the turn of the century America had reason to be proud of the educational progress it had made. The dream of equality of educational opportunity had been partly realized. Any white American with ability and a willingness to work could get a good education and even professional training. The schools were very far from perfect, of course: teachers were inadequately prepared, classrooms were overcrowded, school buildings and equipment were inadequate, and the education of Negroes had been neglected. But the basic institutional framework for a noble conception of education had been created. Free public schools, from the kindergarten through the university, had been established.

The story of the next quarter century of American education — a story of opportunity lost and of the acceptance by educational administrators of an inappropriate philosophy — must be seen within the larger context of the forces and events which were shaping American society. For while schools everywhere reflect to some extent the culture of which they are a part and respond to forces within that culture, the American public schools, because of the nature of their pattern of organization, support, and control, were especially vulnerable and responded quickly to the strongest social forces. In this period as in the decades immediately preceding it, the most powerful force was industrialism — the application of mechanical power to the production of goods — and along with that the economic philosophy of the free enterprise, capitalistic system under which industrialism developed in America.

The material achievements of industrial capitalism in the late nineteenth century were responsible for two developments which were to have a great effect on American society and education after 1900.

One of these was the rise of business and industry to a position of prestige and influence, and America's subsequent saturation with business-industrial values and practices. The other was the reform movement identified historically with Theodore Roosevelt and spear-headed by the muckraking journalists. These two developments, and the vulnerability of the school administrator, contributed to the conditions in American society which explain the tremendous impact of Frederick Taylor and his system of scientific management, and the continuing influence of the business-industrial ideology upon American society and education after 1911.

The rise of the businessman as the figure of leadership in the American community had its roots in the emergence during the seventeenth and eighteenth centuries of the middle class in Europe, where the free enterprise system, with the achievements of science and technology at its disposal, had tangibly demonstrated its advantages. In wealthy America, the tremendous industrial and material growth under the capitalistic system was clearly visible. Visible too, with their vast fortunes, were the great industrial and financial leaders — men such as Andrew Carnegie, John D. Rockefeller, J. P. Morgan, Edward H. Harriman, and the rest. By 1900 these men had been accorded top status by most of their countrymen, and quite naturally their values and beliefs (including the economic philosophy which had made it all possible) were widely admired and accepted. Indeed, the acceptance of the business philosophy was so general that it has to be considered one of the basic characteristics of American society in this period. Calvin Coolidge was not overstating the case when he said in 1925: "The business of America is business."

Doubtless, their vast, accumulated fortunes is enough to explain the prestige enjoyed by the leading businessmen and industrialists, but there were other factors partly responsible for their high standing. One of the most important of these was the McGuffey Readers. Millions of Americans in their formative years learned from these books not only the idea that success was a result of honesty and hard work but the idea that success was *material* success; and the successful individuals used as models were usually bankers or merchants. These ideas were bolstered after 1865 by the tempting, materialistic "success" literature (particularly in popular journals) in which businessmen and business values were lauded. Sometimes these materials were written by such influential leaders as Andrew Carnegie or Theodore Roosevelt, but most often they were written by journalists or professional success writers such as Orison Marden.

It was inevitable that these business values would greatly influence the public schools at the turn of the century, but the extent of this influence was furthered by certain aspects of the great reform crusade. This movement was primarily an attempt to cope with the problems which were a product of rapid industrialization: the consolidation of industry and the concentration of wealth; the ruthless exploitation of the country's natural resources; the corruption and inefficiency in government; the tremendous growth of cities; the flood of immigrants who added to the complexity of the social and political problems in the urban areas; and finally, the fear among the middle class that America would react to these problems in an extreme or radical way (this reaction had of course been predicted by Karl Marx and had been realized, to an extent, in the growth of various forms of socialism in America).

That genuine problems existed in American society at the turn of the century there can be no doubt. But the generation of widespread public enthusiasm and indignation necessary to give force to a reform movement in a democratic society required that the public be aroused and informed. This function was performed so effectively by the muckraking journalists through the medium of low-priced periodicals that one historian has stated that "to an extraordinary degree the work of the Progressive movement rested upon its journalism" and that "it was muckraking that brought the diffuse malaise of the public into focus."[1]

The vehicle for muckraking was the popular magazine — *McClure's*, *Munsey's*, the *Ladies' Home Journal*, the *Saturday Evening Post*, and later the *American*, which were attractively printed and directed toward popular appeal. (The *Saturday Evening Post*, for example, emphasized business, public affairs, and romance, while the *Ladies' Home Journal*'s keynote was "intimacy" — "Heart-to-Heart Talks," "Side Talks to Girls," and "Side Talks to Boys.") Most important, the magazines were low in price, and circulations ran to the hundreds of thousands; two of them, the *Ladies' Home Journal* and the *Saturday Evening Post*, sold over a million after 1910.[2] By 1905 there were twenty such magazines with a combined circulation of over five-and-a-half-million. These journals were published not by literary men but by business promoters, and their editors were newspaper editors. Whereas the older monthlies had been books in magazine form, the new journals were newspapers in magazine form.

The most famous of the muckraking journals, *McClure's*, featured Lincoln Steffens, Ida Tarbell, and Ray Stannard Baker as staff writers. S. S. McClure's innovation was to pay his writers for the research necessary to present a thorough, factual exposure. He claimed

[1] Richard Hofstadter, *The Age of Reform* (New York, 1955), p. 185.
[2] Frank Luther Mott, *A History of American Magazines* (Cambridge, 1957), IV, 688.

that none of the articles by Steffens on bossism and the connection between business and corruption in city politics, by Miss Tarbell on the Standard Oil Company, or by Ray Stannard Baker on the railroads, cost less than $1,000, more than half cost $2,500, while each of Miss Tarbell's articles cost about $4,000.[3] But the expenditure paid off handsomely as circulation increased rapidly.

With *McClure's* demonstration in 1902 and 1903 of the profits of exposure, other popular journals joined in the endeavor. In the next decade, America was flooded with muckraker material as every aspect of American life came under attack to such extent that even the most complacent were prodded into discontent. Some of the muckrakers, such as Steffens, Baker, and Tarbell, combined the accuracy and thoroughness of the research scholar with the qualities of a good reporter, but others were neither so painstaking nor so responsible and many of the articles degenerated into sensationalism. The positive result of this effort was legislation curbing monopolies, controlling child labor, establishing conservation agencies, extending the income tax, and, in general, helping to correct the more flagrant abuses of industrial, democratic America. But there were other outcomes which were not so positive. The irresponsible, shot-gun type of criticism hurt many an innocent victim, among them some dedicated schoolmen. Even more unfortunate, this type of criticism in the popular journals stirred the public to clamor for change and often vulnerable school administrators were stampeded into actions which did great harm to American education.

In the course of the reform movement, much of the exposure and criticism of the muckrakers was directed at big business — the "captains of industry." Indeed, some Americans, including one prominent businessman, James P. Munroe, went so far as to label these "captains" as "exalted thieves" and "corrupters of public morals."[4] The result, as one historian put it, was that some of the gilt was scraped "from that favorite idol of the late nineteenth century, the successful big businessman."[5] But, despite the indictment of these business leaders, neither the muckrakers nor Americans generally condemned the capitalistic business system as such. They regarded these evils as the aberrations of a few greedy men and took the view that if these men were controlled, the country would be restored to a healthy condition.

As Richard Hofstadter has pointed out, the muckrakers were moderate men, not radicals, and they were working in a period (despite the problems) of general prosperity. They did not intend to stir the

[3] C. C. Regier, *The Era of the Muckrakers* (Chapel Hill, 1932), p. 16.

[4] James P. Munroe, *New Demands in Education* (New York, 1912), p. 127.

[5] Ralph Henry Gabriel, *The Course of American Democratic Thought* (New York, 1940), p. 331.

American people to drastic action which would transform American society.[6] They did not attack the business system; indeed, and very important to our story, their solution to many of the problems was the application of modern business methods. This was especially true in regard to corruption and inefficiency in government. For example, in October, 1906, *McClure's* published an article by one of the leading muckrakers, George Kibbe Turner, entitled "Galveston: A Business Corporation" in which he described the new five-man business corporation-type government in the Texas city. Turner judged the experiment a "brilliant success" on the basis of its financial record.[7] The following April in an editorial, *McClure's* compared Chicago unfavorably with Galveston and, to prove its point, printed Charles Eliot's statement that "Municipal Government is pure business and nothing else — absolutely nothing else."[8] In the next three years *McClure's* printed several articles on the same topic — all of them lauding the new plan and claiming great financial saving, the elimination of corruption, and strong popular support. Meanwhile, the *Outlook* published an article on "The Business Mayor of Scranton" in September, 1906. The new mayor ran on a platform of business, not politics, and governed the city by business rules and business principles. For, the author said, "The city is a corporation; why run it any other way than you would a corporation?"[9]

So the business ideology was spread continuously into the bloodstream of American life. It was strengthened, not weakened, by the muckrakers as they extolled "modern business methods" and "efficiency" and connected these in the public mind with progress and reform. It was strengthened, too, by the vigorous conservation movement because the emphasis upon conservation blended into and reinforced a corollary drive to eliminate waste, and the elimination of waste was connected with modern business methods. It was, therefore, quite natural for Americans, when they thought of reforming the schools, to apply business methods to achieve their ends.

The Schools in a Business Society

The business influence was exerted upon education in several ways: through newspapers, journals, and books; through speeches at educational meetings; and, more directly, through actions of school boards. It was exerted by laymen, by professional journalists, by businessmen or industrialists either individually or in groups (e.g., the National

[6] Hofstadter, *Age of Reform*, p. 195.
[7] Vol. XXVII, pp. 610–20.
[8] Vol. XXVIII, p. 686.
[9] Vol. LXXIV, p. 197.

Association of Manufacturers), and finally by educators themselves. Whatever its source, the influence was exerted in the form of suggestions or demands that the schools be organized and operated in a more businesslike way and that more emphasis be placed upon a practical and immediately useful education.

The procedure for bringing about a more businesslike organization and operation of the schools was fairly well standardized from 1900 to 1925. It consisted of making unfavorable comparisons between the schools and business enterprise, of applying business-industrial criteria (e.g., economy and efficiency) to education, and of suggesting that business and industrial practices be adopted by educators. In 1903, for example, the *Atlantic Monthly* published an article which was devoted to an attack on politics in school administration and which recommended the adoption of a business organizational pattern. After warning educators that "school administration should be economical" and that the "peoples' money should not be wasted," the author stated, "The management of school affairs is a large business involving in a city of 100,000 inhabitants an expenditure of probably $500,000 annually; the same business principles adopted in modern industry should be employed here."[10] Evidence of business influence appeared again in 1905 at the annual meeting of the National Education Association; a symposium was held on the question "What Are at Present the Most Promising Subjects for Such Investigations as the National Council of Education Should Undertake."[11] Significantly, the first topic was a "Comparison of Modern Business Methods with Educational Methods," and the first speaker, George H. Martin, secretary of the State Board of Education in Massachusetts, told his audience, "the contrast between modern business methods and the most modern methods in education is so great as to suggest some searching questions. In the comparison, educational processes seem unscientific, crude, and wasteful."[12]

By 1907 there were indications that aspects of the business ideology had been accepted and were being applied by educators themselves. In that year William C. Bagley, one of the leaders in American education for the next three decades, published a textbook on education entitled *Classroom Management*, which was saturated with business terminology. Bagley stated, for example, that the problem of classroom management was primarily a "problem of economy: it

[10] William H. Burnham, "Principles of Municipal School Administration," Vol. XCII, pp. 105–9.
[11] The National Council of Education was a division of the National Education Association. Its membership consisted of leaders from all branches of the educational system. Its function was to study educational issues and to make policy recommendations.
[12] N.E.A. *Proceedings* (1905), pp. 320–21.

seeks to determine in what manner the working unit of the school
plant may be made to return the largest dividend upon the material
investment of time, energy, and money. From this point of view, classroom management may be looked upon as a 'business' problem."[13] In
this book, which was written for teachers in training and which went
through more than thirty reprintings between 1907 and 1927, Bagley,
in stressing the need for "unquestioned obedience" as the "first rule
of efficient service," said the situation was "entirely analogous to
that in any other organization or system — the army, the navy, governmental, great business enterprises (or small business enterprises,
for that matter)."[14]

The commercial-industrial influence was, of course, not limited to
the elementary and secondary school but was felt in higher education
as well. Business pressure upon these institutions from 1900 to 1910
was in fact greater than it was on the lower schools, although it appears that the higher institutions were better able to defend themselves and that the extent of business influence on higher education
was not as great. Even so, the *Atlantic Monthly* stated in 1910, "our
universities are beginning to be run as business colleges. They advertise, they compete with one another, they pretend to give good
value to their customers. They desire to increase their trade, they offer
social advantages and business openings to their patrons."[15]

Although much of the pressure was applied through the journals
and through the appearance of businessmen before educational meetings, it also came very directly through school boards, which were
dominated increasingly by businessmen. Before 1900, most city
school boards had been large, unwieldy organizations governed to
some extent by politics. Gradually they were reorganized along lines
which paralleled the municipal reform movement, e.g., in Galveston.
This meant not only a reduction in membership (in Boston from
twenty-four to five) but, in the spirit of municipal reform, a change
in composition over to businessmen who were to run the schools along
business lines. Thus the superintendent of schools was hired and fired
by and responsible to a small group of businessmen.

All these changes were to have important and far-reaching consequences for the schools and especially for the administrators. The
self-image of these men began to change. All through the nineteenth
century leading administrators such as Horace Mann, Henry Barnard,
and William T. Harris had conceived of themselves as scholars and
statesmen and, in professional terms, the equal of the lawyer or the

[13] *Classroom Management* (New York, 1910), p. 2.
[14] *Ibid.*, pp. 262 and 265–66.
[15] John Jay Chapman, "Learning," CVI, 134.

clergyman. After 1900, especially after 1910, they tended to identify themselves with the successful business executive. That this business orientation was a prerequisite for success and tenure on the job was clear, and the schoolmen knew it. As early as 1900, for example, the President of the National Educational Association prophesied that "the real educational leaders of the age whose influence will be permanent are those who have the business capacity to appreciate and comprehend the business problems which are always a part of the educational problem."[16]

Another aspect of the impact of business upon education before 1911, and one that illustrates the nature and strength of that impact on the one side and the responsiveness of educators on the other, was the effort to make the curriculum of the schools more practical.[17] While the most specific outcomes of this pressure were the establishment of vocational schools and vocational courses in the existing secondary schools and the decline of the classical studies, the utilitarian movement pervaded the entire school system from the elementary schools through the universities. A less tangible but more important corollary of the practical movement was a strong current of anti-intellectualism which, when it was given expression, generally appeared in such phrases as "mere scholastic education" or "mere book learning."

The emphasis upon the practical was of course quite natural to a people who had been engaged in carving a civilization out of a wilderness. Americans, generally tracing their ancestry from the underprivileged of Europe, had little tradition of learning or scholarship, and the opportunity that excited them in the industrial age in their richly endowed new land was economic opportunity — the acquisition of material wealth. When they were fabulously successful (as the great leaders such as Carnegie, Rockefeller, and Vanderbilt were) and reflected upon their pattern of success, they were aware — and through their writing and speaking they made America aware — that the secret of their success was not learning, at least not book learning, but energy, initiative, and, as they would say, good old common sense. These tendencies were reinforced as they reacted against the obvious condescension and even scorn manifested toward them by the educated, cultured group that did exist in America, particularly in New England.

One of the leading critics of the traditional curriculum and one of

[16] N.E.A. *Proceedings*, p. 58.

[17] The word "practical" was generally used in its narrow sense to mean immediately useful. When applied by businessmen and often by educators to the work of the school, it meant changing the program to serve the needs of business and industry.

the strongest proponents of practical education was one of the most influential men in America in the late nineteenth and early twentieth century — Andrew Carnegie. He believed men had been sending their sons to colleges

to waste energies upon obtaining a knowledge of such languages as Greek and Latin, which are of no more practical use to them than Choctaw. . . . They have in no sense received instruction. On the contrary, what they have obtained has served to imbue them with false ideas and to give them a distaste for practical life. I do not wonder that a prejudice has arisen and still exists against such education. In my own experience I can say that I have known few young men intended for business who were not injured by a collegiate education. Had they gone into active work during the years spent at college they would have been better educated men in every true sense of that term. The fire and energy have been stamped out of them, and how to so manage as to live a life of idleness and not a life of usefulness has become the chief question with them. But a new idea of education is now upon us.[18]

Carnegie was right about a new idea of education being upon America. The century was little more than a year old when the Governor of Michigan welcomed the delegates to the N.E.A. convention in Detroit by stating that "the demand of the age is for a practical education" and he was glad to note that Michigan educators were "herding all their energies in that direction."[19] Evidence to support this was quickly supplied by the State Superintendent of Public Instruction in Michigan, who followed the Governor to the rostrum, saying: "The character of our education must change with the oncoming of the years of this highly practical age. We have educated the mind to think and trained the vocal organs to express the thought, and we have forgotten or overlooked the fact that in about four times out of five the practical man expresses his thought by the hand rather than by mere words."[20]

Year by year after 1900, the pressure for a more utilitarian education continued. By 1907, school superintendents were being praised by the President of the Commercial National Bank in Chicago for their contribution to America's great material progress. As a guest speaker at their annual convention, he told them this progress was "a result of getting away, to an extent, from the mere scholastic education, and developing the practical side, making the school the place to learn how to manufacture. . . ."[21] The tempo was increased in 1908 as businessmen appeared before educators at the annual meeting of

[18] Andrew Carnegie, *The Empire of Business* (New York, 1902), pp. 79–81.
[19] N.E.A. *Proceedings* (1901), p. 52.
[20] *Ibid.*, p. 55.
[21] N.E.A. *Proceedings* (1907), p. 166.

the National Education Association advising, urging, and warning them to continue to make education more practical. One business- man urged educators to incorporate commercial and industrial subjects in the elementary school since seven out of ten students did not go on to high school. "The best education for this 70 per cent," he said, "is utilitarian first, and cultural afterward."[22] He recommended that business English be substituted for composition and that students be taught business principles, contracts, and elementary bookkeeping.

Perhaps the climax of the utilitarian movement occurred in 1909, when the Superintendent of the Illinois Farmer's Institute, speaking before the N.E.A., connected utilitarianism with morality, fired some anti-intellectual salvos, and judged vocational efficiency above citizen- ship. Education, he said, should direct the desire of youth toward "acquisition by earning." Then he told his audience that

Ordinarily a love of learning is praiseworthy; but when this delight in the pleasures of learning becomes so intense and so absorbing that it diminishes the desire, and the power of earning, it is positively harmful. Education that does not promote the desire and power to do useful things — that's earning — is not worth the getting. Education that stimulates a love for useful activity is not simply desirable; it is in the highest degree ethical. . . . Personally I would rather send out pupils who are lop-sided and useful, than those who are seemingly symmetrical and useless. A man without a vocation is more to be pitied than "the man without a country." . . . And the country of which he is an inhabitant is to be commiserated, too.[23]

If educators had any doubts by 1910 of what was expected of them, those doubts should have been resolved at the N.E.A. meetings held in that year. First, the results of a survey which had been conducted by the President of the State Normal School at Peru, Nebraska, were presented to them at one of the general sessions. In an analysis of the responses to a question concerning the greatest weakness in the public high school, the first two answers listed by the surveyor as typical were to the effect that "the work is theoretical, visionary, and im- practical."[24] Then secondary teachers and administrators were told by one New York high school principal, "My girls want to study the social amenities that make life more pleasant and enjoyable, they want to know more about algebra, more of present-day Italy than of ancient Rome. They want to get in 1910 something they can use in 1911."[25] And the head of the mathematics department of another New York high school told his audience that "the most urgent ques-

[22] N.E.A. *Proceedings* (1908), p. 888.
[23] N.E.A. *Proceedings* (1909), pp. 492–94.
[24] N.E.A. *Proceedings* (1910), p. 104.
[25] *Ibid.*, p. 455.

tion before the mathematics teachers of today is, What mathematics is practical? All over the country our courses are being attacked and the demand for revision is along the line of fitting the mathematical teaching to the needs of the masses of pupils."[26]

There were educators — generally high school teachers or principals and college professors — who opposed the extreme emphasis upon the narrowly practical and utilitarian in education. One of these, Thomas J. McCormack, a high school principal from LaSalle, Illinois, told the Department of Secondary Education of the N.E.A. that a deeper meaning for the word "practical" must be sought and he reminded them that in their "inordinate zeal to practicalize and popularize education" they were forgetting that the purpose of education was "to make men and women as well as engineers and ropestretchers."[27] Another principal, from Chicago, Oliver S. Westcott, speaking before the same group a few years later, urged his colleagues to give the "almighty dollar at most but secondary influence in regulating our education curriculum."[28] These were more than voices in the wilderness, for they represented the view of a large segment of American educators, and it was this group (with the help of World War I) that succeeded in fighting off the attempt to fasten the German pattern of vocational education upon American schools. Yet they could not stem the tide of narrow utilitarianism for, as the Superintendent of Schools of New Orleans pointed out, "We are living in a practical, money making age. . . . The big thing today is the reward, the dollar, and it is paid for practice and not for the theory and training behind the practice."[29] What must have represented a typical view of the reconciliation of these men with the realities of American life was presented by a superintendent from Hartford, Connecticut, in 1912. Noting that some educators were concerned about the decline of the classics, he went on to say, "we can also see, however, that the so-called 'practical sense' of our people is very strong. The demand for a short, cheap, effective training to meet the demands of the field, shop, conveyance, trade, home, is a real demand. Given a demand, we are disposed in America to meet it."[30]

Along with these demands to make the academic program practical went an intensive campaign to introduce and extend vocational education in the public schools. Although the adoption of the German system with its early differentiation between academic students and

[26] *Ibid.*, p. 515.
[27] N.E.A. *Proceedings* (1910), p. 506.
[28] N.E.A. *Proceedings* (1914), p. 451.
[29] *Ibid.*, p. 264.
[30] N.E.A. *Proceedings* (1912), p. 175.

vocational students was avoided, the drive for vocational education was quite successful.

On numerous occasions after 1865, businessmen and educators had indicated an interest in developing industrial courses and vocational schools. This interest had been strong enough to be taken into consideration by the Committee of Ten, which had been appointed by the National Education Association in 1892, to study the secondary school program. The committee's recommendations, while broadening the curriculum from its classical base, did not recognize the importance or the necessity of industrial courses or an industrial curriculum. The need that existed was met partly by importing skilled labor. As American industry became more technical, the need for skilled workmen increased and the existing sources of skilled labor were deemed inadequate. Even so, it is doubtful whether the concern of manufacturers would have been as great if Germany had not emerged as an industrial competitor to the United States.

Beginning in 1905, the tempo of the drive for vocational training increased as businessmen began to express their fear of German industrial competition. Almost invariably these men attributed the German success to excellent industrial education and attributed our failure to inadequate provision for such schooling. So, they argued, we should adopt Germany's system of industrial education. This argument was presented to American educators at the N.E.A. Convention in 1905 by Frank A. Vanderlip, vice-president of the National City Bank of New York:

In the group of great industrial nations, there has come forward in recent years one that has taken place in the very front rank among industrial competitors. That nation is Germany. . . . I have had a somewhat unusual opportunity to study the underlying causes of the economic success of Germany, and I am firmly convinced that the explanation of that progress can be encompassed in a single word — schoolmaster. He is the great corner-stone of Germany's remarkable commercial and industrial success. From the economic point of view, the school system of Germany stands unparalleled. . . .[31]

In 1907 the same views were presented again and American educators were reminded of the needs and pressures of business and industry by one of their own group, L. D. Harvey, superintendent of schools in Menomonie, Wisconsin:

Manufacturers and men of affairs have noted the marvelous strides Germany has made in recent years in the industrial world, and have studied the reasons and have found them not in the advantages which Germany possesses in raw material, in means of transportation, or in other of the material things which

[31] N.E.A. *Proceedings* (1905), pp. 141–44.

we possess to a degree far in excess of any other country in the world, but in the development of the educational system of Germany on technical and industrial lines, and they are *demanding* a modification of our educational system on similar lines.[32]

In 1909 the drive for vocational education reached its peak, and it was discussed in almost every session of the annual meeting of the N.E.A. As one speaker put it, "the program of this association bristles with the topic."[33] In that year, too, educators indicated that they would bow to the pressure when the United States Commissioner of Education told the N.E.A., "there can be no doubt that industrial education is needed to perpetuate the prosperity of our industries. This aspect of the case has been widely discussed and may simply be taken for granted here."[34] Even the National Association of Manufacturers was satisfied with the progress that had been made; its Committee on Industrial Education reported in 1909, "Industrial education has taken a firm and lasting hold upon the people of this country, and we are pleased to come before you with the encouraging news that its progress and growth during the past year have been greater than during the year previous."[35] The association continued, however, to press schoolmen to establish more trade schools in the years that followed.

Evidence that the pressure did continue and that it had originated and been maintained primarily by industrialists is provided by an article written in 1913 by William H. Maxwell, superintendent of schools in New York City. In an angry and defiant reaction to unfair criticism and to pressure groups, Maxwell first attacked the "arrogant unreasonableness" of certain educational theorists who periodically made sweeping indictments of the schools and then offered their pet solutions. But nothing, he said, had been as arrogant as the

agitation with which the educational world is now seething for the introduction of industrial or trade teaching in the public schools. That agitation, as every one knows, originated with the manufacturers. They had practically abandoned the apprenticeship system of training workmen. No longer training their own mechanics, they have found it difficult to obtain a sufficient supply of skillful artisans, unless they import them from Europe at great expense. Out of this dilemma the exit was obvious — persuade the State to assume the burden. It was only a new application of Colonel Sellers' definition of patriotism — The old flag and — an appropriation! — let the State do the work that is so oppressive to us. And, as a first step to secure their ends, they and their agents in unmeasured terms denounced the public schools as behind

[32] N.E.A. *Proceedings* (1907), p. 311. (Italics mine.)
[33] N.E.A. *Proceedings* (1909), p. 616.
[34] *Ibid.*, p. 288.
[35] N.A.M. *Proceedings* (1909), p. 18.

the age, as inefficient, as lacking in public spirit. And why? Because the public schools are not training artisans — are not doing the work that had been
done by employers of labor for thousands of years. The arrogance of the
manufacturers was two-fold — first, in condemning the schools for not doing
what thinking men had never before considered it the duty of the schools
to do and what the traditions of thousands of years laid it upon the manufacturers to do; and, second, in demanding that the State, after taxing consumers
for fifty years, through a protective tariff, in order to fill the pockets of manufacturers, should then proceed to pay the bills for training their workmen. To
condemn a great industry — schoolteaching — for not doing what hitherto it
had never been expected to do, and to clamor not only for protection from
competition but for relief at the hands of the state from the duty and expense
of training artisans — could arrogance farther go? [36]

Statements like this were rare. For the most part educators and especially school administrators complied with alacrity to the demands
for vocational training. The immediate result of this drive was that
American education was pushed further into the training of clerks
and factory workers and by that much away from the liberal education of free men. It also made school administrators more aware
of the power of business in American society, and it served to condition them to the pattern of capitulation which was to become prevalent
in educational administration between 1911 and 1925.

Setting the Stage for the Efficiency Expert

At the end of the decade, after years of being subjected to the
steadily growing business influence and about the time that the momentum of reform had reached its peak and Americans had become
accustomed to a critical view of all their institutions, the schools, especially in the larger cities, were facing problems that would have
taxed a professionally excellent, richly endowed educational system.
No such system existed, and the schools and teachers available were
overwhelmed by the new problems which developed. Some fourteen
million immigrants had come to America between 1865 and 1900.
After 1900, they came at a rate of about one million a year. The majority of these people remained in the eastern cities, where their children were entered — with increasing frequency because of the
improvements in child labor laws and compulsory school attendance
legislation — in the public schools. Coming predominantly from the
poorest socioeconomic groups in southern and eastern Europe, these
uprooted, non-English-speaking children from semiliterate families

<hr>

[36] *Educational Review*, "On a Certain Arrogance in Educational Theorists," XLVII
(February, 1914), 175–76.

with diverse cultural backgrounds constituted an educational problem unparalleled in human history.

The physical problems alone were tremendous, for this increased school population meant that thousands of additional classrooms and teachers were needed. Even without the flood of immigration, greater expenditures for education had become necessary because of the normal growth of population and the increasing responsibilities placed upon the schools. Obviously taxes had to be increased to meet even the minimum essentials. Unfortunately, this need for large increases in school funds occurred not only at a time when the country had been roused to a concern for economy and conditioned to suspect that all public institutions were inefficient and wasteful but also in an inflationary period in which the cost of living had risen more than 30 per cent. The result was that hard-pressed educators needing additional funds were forced to deal with a suspicious, economy-minded public wanting to cut costs.

Into this difficult and potentially explosive situation an American educator — not a businessman or muckraking journalist — threw an incendiary bomb in the form of an allegedly scientific study of retardation and elimination, published in 1909, *Laggards in Our Schools*. The author, Leonard Ayres, had collected his data from school records and reports and from statistics collected and published by government agencies. They showed, Ayres said, that the schools were filled with retarded children and that most students dropped out of school before finishing the eighth grade. By retarded children, he meant children who were over-age for their grade regardless of how well they were doing in their work. He claimed that the extent of retardation varied from 7 per cent in Medford, Massachusetts, to 75 per cent for Negro children in Memphis, Tennessee, with the average being about 33 per cent for all pupils in public schools.[37] The figures indicated, he said, that "for every child who is making more than normally rapid progress there are from eight to ten children making abnormally slow progress."[38] Although his data showed only that large numbers of children were over-age for their grade without regard for the social or educational reasons, he held the schools responsible, charging that their programs were "fitted not to the slow child or to the average child but to the unusually bright one."[39]

Ayres did more than simply report the percentages of "retarded" children in the schools. He was one of the first educators to picture the school as a factory and to apply the business and industrial values

[37] Leonard Ayres, *Laggards in Our Schools* (New York, 1909), p. 3.
[38] *Ibid.*, p. 5.
[39] *Ibid.*

and practices in a systematic way. He used the normal year-by-year progress through the schools as a criterion for measuring the relative "efficiency" of a school and he developed a system for presenting this "efficiency" in percentage form. This measure, which he labeled an "Index of Efficiency," was determined through the following procedure:

1. If we can find out how many children *begin* school each year we can compute how many remain to the final elementary grade. Such a factor would show the relation of the finished product to the raw material.

2. The number of beginners tells us of the number of children who under conditions of maximum theoretical efficiency should be in each grade. Hence we may readily calculate the size of the school system under ideal conditions and compare it with the actual size. Pursuing our industrial analogy still further, this gives us the relation of the actual plant in size to the theoretical requirements. This we may call the economic factor.

3. Comparing not theoretical but actual size with the actual not theoretical product, we reach an index of efficiency which will express both the educational and economic results in combination and give us a means of rating different school systems on the basis of efficiency.

To illustrate, suppose we had a factory which instead of utilizing all its raw material (100 per cent) embodied only 50 per cent in its finished product. It appears that the 50 per cent is the measure of its efficiency. But suppose the plant is not economically organized. Suppose that for a theoretical product of 100 per cent it requires an organization represented by 8000 units, but it actually comprises 9000 units, an organization which may be represented by 9/8 or 112.5 per cent of the standard. What then is its real efficiency? Its plant is 9/8 as large as it should be theoretically. From the viewpoint of plant then, the efficiency is 8/9. But its product is only ½ as large as it should be. From the viewpoint of product then the efficiency is only ½.

Looking at our plant now from the two viewpoints, it is obvious that its efficiency is expressed by the product of these fractions or ½ × 8/9 = 4/9 = 44.4 per cent.

Now suppose these conditions are found not in a factory but in a school system. For each 1000 children who enter only 50 per cent reach the eighth grade. The efficiency from the viewpoint of product is ½ or 50 per cent. Moreover, instead of finding 8000 pupils in the eighth grades we find 9000. From the viewpoint of plant, efficiency is 8/9 or 88.8 per cent. The figure representing the efficiency of the school system is then ½ × 8/9 = 4/9 or, in terms of percentages, 44.4 per cent.[40]

Ayres did more than use this as a hypothetical illustration. He applied it to the school systems of fifty-eight cities, which he named. The schools were rated according to their "efficiency" and then the financial consequences of the inefficiency were presented. It turned out that

[40] *Ibid.*, pp. 176–77.

the most "efficient" school system was spending $24,033 or 6.5 per cent of its annual budget on repeaters, and the least "efficient" was spending $120,584 or 30.3 per cent on these students.[41] In preparing these findings, the only evidence Ayres had was the grade and age distribution of the children; he did not have data on when the children had started to school. Thus, if a school had pupils who were eight years old and in the first grade or ten years old and in the second grade, the institution was noted as being inefficient, with the degree of inefficiency depending on the number of such children. But obviously this mechanical analysis did not necessarily indicate academic failure. Non–English-speaking immigrant children regardless of their age had to be placed in a lower grade than their age would ordinarily warrant. The same problem would occur when a family moved from a rural area into a city or from certain areas of the south to the north. There were numerous other reasons which were social and economic in nature and beyond the control of the school, to explain why, in 1907 and 1908, many children were over-age and did not fit into a neat, mechanical age-grade schedule.

That Ayres had an opportunity to make a genuine contribution to the solution of educational problems is evident in his report. Although he ignored or discounted the social and economic conditions which contributed to the complexity of the education problems, he did note the deplorably overcrowded condition of the schools, citing several newspaper comments which indicated that elementary classes of over one hundred children were common. But instead of pointing out that the schools were caught in a vicious circle, with overcrowding causing retardation and retardation contributing to overcrowding, he centered his attention on "the money cost of the repeater" and charged, "It cannot be denied that we are spending money in teaching large numbers of children the same things over again."[42] This "wasteful process of repetition," he claimed, cost the American taxpayers "about twenty-seven millions of dollars in our cities alone."[43] Since this material was written by a prominent educator and presented in a form that gave it the appearance of scientific respectability, it is not surprising that an economy-minded public was critical of its schools and their administrators.[44]

The concern with the money cost of the repeater and the mechanical

[41] *Ibid.*, pp. 96–97.
[42] *Ibid.*, p. 90.
[43] *Ibid.*, p. 95.
[44] Ayres was especially prominent in education between 1910 and 1916. In 1915 he was appointed to direct the giant survey of the Cleveland public schools. In 1920 he left education to accept an appointment as vice-president of the Cleveland Trust Company. An account of his further activity in studying retardation is presented in chapter vii.

conception of education manifested in the "index of efficiency" represented ominous warnings to American education. Certainly Ayres' book, together with the other developments described in this chapter, helped set the stage for the spectacular debut of the efficiency expert on the American scene in the fall of 1910. The dominance of businessmen and the acceptance of business values (especially the concern for efficiency and economy); the creation of a critical, cost-conscious, reform-minded public, led by profit-seeking journals; the alleged mismanagement of all American institutions; the increased cost of living: all these factors created a situation of readiness — readiness for the great preacher of the gospel of efficiency, Frederick W. Taylor, and his disciples. And school administrators, already under constant pressure to make education more practical in order to serve a business society better, were brought under even stronger criticism and forced to demonstrate first, last, and always that they were operating the schools efficiently.

2

REFORM-CONSCIOUS AMERICA
DISCOVERS THE EFFICIENCY EXPERT

In the fall of 1910 America was dazzled by a new idea that came out of the nation's capital and found its way increasingly into the country's newspapers and journals. That idea was a new system of industrial management known as "scientific management," or the "Taylor System" after the man generally credited with its origin and development. It was brought dramatically before the public eye through what started out to be an important, but routine, hearing before a government commission. In the years that followed, this new system became known throughout the world, even finding its way into China and the Soviet Union, where it was endorsed by that old friend of capitalism, Lenin.

The occasion for the emergence of the new system was a hearing before the Interstate Commerce Commission in September, October, and November of 1910. The railroads of the Northeast had applied to the Commission for an increase in freight rates to compensate for higher wages granted to railroad workers in the spring of 1910. The merchants of the area opposed this action because it would increase their shipping costs. Each side was represented by teams of lawyers. The trade association, led by lawyer Louis Brandeis, argued that the railroads were being operated inefficiently and that it was possible for them to make a larger profit without raising rates. At a crucial point in the hearing, Brandeis introduced as witnesses a number of engineers and industrial managers who testified that through the introduction of "scientific management" the railroads should be able to *increase wages* and *lower costs*. Some of these men stated that they had actually reduced costs while raising wages from 25 to 100 per cent. One of the witnesses, efficiency expert Harrington Emerson, who had successfully put efficiency practices into operation for the Santa Fe railroad, estimated that through this system the railroads could save up to one million dollars a day!

Taylor himself, although he was frequently referred to by witnesses who credited him with being the originator of the system, did not appear as a witness. But the impact of the testimony apparently was tremendous, as evidenced by this description of the scene by Ray Stannard Baker:

To those who heard this testimony there seemed at first something almost magical about the new idea; but as one sober, hard-headed businessman after another testified as to what had been actually accomplished in his plant, when it appeared that Scientific Management had been applied with extraordinary results to widely diversified industries from steel plants to bleacheries and cotton mills and including railroad repair shops, the spirit of incredulity changed to one of deep interest. Another factor in carrying conviction to the hearers was the extraordinary fervor and enthusiasm expressed by every man who testified. Theirs was the firm faith of apostles: it was a philosophy which worked, and they had the figures to show it.[1]

And the *Outlook*, commenting on the "magic power" most aptly described as "scientific management," noted that its effect upon industry "has been compared to that made by the change from the use of hand tools to the use of machinery."[2]

Magic indeed, or at least a panacea for the economic ills that beset America. Here was a means whereby production could be increased, wages raised, and prices lowered. Here was American mechanical genius at its best, solving the problem of competition from Germany, the high cost of living, and the conservation of national resources at one blow. Theodore Roosevelt saw in this last point a great patriotic contribution even though its motivating force was economic self-interest. "Scientific Management," he said, "is the application of the conservation principle to production. It does not concern itself with the ownership of our natural resources. But in the factories where it is in force it guards these stores of raw materials from loss and misuse. First, by finding the right material — the special wood or steel or fiber — which is cheapest and best for the purpose. Second, by getting the utmost of finished product out of every pound or bale worked up. We couldn't ask more from a patriotic motive, than Scientific Management gives from a selfish one."[3]

[1] *American Magazine*, LXXI (March, 1911), 564–65.

[2] *Outlook*, XCIV (December, 1910), 751–52.

[3] Quoted in Frank B. Gilbreth, *Primer of Scientific Management* (New York, 1912), p. 2.

Despite the spectacular nature of the testimony and the effectiveness of Mr. Brandeis' strategy, the testimony dealing with scientific management apparently had little effect upon the Interstate Commerce Commission. The Commission did decide against permitting an increase to the railroads, but the reason was that their earnings had been so high in the past it was felt that they could allow higher wages and still pay adequate dividends. The Commission, mentioning scientific management in only two paragraphs of its sixty-four page report, stated that it was everywhere in an experimental stage, that representatives of labor had testified against it, and that upon this record they could not find that the railroads could make good any part of wage advances by the introduction of scientific management.

Prior to the hearings scientific management was little known in the United States, outside of the field of engineering and perhaps business. In fact, the term scientific management had not been generally used even in the field of engineering. Taylor had used the term, apparently accidentally, a few times, but he had not used it regularly to describe his system. The phrase was coined by a group called together by Brandeis in preparation for his legal efforts at the hearing. At this meeting, held in the New York apartment of H. L. Gantt, one of Taylor's close associates, the terms "Efficiency," "Functional Management," and "Taylor System" were suggested and rejected before the final choice was made. Taylor's biographer, Frank Copley, after describing this conference, states that although Taylor "made bold to use it formally," he disliked it because "it had a pretentious sound" and because he thought that "its connotations would seem academic to most people." Taylor was not present at the meeting but it was attended by two of his close associates and admirers — Gantt and Gilbreth.[4]

The hearings had the effect of propelling the phrase scientific management and the name Frederick W. Taylor into prominence. Almost immediately, Taylor was besieged by newspapermen and editors of magazines eager to capitalize on the widespread interest.[5] He received two offers to publish a paper which he had prepared and submitted to the American Society of Mechanical Engineers, but which that organization had not yet published, one from the *American Magazine* and one from the *Atlantic Monthly*. He decided to publish the work in the *American Magazine*, choosing this journal in preference to the *Atlantic Monthly* partly because of his high regard for Ray Stannard Baker, who was associated with it, and partly because he wanted to

[4] Frank B. Copley, *Frederick W. Taylor* (New York, 1923), II, 372.
[5] *Ibid.*, p. 373.

reach "those who are actually doing the practical work of the world." [6]
The first of three instalments of his "Principles of Scientific Management," preceded by a personal sketch by Baker, appeared in March,
1911. Harper's published the three articles in book form in the summer of 1911 and in 1912 published his earlier paper on "Shop Management," which had been presented before the American Society of
Mechanical Engineers in 1903.

Even though Taylor and his system of management were not widely
known in America prior to 1910, he had already won recognition
within the field of engineering. His first formal statement of the system was made before the American Society of Mechanical Engineers
in June of 1895 and entitled, "A Piece-Rate System, A Step Toward
the Partial Solution of the Labor Problem." This paper was deemed
by the editor of the *Engineering Magazine* to be "one of the most valuable contributions that have ever been given to technical literature" and
was published in that journal in January of 1896. [7] Five years later, in
1900, Taylor received world-wide recognition for his part in the development of high-speed steel. In 1903, he presented his first complete
statement of the system, again before the American Society of Mechanical Engineers, under the title "Shop Management." In 1906,
he was elected President of the engineering society and read his third
major work "On the Cutting of Metals" as his presidential address.

After 1906, he lectured frequently to industrial groups and to engineering schools, including those of the University of Pennsylvania
in 1906 and the University of Illinois in 1908, and to the Harvard
Business School in 1909. In 1910, Taylor's system was taught in
formal courses in the business schools of Harvard and Dartmouth.
By the summer of 1910, therefore, the Taylor system was known, but
only within engineering circles and, to some extent, in business, industry, and education.

The railroad hearings in the fall of 1910 changed this very rapidly.
The most obvious manifestation of the great change was in the number
of books and articles written on scientific management in 1911 and
the years immediately following. There were in 1911, according to a
list of references compiled by the Technology Division of the New
York Public Library, 219 articles on the subject. [8] In the years immediately following there were hundreds of articles and scores of books
published on various aspects of scientific management. C. Bertrand
Thompson, a lecturer on manufacturing at Harvard University, in his
book *The Theory and Practice of Scientific Management*, published

[6] *Ibid.*, p. 381–82.
[7] *Engineering Magazine*, X (January, 1896), 690.
[8] Copley, *op. cit.*, I, 410.

in 1917, has a bibliography of 38 pages with more than 550 references on scientific management and closely related subjects; the vast majority of these references have publication dates between 1910 and 1916.[9]

In the flood of enthusiasm, an attempt was made to apply the principles of scientific management to many aspects of American life,[10] including the army and navy, the legal profession, the home, the family, the household, the church, and last but not least, to education. Harrington Emerson, a scientific management engineer, who had given the spectacular testimony in the railroad hearing, gave an address on "Scientific Management and High School Efficiency" before the High School Teachers' Association of New York City, which was published as one of the association bulletins in 1912. J. M. Rice, a physician-educator, who had done extensive pioneering research in the classrooms of American schools from 1892 to 1904, published a collection of his essays in 1914 under the title *Scientific Management in Education.* The subject was given national recognition at the 1913 convention of the Department of Superintendence when the main topic for discussion was "Improving School Systems by Scientific Management." There were scores of articles, books, and reports during the next decade on economy in education, efficiency in education, standardization in education, and the like. In 1911, a group of seven leading school administrators was appointed to a committee on the economy of time in education. And the World Book Company made available a new series in education under the editorship of Paul Hanus, professor of education at Harvard, under the title "The School Efficiency Series."

Nor was Taylor's influence confined to the United States. Within two years after its publication by Harper and Brothers in 1911, his *Principles of Scientific Management* had been translated into French, German, Dutch, Swedish, Russian, Lettish, Italian, Spanish, and Japanese. And a few years later, it was translated into Chinese. The Taylor system was introduced into French war plants during 1918 upon order of Georges Clemenceau. In France, also, an endowed foundation was established to promote the investigation of scientific

[9] C. Bertrand Thompson, *The Theory and Practice of Scientific Management* (Boston), pp. 270–308.

[10] C. S. Brewer, "Scientific Management in the Army and Navy," *World's Work*, XXIII (January, 1912), 311; Henry W. Jessup, "Legal Efficiency," *Bench and Bar*, IV (March, 1913), 55; J. B. Guernsey, "Scientific Management in the Home," *Outlook*, C (April, 1912), 821; Francis E. Leupp, "Scientific Management in the Family," *Outlook*, XCVIII (August, 1911), 832; Frank B. Gilbreth, "Scientific Management in the Household," *Journal of Home Economics* (December, 1912), IV, 438; Shailer Matthews, *Scientific Management in the Churches* (Chicago, 1912).

management and the Taylor system through courses in higher technical schools, through public lectures, and through sending young
French engineers to America to study the system in operation. In Austria, a periodical devoted to the Taylor System, the *Taylor Zeitschrift*,
was established.[11] And in the Soviet Union, Lenin, in an article published in *Izvestia* in April of 1918, urged the system upon the Rus-
sians.

In these years America was enormously preoccupied with Taylor,
scientific management, and the idea of efficiency. Taylor societies
were formed and efficiency societies were formed and a National Efficiency Exposition was held, until Taylor himself thought that it was
"very much overdone" and that the trouble was that "a great army of
cranks and charlatans, who wished to make money out of the new efficiency enthusiasm, joined the society and received endorsement from
its secretary, and printed on their cards 'Member of the Efficiency Society' so as to help them gain customers."[12]

Taylor was not alone in feeling that the whole thing was overdone;
A. G. Webster of Clark University expressed his weariness in a letter
to the editor of the *Nation*, saying, "I am tired of scientific management, so-called. I have heard of it from scientific managers, from university presidents, from casual acquaintances in railway trains; I
have read of it in the daily papers, the weekly papers, the ten-cent
magazines, the fifteen-cent magazines, the thirty-five-cent magazines,
and in the *Outlook*. Only have I missed its treatment by Theodore
Roosevelt; but that is probably because I cannot keep up with his
writings. For fifteen years I have been a subscriber to a magazine
dealing with engineering matters, feeling it incumbent on me to keep
in touch with the applications of physics to the convenience of life,
but the touch has become a pressure, the pressure a crushing strain,
until the mass of articles on shop practice and scientific management
threatened to crush all thought out of my brain, and I stopped my
subscription."[13]

For this condition Taylor and his associates were partly to blame
because they claimed that his principles could be applied to all institutions. It is true that Taylor attacked the "cranks and charlatans"
but in his efforts to sell his system to the public as well as to industry
he had made extravagant claims, as Robert F. Hoxie's investigation
for the U.S. Commission on Industrial Relations was to prove. And
Emerson, the great popularizer of the movement and never one to
understate his case, not only spoke of the efficiency movement in

[11] Copley, *op. cit.*, I, xx–xxiii.
[12] Copley, *op. cit.*, II, 387–88.
[13] A. G. Webster, *Nation*, XCIII (September, 1911), 238.

glowing terms but continually presented it as a panacea for the ills of mankind. Moreover he gave the movement a moral fervor that had all the earmarks of a religious revival. His writing is so saturated with this quality that it is difficult to select an example. But consider a passage from his chapter on "The Cure of Wastes" in his book *Twelve Principles of Efficiency* printed originally in 1911:

If man's progress is slow, it is because of wastes — solely because of wastes — wastes of everything that is precious. How inconceivably slow has been human progress — waste of time; how the accumulated stores of nature have been looted, the forests, the fertility of the soil, the minerals below the surface — wastes of national resources; how inconceivably hard our tasks have been made for us! Cursed has been the ground; in sorrow has humanity eaten all the days of its life, thorns and thistles have we reaped and in the sweat of our faces have we worked. Wasted lives, sorrow instead of joy, painful, ignorant effort instead of glad, intelligent activity! . . . Elimination of all wastes may indeed be a Utopian ideal, not to be realized in the life of our planet, but any waste elimination brings its immediate reward.[14]

The Principles of Scientific Management

What was the nature of this new system which was so enthusiastically received and at the same time so bitterly opposed? It was essentially a system for getting greater productivity from human labor; and Taylor, in describing the system, took great pains to differentiate between the basic principles of the system and its mechanics. He pointed out that a person unfamiliar with industry would seem surprised that such a system should be necessary since it would be taken for granted that both workers and management in their own self-interest would be already producing to their maximum. But, he said, this was not the case. In most plants, production was far below what it could have been and should have been, with many plants producing only one-third to one-half of their maximum output.

The reasons for this wasteful situation were, first, faulty management; and second, soldiering on the part of the workers. In most plants the two factors were interrelated causes of low productivity. Management was at fault for permitting workmen to use rule of thumb methods (as he termed them) in plants. These methods, handed down from generation to generation, were sometimes good, sometimes bad, but always unscientific. According to Taylor, there was always one best method for doing any particular job and this best method could be determined only through scientific study. He complained that even the manufacturers of machines such as lathes had not

[14] Harrington Emerson, *The Twelve Principles of Efficiency* (New York, 1913), p. 372–73.

bothered to determine the best running and feeding speeds to be used on different kinds of metals. Workers were at fault because they deliberately did less work than they were capable of doing — in other words, they were guilty of "soldiering." He believed there were two types of soldiering: "natural," the innate laziness of men,[15] and "systematic."

Taylor admitted that the natural laziness of men was serious, but it could be handled by "external pressure." It was systematic soldiering that was the real evil. This he described as the deliberate slowing down of production while, at the same time, giving the appearance of working at full speed. One of the reasons for this type of soldiering, he said, was the mistaken idea workmen had that an increase in their output would result in unemployment, both for themselves and other workmen. This was a fallacy, he said, because increasing production resulted in lower costs and, therefore, lower prices. Lower prices meant greater sales and greater sales meant more work for more men. Despite this fact which, he said, had been proven in the shoe industry as well as others, "Almost every labor union had made, or is contemplating making, rules which have for their object curtailing the output of their members; and those men who have the greatest influence with the working-people, the labor leaders, as well as many people with philanthropic feelings who are helping them are daily spreading this fallacy and at the same time telling them that they are overworked."[16] Taylor then gave his opinion as follows:

A great deal has been and is being constantly said about 'sweat shop' work and conditions. The writer has great sympathy with those who are overworked, but on the whole a greater sympathy for those who are *under paid*. For every individual, however, who is overworked, there are a hundred who intentionally underwork — greatly underwork — every day of their lives, and who for this reason deliberately aid in establishing those conditions which in the end inevitably result in low wages.[17]

The other major cause for systematic soldiering was faulty management. The workers had learned from bitter experience that if an employer found that a worker could do more work a day he would be forced to do more work for the same pay. It was for this reason that ordinary piece work had failed. Employers used the piece work system as an incentive to get men to show how much they could produce when working at top speed. When they discovered this, they lowered the price per piece, and the workman ended up working at top speed

[15] Frederick W. Taylor, *The Principles of Scientific Management* (New York, 1911), p. 19.
[16] *Ibid.*, p. 17.
[17] *Ibid.*, pp. 17–18.

for the same wages he had received before. For this reason the men decided on the amount of work that should be done and would not permit any worker to do more.

But he said that even under the very best system of management, which he described as a system of initiative and incentive, maximum production was not uniformly attained. Under this system men were given freedom, urged to produce more, and rewarded with higher wages, shorter hours, promotions, and better working conditions. This system was not as good as scientific management because the men who did the work were incapable, either through lack of education or mental ability, of understanding the scientific basis which underlay the job.[18] Therefore, the management must step in and assume new duties and these duties, listed below, constituted the basic principles of scientific management:

First. They develop a science for each element of a man's work, which replaces the old rule-of-thumb method.

Second. They scientifically select and then train, teach, and develop the workman, whereas in the past he chose his own work and trained himself as best he could.

Third. They heartily cooperate with the men so as to insure all of the work being done in accordance with the principles of the science which has been developed.

Fourth. There is an almost equal division of the work and the responsibility between the management and the workmen. The management take over all work for which they are better fitted than the workmen, while in the past almost all of the work and the greater part of the responsibility were thrown upon the men.[19]

The first three new duties constituted what management was to do step by step under the Taylor system, whereas the fourth duty was really the heart of the whole approach. It was a new role for management — an active role of analyzing, planning, and controlling the whole manufacturing process *in detail.* When Taylor said that there was an almost equal division of the work and responsibility, he was probably literally correct, but the statement was misleading. It certainly had the implication that the workmen would have some share in *all aspects* of the work and some responsibility for *all aspects* of it. However, this was not Taylor's intent. The worker's equal division of work was to do what he was told to do by management and his share of the responsibility was that responsibility to do what he was told. In his system the judgment of the individual workman was replaced by the laws, rules, principles, etc., of the science of the job which was

[18] *Ibid.,* pp. 25–26.
[19] *Ibid.,* pp. 36–37.

developed by management. Taylor justified this on the ground that "one type of man is needed to plan ahead and an entirely different type to execute the work."[20] The whole attitude of Taylor in this respect was described by a mechanic who worked under him. In the discussion of the problems that came up in the shop, Taylor would tell him that he was "not supposed to think, there are other people paid for thinking around here." Apparently this mechanic was a rugged individualist, because he added, "I would never admit to Mr. Taylor that I was not allowed to think."[21]

The Mechanisms of Scientific Management

The first element in the mechanism of scientific management listed by Taylor was time and motion study and the development of unit times for the various components of any job. This Taylor regarded as "by far the most important element in scientific management," and it was the basic element in achieving his first principle of the development of a true science for a particular job.[22] Frank Gilbreth testified on this point by stating that "any plan of management that does not include Taylor's plan of time study cannot be considered as highly efficient. We have never seen a case in our work where time study and analysis did not result in more than doubling the output of the worker."[23] Not only was time and motion study thus conceived by the engineers themselves, but also it was apparently identified in the mind of the average American as the key element of the system. Milton Nadworny notes, "Although scientific management employed many identifiable and characteristic mechanisms, its most prominent tool was a stopwatch, the popular symbol of the scientific management movement. The stopwatch symbolized the new approach to management: 'management based on measurement.' "[24]

When Taylor introduced his system into any shop, his first step was to make a careful, detailed, and exhaustive study of the various aspects of the jobs being done. For example, in a machine shop Taylor would observe, time with a stop watch, and record the times of various motions of a group of the most skilful men in the shop. After studying his data, he would then select a worker he regarded as being potentially a first-class man, offer him a bonus for working faster, and experiment. He would combine what he regarded as the best and fastest movements for each phase of the work that he had observed,

[20] *Ibid.*, pp. 37–38.
[21] Copley, *op. cit.*, I, 189.
[22] Frederick W. Taylor, *Shop Management* (New York, 1912), p. 58.
[23] Gilbreth, *op. cit.*, p. 12.
[24] Milton J. Nadworny, *Scientific Management and the Unions 1900–1932* (Cambridge, 1955), p. vi.

and eliminate all useless motion. The experimental first-class man would then be taught all the proper motions and Taylor would have him repeat the process until he had satisfied himself that the job was being done in the best and fastest manner. This procedure would then be standardized and one by one the other workers would be taught and required to use this system. His belief was that there was one best way of doing any job and this method could be determined only through the scientific study of that job by experts with proper implements, i.e., a stop watch and recording card.[25]

The actual time and motion study was only a part of developing a science of a particular job, although its relative importance depended, to some extent at least, on the nature of the job. Equally important was the study and analysis and improvement of the tools and machines. For example, in his early efforts to increase productivity at Midvale Steel Company in Philadelphia, Taylor soon found that metal-cutting tools needed improvements which involved, among other things, exhaustive experiments on the proper speeds for cutting various metals. He spent some twenty-five years experimenting in this field, and he carried out more than forty thousand recorded experiments.[26] As a result of these efforts he made important contributions to technology and received world-wide acclaim.

Frequently, in the attempt to increase productivity, Taylor encountered difficult technical problems which he himself could not solve. When these problems involved higher mathematics, his response was to call upon experts. Thus it happened that he and Carl Barth, a Norwegian mathematician, became close associates, and Barth was consulted on many occasions by Taylor. In the summer of 1899 Taylor was attempting to solve some of the difficult calculating problems involved in the operation of lathes in the machine shop at Bethlehem Steel, and in December of 1899, a slide rule developed by Barth was put into operation in the machine shop.[27] Through its use, an ordinary lathe-hand with little knowledge of mathematics could solve the most complicated mathematical problem necessary in a matter of minutes. It was this kind of result that Taylor claimed could never be achieved under even the best of the ordinary systems of management.

[25] Taylor, *Scientific Management*, p. 25. Strangely, Taylor opposed the use of motion pictures in time and motion study, believing the stop watch to be adequate. Frank Gilbreth did the pioneer work in this field and as early as 1912 devised a system that he described as micromotion study. Until his death in 1924 Gilbreth "waged an intensive campaign" for the acceptance of his system, and in the early twenties both he and his wife Lillian criticized the "unscientific pretensions of the proponents and advocates of the stop watch method." Nadworny, *op. cit.*, p. 108.

[26] Copley, *op. cit.*, I, 246.

[27] *Ibid.*, II, 35.

After a careful, intensive study of a particular job, the second element in the mechanism of scientific management was introduced, that
of standardization. Actually, this process was interrelated with the
time and motion study since in each step of the job analysis certain
tools and work motions were adopted and made a standard part of the
job, and these standard elements were necessary in determining the
best and fastest way of doing the job.[28] The tools and motions thus
standardized on the pilot analysis were then introduced for all similar
jobs in the plant. Taylor pointed out that these standards were not
absolute or immutable, and he urged a continual search for better
and faster methods. But until improved methods were discovered,
the implements and practices that had been found best were to be the
standard. When improved methods were developed, they would replace the older methods and would then become the standard. Taylor's
idea was that every aspect of the job from the minute details for operating machines to the selection of "first class men" should be standardized.[29] He claimed that since these standards had been determined
objectively and scientifically they not only eliminated any chance of
soldiering but also prevented clashes between workers and employers
over what constituted a fair day's work.[30]

The third element in the mechanism of scientific management, and
one that Taylor described as "perhaps the most prominent single element," was the task idea.[31] Taylor believed that it was necessary and
desirable for management to set definite tasks each day for each
worker, and in seeking justification for this practice, he turned to the
schools:

There is no question that the average individual accomplishes the most when
he either gives himself, or some one else assigns him, a definite task, namely,
a given amount of work which he must do within a given time; and the more
elementary the mind and character of the individual the more necessary does
it become that each task shall extend over a short period of time only. No
school teacher would think of telling children in a general way to study a certain book or subject. It is practically universal to assign each day a definite
lesson beginning on one specific page and line and ending on another; and
the best progress is made when the conditions are such that a definite study
hour or period can be assigned in which the lesson must be learned. Most of
us remain, through a great part of our lives, in this respect, grown-up children,
and do our best only under pressure of a task of comparatively short du-
ration.[32]

[28] Taylor, *Shop Management*, p. 123.
[29] Taylor, *Scientific Management*, p. 65.
[30] Taylor, *Shop Management*, p. 40.
[31] Taylor, *Scientific Management*, p. 39.
[32] Taylor, *Shop Management*, p. 69.

Under scientific management each man's task was worked out by the planning department. Each worker received an instruction card which described in minute detail "not only what is to be done, but how it is to be done and the exact time allowed for doing it."[33] The task for an individual worker was theoretically regulated to get the maximum output from a man without injuring his health. If the job were found to be injurious to the worker's health the task had to be revised. Taylor stated that if the worker was "overtired by his work, then the task has been wrongly set and this is as far as possible from the object of scientific management."[34]

The second half of the task mechanism was the bonus plan. Taylor claimed that his development of the bonus plan resulted from "a series of experiments made upon workmen."[35] These experiments proved, he said, that it was impossible to get men to work at a high rate of speed for any length of time unless they were paid more than they received for an easier pace and, furthermore, they had to be assured that the pay increase was permanent.[36] This latter condition was necessary because employers had often offered workers higher wages as an inducement to step up production in order to find out what the men could produce. Then the men were forced to produce at this level for the wages they had received before and, what was worse, they frequently worked themselves out of a job. That this condition existed even in the plants where scientific management had been introduced was discovered by Hoxie in his investigation of the actual operation of the Taylor system for the U.S. Commission on Industrial Relations. Reporting on the bonus systems as he saw them, he noted that there was "a strong tendency then, under all these systems of payment, to keep the workers going at top speed as long as the work lasts, and then to send them home or lay them off; or where this is not done, they are put temporarily on day work. In the one case, continuity of employment is sacrified, in the other stability of income."[37]

There were other aspects of the bonus plan that Taylor emphasized. One of these was that the bonus or reward, to be effective, had to be given immediately after the work had been done. And with "more elementary characters" such as young girls or children, the reward, or evidence of achievement which indicated reward, might be necessary as "often as once an hour."[38] Taylor believed that many workmen were incapable of looking very far ahead and, therefore, they

[33] *Ibid.*, p. 39.
[34] *Ibid.*, p. 137.
[35] Taylor, *Scientific Management*, p. 121.
[36] *Ibid.*
[37] Robert F. Hoxie, *Scientific Management and Labor* (New York, 1921), p. 83.
[38] Taylor, *Scientific Management*, p. 94.

would not work hard for a bonus at the end of six months. For this reason he thought that profit-sharing plans were ineffective. On the other hand "if they see a definite opportunity of earning so many cents by working hard for so many minutes, they will avail themselves of it." [29] But there was also the negative side, and rewards in the form of better pay were only half of his plan for getting men to achieve the task assigned by management. The other half was punishment for failure to complete the task in the established time. This punishment took the form of lowered pay and, if the failure continued, of eventual discharge. As he said, "All of those who, after proper teaching, either will not or cannot work in accordance with the new methods and at higher speed must be discharged by the management." [40]

The fourth element was what Taylor called functional foremanship. After a job has been studied scientifically and all of its aspects had been standardized and tasks had been assigned, it was necessary to teach the new methods to the men and to see that the job was done by the men in the right way. According to Taylor, this was so because "Human nature is such . . . that many of the workmen, if left to themselves, would pay but little attention to their written instructions. It is necessary, therefore, to provide teachers (called functional foremen) to see that the workmen both understand and *carry out* these written instructions." [41] The number and type of foremen who would be used under the Taylor System depended on the size of the shop or plant, and to some extent upon the nature of the work being done. But in every instance the principle was that of extreme specialization. Management should arrange the work so that each man should have as few functions as possible to perform and Taylor's goal was that "the work of each man in the management should be confined to the performance of a single leading function." [42]

Taylor criticized the arrangement prevailing in most shops, which he called the military type, not on the ground that it was authoritarian, but because it expected too much of one foreman. Under this system, one man was in charge of one entire shop, and Taylor believed this man was likely to be a jack-of-all-trades and a master of none. Under his system, this single military-type foreman would be replaced by "eight different bosses." [43] These functional foremen who were the "expert teachers" chosen for their knowledge and skill in special fields were, first, the inspector, who helped the worker under-

[39] Taylor, *Shop Management*, p. 84.
[40] Taylor, *Scientific Management*, p. 83.
[41] Taylor, *Scientific Management*, p. 123.
[42] Taylor, *Shop Management*, p. 99.
[43] *Ibid.*

stand his instruction card and drawings; second, the gang boss, who taught the worker how to set up the work in his machine and how to make all of his personal motions in the quickest and best way; third, the speed boss, whose job was to see that the machine was run at right speed, that the proper tools were used, and that the machine turned out the product in the least possible time; fourth, the repair boss, who attended to the adjustment and maintenance of the machine; fifth, the time clerk, who kept written records of output and of pay due the men; sixth, the route clerk, who supervised the routing of the work from one part of the shop to another and determined the order in which work would be done; and seventh, the disciplinarian, whose job it was to "interview" the worker in case he got into difficulty with any of his other bosses.[44] These foremen were to be in the shop at all times, instructing, helping, and checking on the men. Each foreman had to be able to demonstrate that he could practice what he taught if this were necessary.

One last major element of the mechanism of the Taylor System needs to be described and that is the planning department. Taylor's idea was that "the shop and indeed the whole works, would be managed, not by the manager, superintendent or foreman, but by the planning department."[45] The job of the planning department, through its scientific time and motion study, was to develop the science of the job, which involved the establishment of many rules, laws, and formulae to replace the judgment of the individual workman.[46] This planning and developing the science of the job was done even with elementary laboring jobs. At Bethlehem Steel, for example, a labor office was established for the work in the yards where "every laborer's work was planned out well in advance, and the workmen were all moved from place to place by the clerks with elaborate diagrams or maps of the yard before them, very much as chessmen are moved on a chessboard. . . ."[47]

Taylor was criticized on the ground that under his system there were too many unproductive persons, i.e., planners, functional foreman, and clerks, eating up the profits of the plant. He answered this criticism by showing what he said were the results of his system. The figures he gave, which indicated the success of his work at the end of his third year in the yards at Bethlehem, were as follows: *The number of yard laborers had been reduced from approximately 500 to 140; the average number of tons moved per man per day was increased*

[44] Taylor, *Scientific Management*, pp. 124–25. Taylor does not mention the eighth foreman's role.

[45] Taylor, *Shop Management*, p. 110.

[46] Taylor, *Scientific Management*, p. 37.

[47] *Ibid.*, p. 69.

*from 16 to 59; the average earnings of these men were increased from
$1.15 per day to $1.88; and the average cost of handling a ton of
material was reduced from 7 cents to 3 1/3 cents, and this figure included the costs of wages of foremen, clerks and time study men and
all other costs of his system. Overall, he claimed that in a six months'
period when all of the work in the yard was under his system, the
company was saving at a rate of between seventy-five and eighty
thousand dollars per year.*[48]

There were other elements in the mechanism of scientific management — in fact, Taylor listed thirteen. Some of these, such as the slide
rule and instruction cards for workers, have been discussed under the
four elements already described, while one other, his mnemonic system for classifying and numbering tools, was an extension of the
standardization process. Likewise, the differential rate plan was a
variation of the bonus plan. Other elements, such as his routing system and his cost accounting, were important but not central in his
system.

In describing his system in his writing Taylor used three major
examples. One was the bricklaying experimentation done by Frank
Gilbreth. A second was the work done by Taylor himself at a ball-
bearing plant in Fitchburg, Massachusetts. The third was a part of
his work done in the yards at Bethlehem Steel from 1897 to 1900.
This third example, which involved the lifting and loading of pig
iron, was given a central part in his last book, where it was described
and discussed in detail. The pig iron example will be described here
because it was given such a prominent place by Taylor in both of his
books and was considered by him to be an excellent example of the
nature and operation of his system of scientific management.

Schmidt, Pig Iron, and First-Class Men

According to Taylor, Bethlehem Steel had been having difficulty in
the 1890's selling its pig iron for a profit and as a result had stored
some 80,000 tons of this material in piles in the company yards.
When the Spanish-American War started, the price of pig iron rose
and Bethlehem began to sell its surpluses. The job of moving this pig
iron gave Taylor "a good opportunity to show the workmen, as well
as the owners and managers of the works, on a fairly large scale the
advantages of task work over the old fashioned day work and piece
work, in doing a very elementary class of work."[49] This work had
been done before, of course, and Bethlehem had a regular gang of

[48] *Ibid.*, p. 71.
[49] *Ibid.*, pp. 41–42.

pig-iron handlers. Taylor reported that when he arrived there were some 75 men in this group and they were, he said, "good, average pig-iron handlers"; they worked under an "excellent foreman who himself had been a pig-iron handler"; and the work was being done as fast and as cheap as it was in other plants.[50]

The job itself was very simple. It consisted of lifting a pig of iron which weighed 92 pounds, carrying it some 30 or 40 feet and then up an inclined plank into a railway car, and depositing the pig of iron on the floor of the car. When Taylor began his work the men were loading an average of $12\frac{1}{2}$ long tons per day. This meant that each man was lifting, carrying, and loading some 304 pigs in his ten-hour day, some thirty pigs each hour, one every two minutes. He had been warned that these men were "steady workers, but slow and phlegmatic, and that nothing could induce them to work fast."[51]

His first step was to make a time and motion study of the job. Because he was busy with other work, Taylor placed an "intelligent, college-educated man" who was not familiar with pig-iron handling, although "he understood handling workmen," in charge of the study. This person, who apparently had been trained in engineering, was not familiar with Taylor's methods and therefore had to be taught "the art of determining how much work a first-class man can do in a day."[52] This was done by dividing the work into its elements, and then timing each element with a stop watch. With the pig-iron handlers these elements were described as follows:

(a) picking up the pig from the ground or pile (time in hundredths of a minute); (b) walking with it on a level (time per foot walked); (c) walking with it up an incline to car (time per foot walked); (d) throwing the pig down (time in hundredths of a minute), or laying it on a pile (time in hundredths of a minute); (e) walking back empty to get a load (time per foot walked).

In case of important elements which were to enter into a number of rates, a large number of observations were taken when practicable on different first-class men, and at different times, and they were averaged.[53]

As a result of this study, it was determined that a first-class man should be able to handle 48 tons of pig iron per day instead of $12\frac{1}{2}$. This figure seemed so high, even to Taylor, that he checked and re-checked his figures, but finally decided that they were correct. Once he and his associates were sure, Taylor felt that it was their duty as "managers under the modern scientific plan" to see that the pig iron

[50] *Ibid.*, p. 42.
[51] Taylor, *Shop Management*, p. 48.
[52] *Ibid.*
[53] *Ibid.*, pp. 48–49.

was loaded at the rate of 47 to 48 tons per day.[54] But this was not all, for Taylor said, "It was further our duty to see that this work was done without bringing on a strike among the men, without any quarrel with the men, and to see that the men were happier and better contented when loading at the new rate of 47 tons than they were when loading at the old rate of 12½ tons."[55]

The problem of determining the amount of work a first-class man could do in a day was solved quickly by Taylor after the time and motion study had been done, because of a series of experiments he had conducted in human fatigue over a period of years preceding his work at Bethlehem Steel. By combining the knowledge of the time a first-class man could stand under strain, and the speed with which the various motions required on the job could be performed, he arrived at his figure of 47½ tons to be set as the task to be achieved. Under this schedule, the worker would lift, carry, and load 106,400 pounds per day compared with 28,000 pounds per day on the regular basis. At this new rate, the worker would handle 1,156 pigs instead of 304 in a ten-hour day. And the worker would handle 115 pigs per hour, or almost two each minute, as compared with 30 pigs per hour, or one every two minutes, under the old plan. The bonus that was "scientifically" decided upon for this task was a 60 per cent increase, or, from $1.15 per day to $1.85 per day.

After the "science of the job" had been developed, the next step was to select a first-class man and induce him to work at the desired speed, then to train him for the job. Taylor and his associate spent three or four days watching the gang of 75 pig-iron handlers. Four were selected who "appeared to be physically able to handle pig-iron at the rate of 47 tons per day."[56] After a careful study was made of these four, including a study of their "character," "habits," and "ambition," one was selected. Taylor describes this man and his characteristics and then the way in which he was handled under scientific management as follows:

He was a little Pennsylvania Dutchman who had been observed to trot back home for a mile or so after his work in the evening about as fresh as he was when he came trotting down to work in the morning. We found that upon wages of $1.15 a day he had succeeded in buying a small plot of ground, and that he was engaged in putting up the walls of a little house for himself in the morning before starting to work and at night after leaving. He also had the reputation of being exceedingly "close", that is, of placing a very high

[54] Taylor, *Scientific Management*, pp. 42–43.
[55] *Ibid.*, p. 43.
[56] *Ibid.*

value on a dollar. As one man whom we talked to about him said, "A penny looks about the size of a cart wheel to him." This man we will call Schmidt.

The task before us, then, narrowed itself down to getting Schmidt to handle 47 tons of pig-iron per day and making him glad to do it. This was done as follows. Schmidt was called out from among the gang of pig-iron handlers and talked to somewhat in this way:

"Schmidt, are you a high-priced man?

Vell, I don't know vat you mean?

Oh yes, you do. What I want to know is whether you are a high-priced man or not.

Vell, I don't know vat you mean?

Oh, come now, you answer my questions. What I want to find out is whether you are a high-priced man or one of these cheap fellows here. What I want to find out is whether you want to earn $1.85 a day or whether you are satisfied with $1.15, just the same as all those cheap fellows are getting.

Did I vant $1.85 a day? Vas dot a high-priced man? Well, yes, I vas a high-priced man.

Oh, you're aggravating me. Of course you want $1.85 a day — everyone wants it! You know perfectly well that that has very little to do with your being a high-priced man. For goodness sake answer my questions, and don't waste any more of my time. Now come over here. You see that pile of pig-iron?

Yes.

You see that car?

Yes.

Well, if you are a high-priced man, you will load that pig-iron on that car tomorrow for $1.85. Now so wake up and answer my question. Tell me whether you are a high-priced man or not.

Vell — did I got $1.85 for loading dot pig iron on dot car tomorrow?

Yes, of course you do, and you get $1.85 for loading a pile like that every day right through the year. That is what a high-priced man does, and you know it just as well as I do.

Vell, dot's all right. I could load dot pig-iron on the car tomorrow for $1.85, and I get it every day, don't I?

Certainly you do — certainly you do.

Vell, den, I vas a high-priced man.

Now, hold on, hold on. You know just as well as I do that a high-priced man has to do exactly as he's told from morning till night. You have seen this man here before, haven't you?

Well, if you are a high-priced man, you will do exactly as this man tells you tomorrow, from morning till night. When he tells you to pick up a pig and walk, you pick it up and you walk, and when he tells you to sit down and rest, you sit down. You do that right straight through the day. And what's more, no back talk. Now a high-priced man does just what he's told to do, and no back talk. Do you understand that? When this man tells you to walk, you walk; when he tells you to sit down, you sit down, and you don't talk back at him. Now you come on to work here tomorrow morning and I'll know before night whether you are really a high-priced man or not. . . ."

Schmidt started to work, and all day long, and at regular intervals, was told by the man who stood over him with a watch, "Now pick up a pig and walk. Now sit down and rest. Now walk — now rest," etc. He worked when he was told to work, and rested when he was told to rest, and at half past five in the afternoon had his 47½ tons loaded on the car. And he practically never failed to work at this pace and do the task that was set him during the three years that the writer was at Bethlehem. And, throughout this time he averaged a little more than $1.85 per day, whereas before he had never received over $1.15 per day, which was the ruling rate of wages at that time in Bethlehem. That is, he received 60 per cent higher wages than were paid to other men who were not working on task work. One man after another was picked out and trained to handle pig-iron at the rate of 47½ tons per day until all of the pig-iron was handled at this rate, and the men were receiving 60 per cent more wages than other workmen around them.[57]

Taylor apparently anticipated that this manipulation of Schmidt and especially the cavalier manner in which it was done would evoke some criticism so he defended his actions: first, on the ground that Schmidt was a pretty dull fellow anyway; and second, on the ground that his procedure was the only one that would work since it was effective "in fixing his attention on the high wages which he wants and away from what, if it were called to his attention, he probably would consider impossibly hard work."[58]

After getting Schmidt up to this level of achievement, which a more thoughtful man than Schmidt might have considered a groove or even a deep rut, Taylor's *duty* was to teach and train the other pig-iron handlers. One after another of the men were given the opportunity of improving themselves as Schmidt had done. If they failed they "were either persuaded or intimidated into giving it up."[59]

Those who hold the view that in the western world we are on the downward path from a golden age somewhere in the distant past will probably sigh nostalgically and say that men cast from Schmidt's mold are gone forever. They will be even more disposed to do this when they learn that he not only was not a giant of a man but actually weighed only 130 pounds![60] But, as usual, cruel facts are the killers of the dream, and the fact is that even in those days only one man in eight was able to handle 47½ tons of steel per day. Other readers, with more human interest, will want to know what happened to Schmidt the man. Did he continue to be a first-class man for Beth-

[57] *Ibid.*, pp. 43–47.
[58] *Ibid.*, p. 46.
[59] Taylor, *Shop Management*, pp. 50–51.
[60] *Ibid.*, p. 50.

lehem Steel and scientific management? Or did he eventually die of exhaustion after having reached his peak so quickly? Taylor reports that Schmidt stayed on the job all the time that he (Taylor) was at Bethlehem, "and some years later was still at the same work."[61] Taylor claimed that all the men who succeeded and worked under the task and bonus system became "not only more thrifty but better men in every way; that they live rather better, begin to save money, become more sober, and work more steadily."[62] For Taylor to point out that these men worked *more steadily* was, perhaps, under the circumstances, unnecessary. And some pundit might remark that they saved money and were more sober because they were too tired to spend or drink.

Unfortunately for posterity, Taylor did not answer what, to many, will seem the most interesting questions of all about Schmidt. These were whether, after raising his output from $12\frac{1}{2}$ to 48 tons, he continued to trot back and forth to work and, most important of all, whether he ever finished building the walls of his little house.

In some respects it was unfortunate that Taylor placed so much emphasis and gave such a prominent place in his writing to his work with the pig-iron handlers at Bethlehem Steel. Schmidt, the living embodiment of Taylor's ideal of the first-class man and the epitome of human efficiency, came to be a well-known and controversial figure. Labor leaders and humanitarians were shocked and then indignant at the way he had been treated. It got so bad that Taylor stopped using Schmidt, and some of the proponents of scientific management refrained from using Taylor's name in connection with the system. A few years after this controversy over Schmidt, rumors were circulated that Schmidt had died, presumably from overwork. A year or so later, labor leaders brought the matter up again and Taylor, harassed and distraught, hired a person to locate the famous pig-iron handler and get the facts. Finally the man was located, and Taylor had him examined by a physician who declared him to be healthy and thriving.[63]

Nor was the fear of and hostility toward the Taylor system limited to the United States. It will be remembered that Taylor's work had been translated into French and so enthusiastically received by industrial managers there that a foundation had been established to further his system. But the workers were not quite so enthusiastic. In February of 1913, an article on the Taylor system appeared in the French sporting journal, *L'Auto*. This article received wide attention

[61] *Ibid.*
[62] Taylor, *Scientific Management*, p. 74.
[63] Copley, *op. cit.*, II, 55.

and after being "passed from hand to hand among the workers" made the Taylor system the focus of "the liveliest indignation." The article concluded with this interesting account:

The Taylor System is pitiless; it eliminates the unfit and those who have passed the age of the greatest muscular activity. Here we are reminded of a story formerly related by Fraser.

On visiting Pittsburgh, the English engineer, struck by the fact that he encountered only young and vigorous workers, asked the American who was guiding him, "Where are your old workers?"

At first the American did not answer; but finally, on the insistence of Fraser, he offered him his cigar case and said casually, "Have a cigar, and while we are smoking we will go visit the cemetery."[64]

Taylor's handling of Schmidt was unfortunate because it caused Taylor himself so much unpleasantness and because it gave a distorted picture of both the man and his system. The man was an outstanding, creative engineer, as well as a fine scientist. In his work with metals he exhibited the creative imagination, the persistence, and the singleness of purpose of a scientist. *When educational administrators attempted to bring his system into the schools, they showed no real interest in, or ability to carry out, such painstaking research.*

Nevertheless there was a genuine basis for the hostility that developed. For Taylor, as the leader of the scientific management movement, had not only openly criticized unions but had given his critics ample cause for questioning his belief in the dignity of man as well as his concern for man's welfare, when he wrote: "Now one of the very first requirements for a man who is fit to handle pig-iron as a regular occupation is that he shall be so stupid and so phlegmatic that he more nearly resembles in his mental make-up the ox than any other type."[65] And speaking of Schmidt, he said: "He merely happened to be a man of the type of the ox, — no rare specimen of humanity. . . . On the contrary, he was a man so stupid that he was unfitted to do most kinds of laboring work, even."[66] It was this kind of language, added to his description of Schmidt's work, that led to the fear, anxiety, and antagonism of labor and to the indignation of humanitarians.[67]

[64] Quoted in H. Dubreuil, *Robots or Men* (New York, 1930), pp. 65–66.

[65] Taylor, *Scientific Management*, p. 59.

[66] *Ibid.*, p. 62.

[67] An example of the hostility of labor was the following statement by Samuel Gompers in the *American Federationst* (XVIII, 116) in February, 1911, in an editorial entitled "Machinery To Perfect the Living Machine": "So, there you are, wage workers in general, mere machines — considered industrially, of course. Hence, why should you not be standardized and your motion-power brought up to the highest possible perfection in all respects, including speed? Not only your length, breadth, and thickness as a machine, but

There were other factors which eventually brought about strong opposition to his system. One was that the claims for the new system were so extravagant that they could not possibly have been realized and some disenchantment was inevitable. Taylor had warned against the tendency to accept his system as a magical cure-all but could not stem the enthusiasm.[68] But he had also been guilty of claiming a universality for his ideas which went far beyond their applicability. Another development which helped to generate hostility toward his system was the appearance (also recognized and criticized by Taylor) of many self-styled efficiency experts. According to Hoxie scientific management as a movement was

cursed with fakirs. The great rewards which a few leaders in the movement have secured for their services have brought into the field a crowd of industrial patent-medicine men. The way is open to all. No standards or requirements, private or public, have been developed by the application of which the goats can be separated from the sheep. Employers have thus far proved credulous. Almost anyone can show the average manufacturing concern where it can make some improvements in its methods. So the scientific management shingles have gone up all over the country, the fakirs have gone into the shops, and in the name of scientific management have reaped temporary gains to the detriment of the real article, the employers and the workers.[69]

Finally, it is clear that much of the difficulty was inherent in the complexities of the human problems involved in modern industry — problems that men like Taylor, Gantt, and Gilbreth only dimly perceived in the early years. Excellent engineers that they were, they were not prepared by their training to cope with such problems.

This, then, ends the account of Frederick Taylor and his system of scientific management and begins the story of the influence of his ideas on varied aspects of American education. His ideas were adopted, interpreted, and applied chiefly by administrators; and while the greatest impact was upon administration, the administrator, and the professional training programs of administration, the influence extended to all of American education from the elementary schools to the universities.

your grade of hardness, malleability, tractability, and general serviceability, can be ascertained, registered, and then employed as desirable. Science would thus get the most out of you before you are sent to the junk pile."

[68] The *Nation* in a most insightful editorial had warned against considering scientific management as a magical formula, pointing to the "infinite care," the "infinite persistence," and the "laborious research" which was required (Vol. XCIII [May 11, 1911], p. 464). Taylor responded with a letter in which he indicated his approval of and his appreciation for these views. *Nation*, XCIV (June 15, 1911), 602.

[69] Hoxie, *op. cit.*, p. 117.

3

CRITICISM AND RESPONSE
IN THE EARLY YEARS OF THE
EFFICIENCY ERA

In the fall of 1910 the efficiency expert made his grand entrance into American society. His debut was a tremendous success and had the effect of propelling Frederick Taylor into national prominence and helping to make the country efficiency-conscious. In the years that followed the words "efficiency" and "scientific management" appeared so frequently in the press that, if Professor Gabriel is correct in stating that "An age is known by its catchwords," it is appropriate to label this period in American history as an "Age of Efficiency."[1]

The rapid spread and acceptance of the ideas associated with scientific management were due in part to conditions which existed in American society (e.g., the rising cost of living, the years of publicity given to conservation and the elimination of waste, and the reform attitude of the public) and in part to the fact that "scientific management" had captured the imagination of the American people. Its enthusiastic reception was, of course, both manifested in and generated by the popular press. But in the process of publicizing "scientific management" writers not only claimed the advantages of its application to all institutions, but they also presented it as a system which could be applied not only by experts but by anyone with common sense. This simplified, non-technical characterization of Taylor's system along with the numerous examples of applying it contributed to its popularity and encouraged people without adequate training to become "efficiency experts."

Taylor was partly responsible for the notion of universal applica-

[1] Ralph Henry Gabriel, *The Course of American Democratic Thought* (New York, 1940), p. 336.

bility, for he had said that his principles could be "applied with equal force to all social activities: to the management of our homes; the management of our farms; the management of the business of our tradesmen, large and small; of our churches, our philanthropic institutions, our universities, and our governmental departments."[2] The same claim was made with greater enthusiasm by Harrington Emerson who, in addition, placed less emphasis on the need for expertness and scientific training in applying scientific management and in achieving efficiency.

But the major assurance that scientific management had universal applicability and could be applied by anyone with common sense came from the popular journals. In July of 1911, shortly after Taylor's articles had been published, the editors of the *Saturday Evening Post* told their readers that there was "nothing fundamentally new about scientific management" and that the important thing was the development of a "persistently critical attitude." With this attitude, said the *Post*, "faults and wastes may be discovered almost anywhere." Significantly, the title of the editorial was "Scientific Management for All."[3] Two months later readers were told that scientific management was neither new nor complicated and that it was in fact "as old as truth itself" and "as simple as the alphabet." "In the ordinary store or office," said the author, "you can apply it yourself. . . . Any average man, with faculties reasonably analytical, can make time-studies and can learn to know goods."[4]

Perhaps as a result of this propaganda, the field of management had become top-heavy with theorists, some of whom were honest and well-intentioned and some outright fakes. This dilemma, said Forrest Crissey, writing in the *Saturday Evening Post*, left several courses open to the factory manager who had become "converted to this modern gospel." One was to hire an efficiency expert and take his chances. Another was to "become his own efficiency expert."[5] After giving detailed instructions on how this could be done, he concluded by pointing out that after all "the keynote to scientific management is cutting costs and that includes the elimination of wastes." The whole thing, he said, "is nothing less than organized common-sense applied to making cost go down instead of up. And it is by far the most effective agency to that end that yet has been discovered."[6]

[2] Frederick Taylor, *The Principles of Scientific Management* (New York, 1911), p. 8.

[3] *Saturday Evening Post*, CLXXXIV (July 29, 1911), 8.

[4] Edward Mott Woolley, "Cutting Out the Motions in Business," *Saturday Evening Post*, CLXXXIV (September 9, 1911), 28.

[5] "The Selfmade Efficiency Expert," *Saturday Evening Post*, CLXXXV (November 2, 1912), 10.

[6] *Ibid.*, p. 58.

Other popular journals began to feature articles in which suggestions were made for applying the new system. In August of 1911 an article by Francis E. Leupp entitled "Scientific Management in the Family" was published in the *Outlook*. Mr. Leupp suggested that the family be carefully organized with a planned division of labor so there would be no overlapping of functions, and he recommended that someone be made responsible and held accountable for each household task. He also suggested that understudies be trained for each role so that in case of illness or death each job would be taken over quickly. This practice, he said, had been used in "factories and accounting offices, railways, and mining enterprises," and there was no reason why "it should not be extended to the family adminstration."[7]

The response to Leupp's article must have been favorable for in December of 1911 the editors of the *Outlook* began a series of articles on "Home Efficiency." In announcing the series the problem was introduced with some pertinent questions such as: "Does your home pay? Does it make a fair return on the investment of time and strength and money that is put into it? As a factory for the production of citizenship is it a success?"[8] Perhaps the most interesting article in the series appeared in April of 1912. It was written by John B. Guernsey and appropriately entitled "Scientific Management in the Home." "Cannot the management of the average household be conducted as a business proposition?" he asked. His answer was that it could and he claimed, in the tradition of Harrington Emerson, that "enormous economies" could be achieved thereby. As a part of the application of Taylor's ideas Guernsey suggested that the "management" work out ten or twelve standardized meals each with a standard content, a standard procedure, and a standard time. On the question of time studies he demonstrated how they could be used in the making of biscuits, which process he broke down into eighteen operations with the time allotment (in seconds) provided for each step. For those servants who developed into efficient first-class workers, and who, for example, did not waste seconds gazing out of the window while putting the biscuits into the oven, he suggested an appropriate reward.[9]

This article evoked some sharp criticism from readers, one of whom pointed out that for the ordinary family to adopt his scheme would be "about as practical as coupling a steam locomotive to a baby carriage," while another was incensed at the inhumanity of

[7] *Outlook*, XCVIII (August 12, 1911), 836.
[8] *Ibid.*, XCIX (December 2, 1911), 807.
[9] *Ibid.*, C (April 13, 1912), 821–25.

preventing a servant from enjoying the aesthetic experience of gazing out of the window for 102 seconds.[10]

At the same time scientific management was being adapted to the home and family, it was also being applied to the churches. One prominent clergyman, Dr. Shailer Matthews of the University of Chicago, praised Taylor's work as a "practical philosophy destined to replace haphazard, traditional methods."[11] Church workers, he said, had to be taught to "work under direction according to plans" even if this meant the loss of some initiative, for this was what the "philosophy of efficiency demands."[12] Efficiency also demanded, Matthews said, that churches keep proper records:

> A really efficient church should have application blanks for membership which cover pledges to render service, cards for the assignment of particular tasks to the various members, blanks on which they shall report, and a card catalogue, always kept up to date, of church membership and of past members of the church or congregation. . . . If this seems to make the church something of a business establishment it is precisely what should be the case. We have too long regarded the church as capable of performing its possible services to the community without the most elementary means of administration.[13]

When Matthews made some of the same comments before a group of Presbyterian ministers in the fall of 1912, his speech evoked a critical response from the *Nation*. The editorial, entitled "Efficiency Tests for Clergymen," began by asking "As the modern efficiency expert pursues his devastating way, the troubled question is more and more frequently heard: 'Who of us is safe?'" The college professor, said the *Nation*, was no longer immune, for he had been asked to punch time clocks and justify his efforts by daily records. Now the clergy were being subjected to the same treatment. According to the press reports, Matthews had criticized the clergy for their shocking waste of time and, added the *Nation*, "they seem to have as many unnecessary motions as the old-style bricklayer." The editor, speculating on the consequences of his advice, sketched out a theoretical time card which a minister might fill in as follows:

> 9:30 to 10:27, visited the widow and the fatherless in their affliction.
> 10:27 to 11:03, bound up three broken-hearted.
> 11:03 to 12:15, at the hospital. Spoke to ten patients. Repeated twelve verses from the Scriptures. Offered three prayers. Recited four hymns.
> 12:15 to 12:32, lunch.

[10] *Ibid.*, CII (September 14, 1912), 74.
[11] Shailer Matthews, *Scientific Management in the Churches* (Chicago, 1912), pp. 1–2.
[12] *Ibid.*, p. 37.
[13] *Ibid.*, pp. 57–58.

12:32 to 3:10, made a round of the classes in sewing, cooking, athletics, and inspected two companies of boy scouts.

3:10 to 5:20, kept office hours, seeing five book-agents, three applicants for charity, two clerical impostors, a delegation from the Daughters of the Revolution, and six persons with suggestions about enriching the church services and improving the sermons.

Summing up the whole day, I humbly reckon my efficiency percentage at 97.3.

The editor softened his criticism by disclaiming any intention of burlesquing the work of the clergy and by admitting the need for conducting church activities "in a business way." But he warned against the application of efficiency tests in areas of human life where they did not belong. "What way is there," he asked, "of making an arithmetical estimate of the services of Father Damien, or of any clergyman who goes fearlessly where infection or plague is raging?"[14]

An account of the spread of scientific management into American life could go on at great length, but the pattern was much the same whether the analysis was made of the army, the navy, (and in fact many of the governmental agencies or divisions) or of the various professions such as law, medicine, and engineering. Naturally, the greatest impact was upon business and industry. But the new industrial philosophy had received, as one writer in a popular journal put it, "worldwide notice" and had been "discussed from a thousand angles," even finding its way into popular fiction.[15]

In addition, the total impact of scientific management was augmented and was itself made more pervasive by its close association with the more general notion of efficiency which was constantly being stressed by such leaders in American society as Theodore Roosevelt, who, in an address to students which received attention in the popular press, said,

You must be efficient, you must be able to hold your own in the world of politics, the world of business, able to keep your own head above water, to make your work satisfactory, to make it pay. If you do not, you cannot do good to others. You must be efficient. You must never forget for a moment that, so far from being a base theory, it is a vital doctrine, a doctrine vital to good in this country.[16]

Mounting Criticism of Education 1911–13

The publicity given scientific management and the great claims made in its behalf intensified the public's feeling that great waste

[14] *Nation*, XCV (October, 1912), 402–3.
[15] James H. Collins, "Figuring the Net Value of Efficiency," *Saturday Evening Post*, CLXXV (March, 1913), 9.
[16] *Outlook*, CIV (August 2, 1913), 751.

existed everywhere, and at the same time offered a means of eliminating it. One result was that a new wave of criticism was directed against many institutions, especially those large enough to be suspected of gross managerial inefficiency and those supported by public taxation. The schools, particularly in the larger cities, met both of these criteria. Beginning early in 1911 hardly a month passed for two years in which articles complaining about the schools were not published either in the popular or in the professional journals. Gradually the criticism grew in volume, reaching a peak in the spring, summer, and fall of 1912. In these months a series of sensational articles were published in two of the popular journals with tremendous circulations, the *Saturday Evening Post* and the *Ladies' Home Journal*. As the criticism mounted, the efforts of educators increased accordingly to meet the demands.

As early as February, 1911, one superintendent from Iowa wrote that "much criticism" was being directed against the public schools and he testified that the charge was "our system is inefficient and impractical." He placed the responsibility for the "present criticism" on commercial interests who, he said, looked "only for immediate earning capacity." He was against changing the curriculum and insisted that courses in science, history, mathematics, and language constituted the best possible program for American students. Yet, even in defending the schools, he made a concession to the critics by stating, "what we need is more efficient management of the old system instead of something new."[17] The more typical attitude of schoolmen was taken in March by M. C. Wilson of the State Normal School at Florence, Alabama. Noting that there were "signs of discontent," he stated that "one hears many protests from the business house, the factory, the farm, and from every form of industry. . . ." Then he not only joined the critics by agreeing that the school did not fit children to earn a living but also contended that the school failed in moral training and in academic work. Perhaps, he said, it was time to ask whether educators should "discard the old machine for a lighter and a more efficient one?"[18]

In May of 1911, as the final instalment of Taylor's series was appearing in the *American Magazine*, educators were given a preview of the vicious criticism they were to experience the following year. Simon Patten, well-known economist-reformer, writing in the influential *Educational Review* demanded that schools provide evidence of

[17] E. T. Armstrong, "Is Our Present High School System Inefficient?" *American School Board Journal*, XLII, 3–4.

[18] "Some Defects in Our Public School System," *Educational Review*, XLI (March, 1911), 238–44.

their contribution to society or have their budgets cut. "The advocate of pure water or clean streets," said Patten, "shows by how much the death rate will be altered by each proposed addition to his share of the budget. . . . Only the teacher is without such figures." Why, he asked, should New York spend its money on schools instead of on subways, parks, and playgrounds? Why should it "support inefficient school teachers instead of efficient milk inspectors? Must definite reforms with *measurable results* give way that *an antiquated school system may grind out its useless product?*" Patten challenged educators to answer his question by showing results that could be "readily seen and measured."[19]

Patten was irritated by the fact that many educators had remained aloof from the struggle to improve the worst abuses of industrial America and had limited their participation to a pious but safe concern for something they called character-building. Undoubtedly too, there was too little attention given in the schools (as Dewey frequently claimed) to the study of America in the twentieth century. But regardless of these facts his criticism was an intemperate, anti-intellectual attack in which he both misunderstood and grossly oversimplified the educational process. He did not recognize that the social sciences were not at this time sufficiently developed to give valid and reliable measurements of educational outcomes. And in addition to pushing educators prematurely toward attempts to show results quantitatively, his criticism played into the hands of those who wanted to use the schools to train clerks and factory hands as well as those who were seeking excuses to economize regardless of the consequences. In both his demand for tangible results and his threat of cutting funds he hit educators where they were most vulnerable.

In the summer and fall of 1911 the popular journals printed a few articles on the schools which indicated that public criticism was mounting. For example, the *Ladies' Home Journal*, in an editorial entitled "What Is the Matter?" reported that their letters from readers indicated that dissatisfaction with the schools was increasing and, said the editor, "on every hand the signs are evident of a widely growing distrust of the effectiveness of the present educational system in this country."[20] The publicity given the efficiency movement began to have its effect. In Providence, Rhode Island the school board was criticized by the press for declaring a holiday on a Monday preceding Decoration Day to allow students a four-day vacation. This action, said the newspaper, cost the taxpayers five thousand dollars, not in actual ap-

[19] "An Economic Measure of School Efficiency," *Educational Review*, XLI (May, 1911), 467–69. (Italics mine.)
[20] Vol. XXVIII (June, 1911), p. 5.

propriation, but in terms of loss of possible returns on the money invested. The board's action was described as "poor business" and "not scientific economy."[21] Later in the year the Des Moines school board was "found guilty, by the local press, of extravagance and loose business methods on a dozen or more counts."[22] It had become quite clear, as one educator put it, that educators were being "compelled to face a powerful adverse public criticism — a criticism not of the existence or public support of the schools but rather of their efficiency."[23]

Then in February, 1912, school administrators were, one might say, bearded in their own den when this criticism was carried by a lay speaker into the meeting of the Department of Superintendence of the National Education Association held in St. Louis. They were accused of being inefficient, and they were given suggestions for remedying their faults. The speaker, George H. Chatfield, secretary of the Permanent Census Board in New York City, early in his speech reminded his audience that "the efficiency of our school system is questioned" and he added that "not within memory has the attention of schoolmen focused so persistently in this direction." Critics were everywhere and investigations of school systems were increasing. Since the fundamental doctrine of these innovators was the "elimination of waste," he reminded the administrators of the new developments in industry in which "new processes, new labor-saving devices, new methods of planning, more detailed instructions, more exacting records" were being used and production was being doubled and even tripled. Citing several examples of the detailed records kept by certain industrial concerns, and the profits achieved thereby, he urged schoolmen to follow in their footsteps. How else, he asked, could the educator justify himself "when the businessman complains of his product."[24]

As the school superintendents boarded their trains at Union Station in St. Louis to return home, they had reason to be apprehensive, and they probably gave considerable thought during the trip to ways and means of making their schools more efficient. Undoubtedly, some of them entertained fond hopes that the criticism would subside and part of the tension would be relieved. If they did, they were soon to realize that this was only wishful thinking. But it is doubtful that even the most pessimistic among them was prepared for the onslaught of the next nine months.

This assault came from the two popular journals, the *Ladies' Home Journal* and the *Saturday Evening Post* which not only had circula-

[21] Reported in *American School Board Journal*, XLIII (July, 1911), 2.
[22] *Ibid.* (December, 1911), p. 26.
[23] N.E.A. *Proceedings* (1911), p. 519.
[24] N.E.A. *Proceedings* (1912), pp. 387–90.

tions in the millions, but were journals which catered to and were read largely by those middle-class groups who had led the progressive movement and had become reform-conscious in the preceding decade. The *Post* began the serious lay attack with an article published early in March entitled "Our Medieval High Schools — Shall We Educate Children for the Twelfth or the Twentieth Century?" The author attacked the colleges which he said had "Miltonized, Chaucerized, Vergilized, Schillered, physicked and chemicaled the high school." Then he criticized the high schools for their emphasis upon "culture" and what he called a "gentleman's education." Educators in these schools, he said, were agreed that such education "should be of no use in the world — particularly in the business world" and that it should not be "desired by the mob."[25] This article was followed a week later by another entitled "Medieval Methods for Modern Children" in which the author broadened her criticism to include administration. "At present," she said, "there is inefficiency in the business management of many schools such as would not be tolerated in the world of offices and shops."[26]

These criticisms, although the titles were barometric, were mild in comparison with those which appeared in the *Ladies' Home Journal* in the summer of 1912. The attacks began with an editorial entitled "The Case of Seventeen Million Children — Is Our Public-School System Proving an Utter Failure?" The editor pointed out that the people of the United States had invested nearly a billion dollars in their schools and spent four hundred million dollars each year, and he concluded that "surely for so huge an outlay the returns should be stupendous." But what were the returns, he asked? Then he cited statistics on the small number of children who finished high school, on the number of illiterates (conceding, however, that two-thirds of these were Negroes, for whom little or no education had been provided, and immigrants), and on the relatively low (twenty out of twenty-five million) number of children in school. Despite these deplorable facts, said the editor, "our education is really preparing our children for a life of scholasticism — the stress is on a critical pursuit of literature and a dilettante acquaintance with the arts and sciences."[27]

The attack continued with an article entitled "Is the Public School a Failure? It Is: The Most Momentous Failure in Our American Life Today." The author, Ella Frances Lynch, a former teacher who claimed to have spent months of careful investigation in preparing her

[25] William Hughes Mearns, *Saturday Evening Post*, CLXXXIV (March 2, 1912), 18–19.
[26] Maude Radford Warren, *ibid.*, CLXXXII (March 12, 1912), 11–13, 34–35.
[27] *Ladies' Home Journal*, XXIX (August, 1912), 3.

article, stated that "the American public-school system, as at present conducted, is an absolute and total failure." Then she asked,

Can you imagine a more grossly stupid, a more genuinely asinine system tenaciously persisted in to the fearful detriment of over seventeen million children and at a cost to you of over four-hundred-and-three million dollars each year — a system that not only is absolutely ineffective in its results, but also actually harmful in that it throws every year ninety-three out of every one hundred children into the world of action absolutely unfitted for even the simplest tasks in life? Can you wonder that we have so many inefficient men and women; that in so many families there are so many failures; that our boys and girls can make so little money that in the one case they are driven into the saloons from discouragement, and in the other into the brothels to save themselves from starvation? Yet that is exactly what the public-school system is today doing, and has been doing.

The public school system, she said, was not something to be proud of but "a system that is today a shame to America."[28]

After this attack it would be difficult to believe that there would be anything left to say but the critical articles continued to be published. In September the *Journal* introduced an article by Frederic Burk, president of the San Francisco State Normal School, entitled "Are We Living in B. C. or A. D.?", with the "momentous failure" headline it had used previously.[29] The same issue of the *Journal* carried an article by William McAndrew, principal of the Washington Irving High School in New York on "The Danger of Running a Fool Factory," in which the author claimed that American education was "permeated with errors and hypocrisy."[30]

The *Journal* capped its contribution to American education in a November issue in which it presented a series of comments by leading Americans. James E. Russell, dean of Teacher's College, was quoted as saying that "our educational system is wasteful and inefficient." Boris Sidis of Harvard University said:

We desiccate, sterilize, petrify and embalm our youth. Our children learn by rote and are guided by routine. The present school system squanders the resources of the country and wastes the energy and the lives of our children. The school system should be abolished. Our educators are narrow-minded pedants, occupied with the dry bones of textbooks and the sawdust of pedagogics, who are ignorant of the real, vital problems of human interest.

And the indictment was completed by H. Martyn Hart, dean of St. Johns Cathedral in Denver, who, in the spirit of the times, blamed the schools for society's ills and traced it all to inefficiency:

[28] *Ibid.*, pp. 4–5.
[29] *Ladies' Home Journal*, XXIX (September, 1912), 5–6.
[30] *Ibid.*, p. 7.

The people have changed but not the system; it has grown antiquated and will
not meet our present needs; it has indeed become a positive detriment and is
producing a type of character which is not fit to meet virtuously the tempta-
tions and the exigencies of modern life. The crime which stalks almost un-
blushingly through the land; the want of responsibility which defames our
social honor; the appalling frequency of divorce; the utter lack of self-control;
the abundant use of illicit means to gain political positions; are all traceable
to its one great and crying defect — inefficiency.[31]

There the *Journal* ended its attacks. Early in 1913 it began a series
to point out what could be done to correct the evils it had exposed,
and the editor urged parents to see that reforms were introduced.[32]

The Vulnerability of School Administrators

The sudden propulsion of scientific management into prominence
and the subsequent saturation of American society with the idea of
efficiency together with the attacks on education by the popular journals made it certain that public education would be influenced greatly.
But the *extent* of this influence was increased by the vulnerability of
the leaders in the schools — the superintendents — to public opinion
and pressure.

As early as 1900 the professional survival of school superintendents depended on their ability to appease their most powerful and
vocal critics. In that year Superintendent Aaron Gove of Denver,
speaking before the Department of Superintendence of the National
Education Association, said that the reasons why superintendents lost
their jobs were "well in sight." He stated that

Neither scholarship nor executive ability alone had been found ample for
permanent occupation. . . . The school superintendent who, with competent
counsel added to his own expert ability, constructs a course of study, con-
demns the work of a poor teacher, objects to the engagement of inferior talent,
frowns upon the purchase of unnecessary apparatus, or, what is even more
threatening, recommends the substitution of a better text-book for a poor one,
understands full well that, however unanimous may be the support of his
board, many taxpayers, as well as mercantile and commercial interests, are
sure to take a hand either to forward or prevent the execution of whatever
plans he may devise. The inevitable letter to the press, over the anonymous
signature of "Taxpayer" is a reminder that the people propose to allow their
representatives on the school board to act their will only when it coincides
with that of the individual opinion. . . . And so one has a right to assume
that, in addition to the power and skill of the superintendent of great industries, the superintendent of schools needs another qualification — that of mol-

[31] *Ibid.* (November, 1912), p. 9.
[32] *Ibid.*, XXX (January, 1913), 3.

lifying and educating a great and not always prudent or well-informed constituency.[33]

Year by year after 1900 public opinion became a more powerful force as newspapers and popular journals featuring sensationalism and exposure reached an increasingly larger audience. And even though criticism of the schools was *relatively* light before 1911 the power of public opinion and the influence of pressure groups was felt increasingly, and the security of educators declined accordingly. By 1909 the situation was such that a leading administrator wrote, "The professional life of the American schoolmaster is beset by uncertainty. Except in very few cities we are laboriously building houses of cards which no matter how much care and effort we have expended, we may tomorrow surmount with one careless addition that falls flat and tumbles the whole structure to ruin."[34]

Less than two years later in January, 1911, when the efficiency movement was barely underway, the most influential journal in educational administration, the *American School Board Journal*, commented editorially on the professional insecurity of school administrators:

True it is, that the tenure of the school superintendent is an uncertain one and that his position is attended with vexatious conditions. These upheavals are so frequent and the discussions which find their way into the public press, so painful to the victim and disturbing to the school system, as to excite more than ordinary interest. . . . That the official life of the superintendent is a short one has been amply demonstrated. Where he changes from village to small city, from small city to large city he is still in the momentum of promotion, but the crisis is reached where a cold blooded decapitation confronts him. Much more serious becomes the fate of the new man who has reached a high position in school superintendency labors and who is threatened with premature retirement.[35]

[33] N.E.A. *Proceedings* (1900), 221. Additional testimony of the power of public opinion and the vulnerability of schoolmen was given to the same group the next year by John Dewey: "Consider the way by which a new study is introduced into the curriculum. Some one feels that the school system of his [or quite frequently nowadays her] town is falling behind the times. There are rumors of great progress in education being made elsewhere. Something new and important has been introduced; education is being revolutionized by it; the school superintendent, or members of the board of education, become somewhat uneasy; the matter is taken up by individuals and clubs; pressure is brought to bear on the managers of the school system; letters are written to the newspapers; the editor himself is appealed to to use his great power to advance the cause of progress; editorials appears; finally the school board ordains that on and after a certain date the particular new branch — be it nature study, industrial drawing, cooking, manual training, or whatever — shall be taught in the public schools. The victory is won, and everybody — unless it be some already overburdened and distracted teacher — congratulates everybody else that such advanced steps are taken." *Ibid.*, 1901, 334–35.

[34] William McAndrews, "When the Schoolman Fails," *Educational Review*, XLII, 18.

[35] Vol. XLII, p. 10.

This was in January, 1911. In the next two years as the efficiency mania spread and the criticism of education grew, the job security of school superintendents decreased. It will be recalled that the storm of criticism reached its peak in the late summer and early fall of 1912. In June of 1913 the editor of the *American School Board Journal* reported that "no recent year has seen such wholesale changes in superintendencies and other higher school positions as the present year — 1913. In the Middle-west there has been a perfect storm of unrest culminating in wholesale resignations, dismissals and new appointments."[36] Clearly the journals had reaped a harvest for their efforts.

Administrators Respond to the Demands for Efficiency

As early as February, 1911, educators began responding publicly to the demand to apply scientific management to the work of the school. The occasion was the annual meeting of the Department of Superintendence of the National Education Association, and the administrator who initiated the response was J. George Becht, principal of the State Normal School in Claxton, Pennsylvania. Becht told his audience that the nation had been seeking a more scientific basis for the "common arts of life" for the past twenty-five years. This basis had been found, he said, through the pioneering efforts of Frederick W. Taylor, who had shown what miracles could be achieved "by applying the principles of scientific management to the activities that range from carrying a hod to the highest expressions of physical labor." Becht then gave some of the details of the bricklaying experiment and indicated how many useless motions had been eliminated. He also reminded his fellow administrators that the "standard literary journals" were "giving over their columns" to promote the idea that educators should utilize these new methods and thereby become more efficient. Becht optimistically interpreted the layman's widespread discussion of educational practice as "one of the most hopeful signs in the educational firmament."[37]

The effort to introduce scientific management into the educational field gathered momentum at the annual meeting of the N.E.A. held in the summer of 1911. Charles H. Keyes, the president of the National Council of Education, urged the appointment of a committee (which was constituted) on the subject of "Tests and Standards of Efficiency of Schools and School Systems." Keyes told his audience of prominent educators that there was a "very pressing demand" for educators to apply the scientific efficiency procedures that were being used so ef-

[36] Vol. XLVI, p. 28.
[37] N.E.A. *Proceedings* (1911), p. 221.

fectively in industry. In response to "hostile criticism," he said, educators had initiated a few surveys, but this effort involved bringing in outside schoolmen, ostensibly "experts," who worked with the local schoolmen who also had some claim to expertness. But the outcome was merely an expression of "expert opinion," since education had no "scientifically established standards" such as existed in other fields.[38]

Perhaps the most significant and direct effort to introduce and apply the principles of scientific management into the schools in 1911 was made in the fall of that year by the High School Teachers Association of New York City. This group, under the leadership of its president, William T. Morrey, devoted three years to the task of studying "Efficiency in the High Schools through the Application of the Principles of Scientific Management," as these had been "enunciated in the industrial world."[39] The association began its effort by inviting the well-known efficiency expert, Harrington Emerson, to speak at its December meeting on the topic, "Scientific Management and High School Efficiency."

Emerson told his audience that while teaching at the University of Nebraska he had discovered certain fundamentals of organization which were applicable in "all institutions of learning" and "throughout all life." Those "universal" fundamentals he enumerated as follows: each animal or individual must breathe, eat, sleep, and keep its temperature variation within narrow limits or the organism would die. He concluded this paragraph by stating that "one can spend a lifetime and not know all there is to know about any individual animal or insect."

After telling his audience that they knew more about teaching than he did, he told them that he would discuss only those fundamentals of education which were similar to all other activities. These essentials, he said, could be applied "not only to school life but to everything human." Then he turned to the problem of efficiency and began by describing what efficiency was not. First, he said, strenuousness was not efficiency and he pointed out that a man could go faster on a bicycle than he could on foot. Second, efficiency was not system, and he cited an example of a doctor in the Spanish-American war who had filled out the wrong forms, did not receive his medicine, and lost his patient. Finally, efficiency was not the intensive use of such "crude instruments as land, labor, and capital." He summed up this section by asking his audience "Is your work as teachers strenuous? If so it

[38] *Ibid.*, pp. 340–41.
[39] *Efficiency in High Schools: Studies, 1911–14, in the Application of the Principles of Scientific Management to High School Problems* (A Collection of Bulletins of the High School Teachers Association of New York City), p. vii.

is not efficient." "Is your work as teachers systematized? If it is it cannot be efficient." "Does it depend on your school buildings, on the toil and labor of many teachers, on your books? If it does it cannot be efficient."

At this point Emerson shifted his attention to industrial plants and told the educators how he brought the benefits of scientific management to them. He said there were four essential elements necessary for efficiency in every plant. These were: first, definite and clear aims; second, an organization capable of attaining these aims; third, equipment adequate to achieve the aims; and fourth, "a strong executive who is able to carry them out." This last condition (which apparently referred to the aims) must have sounded very pleasant to the administrators in the audience. Then Emerson discussed his twelve principles of efficiency. This section of the speech, although not without its humorous aspects, was so unbelievable (considering the occasion and the audience) that it deserves a verbatim account:

In these matters plants are generally defective, and the conditions cannot be rapidly changed. Assuming, however, that we find a satisfactory condition, we next apply the twelve principles of efficiency.

Take, for instance, a bank burglar. I tell him that the first principle is that of a *high ideal*. I ask him if his ideal is compatible with the first principle of efficiency, a high ideal.

The second principle of efficiency is *common sense*, good judgment. I ask him if it is compatible with common sense to choose as a profession bank burglary.

The third principle of efficiency is *competent counsel*. I ask him where he got counsel to the effect that the business of breaking into banks is a good one.

The fourth principle is *discipline*, which means the welfare of society. I ask him whether breaking into banks is compatible with discipline. Discipline plays a part only when the burglar is caught red-handed and sent up.

The fifth principle is the *fair dealing*. I ask him whether breaking into a bank is a fair deal.

If at the very start of his business a man neglects the five first principles, how can we apply for him the other *practical principles*:

    (6) *Standard records.*
    (7) *Planning.*
    (8) *Standard conditions.*
    (9) *Standardized operations.*
    (10) *Standard instructions.*
    (11) *Standard schedules.*
    (12) *Efficiency reward.*

Then we come down to organization, and we apply to each part the same test of the twelve principles. We apply it to the aim. We apply it to every man and to every movement, and after we finish with the organization we apply the same twelve principles to the equipment — to each machine, to all the materials, to all the methods. Then we go to the executive, and we apply to him the twelve principles.

By the time we have made this survey, the whole organization looks to us like a sieve. There are holes in it everywhere, some of them large, some of them small. The first thing to do is to stop the larger leaks, then we stop the lesser leaks, and we keep busy until all the leaks are stopped. Trying to increase the efficiency of a plant with a sieve-like organization is like carting water in a pail filled with holes. You cannot carry it very far. This is the manner in which the principles of efficiency are initially applied.

By this time it would seem reasonable to assume that the audience was thoroughly confused, but Emerson was to challenge their credulity even further, for he dropped the twelve principles and said no more about them. Instead he told his audience that the rest of the problem would be considered under "three simple categories." These were: materials or supplies, personal services, and general charges. For each of these categories there were four different efficiencies and these, he said "stand to one another in a dependent sequence and this results in efficiency being tremendously low in the end." Before dealing with these new efficiencies, however, Emerson gave examples of what he meant by dependent sequence. If, he said, a man lost half of his fortune on Wall Street one day, and the next day lost half of what remained, and the next day lost half of that "he would very soon come to a very small number of dollars." What possible connection this idea had to anything that had been said previously was not clear and Emerson didn't explain. Instead he listed the four new efficiencies. They were efficiency of price, efficiency of supply, efficiency of distribution, and efficiency of use. He illustrated how these efficiencies worked by citing examples of items such as railroad time tables which were too high in price, too numerous, poorly distributed, and not efficiently used. This resulted, he said, in great waste.[40]

If there was any resentment on the part of the members of the association at Emerson's speech it did not appear in the *Bulletin*. On the contrary, in the January edition the secretary of the group wrote that it was not often "that we are privileged to feel so close a kinship between our problems and those of the world of business surrounding us."[41] And President Morrey did his very best to make some sense out of Emerson's speech in his report to the association in November of

[40] High School Teachers Association of New York City, *Bulletin* No. 32 (January, 1912), pp. 3–9.
[41] *Ibid.*
[42] *Bulletin* No. 35 (November, 1912), pp. 2–4.
[43] *Bulletin* No. 36 (December, 1912), p. 44.

1912, and he advocated continuing efforts to apply his principles.[42] As a result, subsequent meetings were devoted to efficiency in administration and efficiency in the recitation.

In the end not much was accomplished. A recommendation by the Efficiency Committee to introduce a system for rating the efficiency of teachers was tabled,[43] and attempts to introduce double and triple shifts into the high schools were strongly opposed.[44] Apparently the only effort to apply the principles of scientific management that was in any way successful was made within the department of biology in one of the New York high schools. The conclusions which were reached by members of the department, as a result of this effort, were presented to the association by a Mrs. Pingaey. The following abstract of her speech was printed in the Bulletin:

A Purpose or object of "Scientific Management."
    1. To increase the efficiency of the laborer, i.e., the pupil.
    2. To increase quality of product, i.e., the pupil.
    3. Thereby to increase the amount of output and the value to the capitalist.
B Comparisons between schools and mercantile establishments:
    1. The teacher obviously corresponds to planning department, superintendent, manager of a factory.
    2. The elements in the enterprise (the workmen, the raw material, and the finished product) are combined in the pupil. The other elements (tools, etc.), are the text books, charts, and apparatus.
C The teacher should study and know thoroughly all these materials.
D The final responsibility must be put on the pupil, and he should be trained and made to feel this responsibility. The teacher's system of grading a pupil helps him to realize the amount of his progress.
E Difficulties in the way of making exact applications of scientific principles:
    1. So many different elements are combined in one (i.e., the pupil).
    2. The raw material (pupil) is affected by so many outside conditions.
    3. Poor raw material cannot be exchanged for good.
    4. Teacher never sees or deals with a finished product.[45]

This speech was apparently followed by another in which specific recommendations were made for the classroom teacher. These included the use of printed outlines, seating plans, recitation cards, attendance sheets, and other "labor saving devices." The teachers were advised that "Perfected business methods mean that better quality of work should be obtained with less expenditure of energy."[46]

By 1912 evidence of the increasing impact of the public criticism

[44] *Bulletin* No. 44 (May, 1914), p. 190.
[45] *Bulletin* No. 36 (December, 1912), p. 47.
[46] *Ibid.*

of the schools and the growing influence of business and industry upon all aspects of education was abundant. In their February annual meeting (at which they heard the lay criticism of Chatfield) the superintendents listened to the suggestions and self-criticisms of the profession. They were told that "the impulse of this awakening to the call for efficiency is felt everywhere throughout the length and breadth of the land, and the demand is becoming more insistent every day. . . ."[47] And they were warned by another educator that "the schools *as well as other business institutions* must submit to the test for efficiency."[48] At the same time they were being told by an administrator in an article in the *American School Board Journal* that there was a "tremendous lot of waste in school administration," and that "if it is worth while in the business world to devote careful, painstaking study to the number of motions necessary to laying bricks, handling pig iron, or painting a structure, it is not worth far more to conserve human endeavor in developing the human product."[49]

These warnings may have been unnecessary, for the program of this meeting indicated that the superintendents were already responding. For example, one entire meeting was devoted to "The Determining of School Efficiency," and speeches were given by administrators in other meetings on such topics as "Waste and Efficiency in School Studies" and "The Standardization of Janitor Service." In the same month, Franklin Bobbitt of the University of Chicago, in an article published in an educational journal, connected the platoon school organization developed in Gary, Indiana with scientific management.[50]

As might have been expected, the program of the annual meeting of the National Education Association, held in Chicago in July, 1912, was sprinkled with topics relating to business efficiency. At one of the general sessions an address was given on "What the Public May Expect in Dividends: Material, Civic, and Social," and practically every department or division had at least one meeting or address connected with efficiency. For example, a major meeting of the National Council of Education was devoted to the question "By What Standards or Tests Shall the Efficiency of a School or System of Schools Be Measured?" In the Department of Secondary Education a speech was given on "Progress in Standardizing the Measurement of Composition." The Department of Normal Schools had one address on "Standards of Measuring the Efficiency of Normal-School Students," and

[47] N.E.A. *Proceedings* (1912), p. 427.
[48] *Ibid.*, p. 492. (Italics mine.)
[49] Walter I. Hamilton, "Some Waste Motion in School Administration," XLIV (February, 1912), 23–24.
[50] "The Elimination of Waste in Education," *Elementary School Teacher*, XII (February, 1912), 260.

another on "Securing and Maintaining Efficiency in the Teaching Force of Normal Schools." The Department of Business Education was concerned with topics such as "Efficiency in the Business Department of the High School." Even the Department of Science Instruction had an address entitled "A Study in Adolescent Efficiency" and the Library Department had one on "Educational By-Products in Library Work." Perhaps the most surprising feature of the entire program, however, was an address in the Department of Music Education on "The Principles of Scientific Management Applied to Teaching Music in the Public Schools." Even more surprising was the fact that the speaker, C. A. Fullerton of Iowa State Teachers College, had obviously studied Taylor's writing very carefully and manifested a much clearer conception of the real nature of scientific management than any other educator I have encountered.

Fullerton began by lauding scientific management, stating that it was "One of the most significant movements of the present generation. . . ." By applying its principles, he said, "the quality of the laborer is improved, the quantity is greatly increased, and [showing that he accepted Taylor's testimony uncritically] the laborer is in better condition after his day's work." He then went on to describe Gilbreth's work and the revolution that had been brought about in the bricklaying trade, and he mentioned Taylor's contribution in increasing the productivity of shovelers. Then, again indicating that he took Taylor at his word or at least agreed with it, he said that the new system could be applied with equal effectiveness to higher types of human activity. The question was, he said, whether scientific management could be applied by music teachers to enable them to increase their efficiency. He answered this question in the affirmative, and he believed that the more educators studied Taylor's system the more they would be "convinced that it has a great deal to offer for the improvement of all educational work." He granted that educators were dealing with "immortal souls instead of bricks and steel," but he thought this fact was "no argument in favor of false and clumsy methods." Although he was not as willing as some other educators to concede the backwardness of education, he did join the majority in placing it behind industry. "We are," he said, "clearly running our schools on a lower plane of efficiency than we are some of our factories. As a nation we cannot afford to do this." Then he added a prediction. "As sure as daylight follows the dawn," he said, "this higher standard of efficiency will be applied to all phases of education, including religious education, and the sooner the better."

He turned his attention then to the application of the principles of scientific management to teaching music. He conceded that the task would not be easy but he believed this was not sufficient "reason for backing away from it." To illustrate his point he discussed the problem of determining the "best method for teaching sight-reading." This was, he said, an "inviting problem for the efficiency expert" but a difficult one, for

it includes all that there is in a bricklaying problem and much more, for technical skill is only part of the object sought. One reason why better progress has been made in reducing the technique of the factory to a scientific basis than in the technique of public school music is that success in the technique of the factory is measured by dollars and cents and the results are not questioned. It is not so easy to measure success in the development of an art — and the appreciation of beauty. Technical skill in the factory means the ability to turn out so many articles per day. Technical skill in music means the ability to perform music, but its value depends on the power to interpret music in an artistic manner and also on the taste used in selecting music that is worth performing.[51]

In this passage as well as in the rest of his speech, Fullerton's insight went beyond that of other educators who attempted to apply scientific management to education. He realized that the problems in education were vastly more complex. He realized that exceptional knowledge and training would be required of the expert. He realized that a great deal of time would be required. And he realized that the essence of the Taylor system was its intensive and persistent study of problems, and he stated that this was the important contribution that men such as Taylor and Gilbreth had made to education. Whether his ideas on improving music teaching were reasonable or not, he put his finger on the problem. As we shall see, the administrators who attempted to apply scientific management to education did not have the training necessary to study education, nor did they perceive the time and effort such study would require. And, of course, they did not have the time or money for painstaking, thoughtful, thorough research.

Although educators were making efforts in 1912 to respond to the demands being made upon them, their critics were not satisfied. In the autumn of 1912 the attacks in the popular journals subsided, but other critics appeared. Two of the most important of these were men who were not professional educators but were active in educational work. They were important not only because they were men of considerable status and influence but also because of the nature of the recommendations they made.

[51] N.E.A. *Proceedings* (1912), pp. 1017–20.

The first of these men was James P. Munroe, who was a kind of industrialist-educator. He was, in 1912, president of the National Society for the Promotion of Industrial Education, chairman of the Massachusetts Commission for the Blind, chairman of the Committee on Education of the Boston Chamber of Commerce, and secretary of the Corporation, Massachusetts Institute of Technology. In addition to holding these positions, he had written extensively on education and had served as editor of *Walker's Discussions in Education*. His criticisms and suggestions were made to educators in a book published late in 1912 and significantly entitled *New Demands in Education*. Since Munroe was prominent in the Boston area his ideas were almost certainly well known to Frank Spaulding, who was superintendent at Newton, Massachusetts and one of the men who led in the effort to adapt scientific management to education. The similarity between Munroe's recommendations and Spaulding's ideas will be apparent when Spaulding's speech to the Department of Superintendence of the N.E.A. in February, 1913, on applying scientific management to education, is presented in chapter four.

Munroe opened his book by stating: "The fundamental demand in education, as in everything else is for efficiency — physical efficiency, mental efficiency, moral efficiency." [52] After a scathing indictment of the American schools, whose inefficiency, he said, resulted in a "colossal and needless waste of human energy," he asked:

What is to be done? What every other business does when it finds itself confronted with possible bankruptcy through preventable waste, losses, and inferiority of output. It calls in engineering and commercial experts to locate causes and to suggest reforms. We need 'educational engineers' to study this huge business of preparing youth for life, to find out where it is good, where it is wasteful, where it is out of touch with modern requirements, where and why its output fails; and to make report in such form and with such weight of evidence that the most conventional teacher and the most indifferent citizen must pay heed.

Such engineers would make a thorough study of (1) the pupils who constitute the raw material of the business of education; (2) the building and other facilities for teaching, which make up the plant; (3) the school boards and the teaching staff, who correspond to the directorate and the working force; (4) the means and methods of instruction and development; (5) the demands of society in general and of industry in particular upon boys and girls — this corresponding to the problem of markets; and (6) the question of the cost, which is almost purely a business problem." [53]

[52] James Phinney Munroe, *New Demands in Education* (New York, 1912), Preface, p. v.

[53] *Ibid.*, pp. 20–21.

The other individual who prodded (or pushed) educators toward taking action to achieve efficiency was William H. Allen, director of the Bureau of Municipal Research in New York City. Allen was an efficiency advocate of long standing and had written a book on *Efficient Democracy*, which included a chapter on efficiency in education. His advice to the educational world was given in a speech to the Wisconsin Teachers Association in the fall of 1912 and was printed in the *American School Board Journal* — a journal so influential that one schoolman described it as the school administrator's "Bible."[54] Allen told his audience what they undoubtedly already knew when he stated, in the first paragraph of his speech, "efficiency is in our vocabulary. It is almost a shibboleth." He added that while a "few reactionaries claim that we cannot measure efficiency, the rank and file of us know that there are so many things we can measure, that we do not need to worry about the fewer things which we cannot measure." Therefore, he stated, the first important step had been taken — people wanted efficiency. Unfortunately, he said, everyone wanted it for someone else and no one was willing to take action in his own school or classroom. "We like," said Allen, "to use the word and to proclaim our allegiance to the newer ideals of scientific management; but saying 'efficient' and being efficient are two different things."[55]

Clearly this apostle of the gospel of efficiency had no intention of permitting educators to respond to their critics by simply *talking* about efficiency. He demanded that they stop talking and begin acting. More than this, Allen characterized and held up to ridicule eight kinds of schoolmen who for one reason or another were not enthusiastically adopting the efficiency measures. These men turned out to be not only stupid but also weak, dishonest, and of course undemocratic. These views were supported by the editor of the *American School Board Journal*, who commented at the end of the article that Allen had pictured "conditions so accurately that every school superintendent and school board member who reads it, may well ask himself: To which of the eight classes of schoolmen do I belong."[56]

There were two events, both of which occurred in February of 1913, which indicated that administrators were acting promptly to appease their critics. One was a major session devoted to "Improving School Systems by Scientific Management" at the annual meeting of the most powerful group of educators in America — the Department of Super-

[54] Ward G. Reeder, *The Business Administration of a School System* (Boston, 1929) p. vi.
[55] "Next Steps in School Efficiency," *American School Board Journal*, XLV (December, 1912), 15.
[56] *Ibid.*, p. 57.

intendence of the National Education Association.[57] The other was the publication of the Twelfth Yearbook of the National Society for the Study of Education, Part I of which was devoted to the application of scientific management to city school systems. The significance of the meeting of the superintendents was heightened by the fact that the first two speeches were delivered by men who had to be classified as among the most prominent in American education. The publication by the National Society was perhaps even more significant, for the society's membership consisted of the leading educators in America, and its yearbook was certainly the most prominent professional publication at that time. It is difficult to see how the leaders in education could have done more to acknowledge the urgency and importance they attached to the need to apply scientific management to the schools.

[57] The professional importance and significance of this annual meeting of the Department of Superintendence may be judged from the words of an editorial in *American School Board Journal*, written specifically about the Cincinnati convention the next year: "The meeting of the Department of Superintendence is the big annual event to which every superintendent who is alive to the responsibilities of his office and the opportunities of his profession must look forward to as the convention which will determine for him educational policies and offer solutions for administrative problems. It is a school for superintendents, a clearing house where educational ideas are exchanged, where difficult questions are answered; it is a post-graduate course for superintendents who would stand in line for promotion in their profession and who would keep up with the everchanging, growing and rising standards in school work.

The Cincinnati convention reminds one very much of important conferences which are held each year in a number of professions and industries. Great business corporations send their presidents and superintendents for the direct benefit which they expect to derive. Every manufacturer knows how these gatherings fix trade policies, make possible a better understanding between houses, reduce abuses and evils of competition, have a tendency for making prices and credits more stable, improve manufacturing methods, etc." "The Cincinnati Convention" L (February, 1915), 30.

4

AMERICAN EDUCATORS
APPLY THE GREAT PANACEA

The superintendents arriving in Philadelphia in February of 1913 for their annual meeting and greeting the colleagues they had not seen for a year may well have sought solace from one another, for 1912 had been a trying year. They had received enough criticism and enough advice to last a lifetime, and the question they undoubtedly asked eagerly of each other was: "What is to be done?" It is also probable that they studied the program topics and the speakers carefully in the hope that a prophet would appear to lead them out of the wilderness. The chances are that they were most expectant about the session devoted to scientific management, for, after all, if this new system could work such miracles in industry, perhaps it could help solve their problems in education. Besides, they had been advised, urged, and even warned by businessmen and by some of their leaders to use the new panacea.

The meeting opened in the usual way with greetings from the mayor and the host superintendent of schools, and the visiting administrators probably were grateful that no unpleasant note of criticism was sounded. They were brought back to earth quickly, however, when their representative who had been appointed to present their official response to the welcome, O. T. Corson, former president of the N.E.A. and editor of the *Ohio Educational Monthly*, immediately began discussing the widespread criticism of the schools. Some of this criticism, he said, was due to ignorance or prejudice but he was strongly tempted to believe that some of the criticism of the *Ladies' Home Journal* type was "part of a business policy, both keen and conscienceless, which recognizes that increased revenues may result from sensational attacks

upon an institution dear to the hearts of the people."[1] This statement
was certainly warmly received, but it provided little consolation and
no help.

They got even less consolation and no practical help from Charles
Judd, who spoke at the evening meeting that same day. In fact, Judd,
who was director of the School of Education at the University of Chicago, probably caused a good deal of uneasiness. He told his audience
that despite the large number of educational organizations, the profession was very weak and unable to defend itself. The result was that
"if the school board objects to what they call fads and innovations, I,
their educational expert, must look cheerfully upon my critics and re-
ply that the cost of living is going up. If the manufacturers tell me that
I do not know how to conduct schools, and that they are going to have
a new deal and a separate system of schools, I must admit all of their
criticisms and ask for a job in the right school." Then he raised an
interesting question. "Do the lawyers allow themselves to be managed
by outside agencies? No, they have a bar association." He pointed out
that the bar association did not spend its time discussing "chiefly
economic matters" and listening to "long inspirational addresses."
Instead, it spent its time on professional matters, as he urged the
teaching profession to do. This was not being done because the teacher
had been, and was expected to be, timid.[2] Of course, Judd was speaking from the relatively safe vantage point of the private university,
and it is probable that his audience of administrators, while admitting
the correctness of his analysis, muttered to themselves something to
the effect that professors in ivory towers should come down on the
firing line and see what it was like.

The session devoted to improving school systems through scientific
management was begun with an address by Paul Hanus on the "Underlying Principles of Scientific Management."[3] The title of his address
was somewhat misleading since he did not deal with these but with
the general problems facing American educators in 1913 and the
steps which might be taken to solve them. His main point was that
more emphasis had to be placed upon research so that educational
activity could be based on "verifiable data which any technically in-

[1] N.E.A. Proceedings (1913), p. 108.

[2] Ibid., pp. 151–52.

[3] Hanus was well known in American education and, judging from his appointment
to important national committees and his frequent speaking appearances at national
meetings, was a recognized leader in the field of educational administration. He had
been brought to Harvard in 1891 by Charles Eliot, as assistant professor of the History
and Art of Teaching, to give the first systematic instruction in education, and he was
head of the Division of Education until the Graduate School of Education was established in 1920. He had received wide recognition within the profession as a result of
his work as director of the survey of the New York Schools in 1911.

formed person can appeal to. . . ." Until this was done, he said, "we are practically helpless." He attempted to console his audience by stating that some progress had been made. He was especially encouraged by the fact that educators were "no longer disputing whether education has a scientific basis; we are trying to find that basis."[4]

Hanus devoted the major portion of his speech to ideas which bore little or no relation to Frederick Taylor's basic principles. If he had read or knew about the basic ideas of Taylor or others of the scientific-manager group in industry, he did not accept them for education. Yet, in his emphasis upon the need for the scientific study of education, Hanus was much closer to the spirit of Frederick Taylor than many other educators, especially other administrators in whose hands scientific management became cost accounting.

While his recommendations were general in nature and did not provide the administrators in the audience with practical suggestions which were immediately useful, he probably did strengthen the tendencies to use standardized tests, school surveys, and other procedures such as efficiency ratings, score cards for buildings, and elaborate systems of records and reports which gave at least the impression of providing a "factual" basis for education. But if Hanus spoke in generalities, the speaker who followed dealt with the problem in a concrete, practical, dollars-and-cents way that every superintendent could not only understand but could apply very quickly in a troubled situation. That speaker was Frank Spaulding, superintendent of schools at Newton, Massachusetts, and a man who since 1910 had been assuming a position of leadership among school administrators.

The Dollar as Educational Criterion

Spaulding had studied in Germany and received his Ph.D. there in 1893 and had served as superintendent of schools in Passaic, New Jersey, before moving to Newton. Later he served as superintendent in Cleveland, and in 1920 he became head of the newly formed Department of Education at Yale University. He opened his speech[5] by stating that Professor Hanus had outlined the principles whose observance "makes theoretically possible the unhampered practice of scientific management within the school." His effort, he said, would be directed toward showing how scientific management could be applied in the schools by reporting on how it had been done in the Newton schools.

While Hanus made no mention of the Taylor system and it had obviously had little impact on his conception of scientific management,

[4] N.E.A. *Proceedings* (1913), pp. 247–48.
[5] N.E.A. *Proceedings* (1913), pp. 249–79.

Superintendent Spaulding mentioned it early in his speech and made it clear that it was this system which he had attempted to apply to the Newton schools. He believed the superintendents were well informed not only of Taylor's work but also of the "marvelous results" of the system. Still, he said,

As we recall the familiar stock examples of scientific management that came to us from the material industries — *such as the mining of pig iron, the laying of bricks, and the cutting of metals* — as we recall the multitude of stop watch observations and experiments, the innumerable, accurate measurements and comparisons of processes and results, out of which after many years these examples have grown, we may be pardoned if we felt a *momentary doubt* of the applicability to the *educational industry* of any *management* worthy to be characterized as scientific.[6]

Spaulding's "momentary doubt" was caused not only by an awareness of the "multitude of stop watch observations" and the "innumerable, accurate measurements" that were a part of the Taylor system but also by a strong belief on the part of many educators, as evidenced in numerous books, articles, and speeches, that some of the aspects of education such as the development of attitudes or of appreciations were not measurable. Spaulding countered the doubt by conceding the difficulty but reminding his audience of the rewards. It would be difficult, he said, "but when we learn of the marvelous results achieved in some material industries through the elimination of waste motions . . . we are somewhat reassured." Then he countered the argument that some aspects of the educational endeavor were not measurable, by saying, "Let us waste no time over the obvious but fruitless objection that the ultimate and real products of a school system — those products that are registered in the minds and hearts of the children that go out from the schools — are immeasurable, and hence incomparable." Spaulding defined scientific management as a "method" which was, he said, "characterized by its spirit quite as much as by its accuracy." The "essentials" of the method were:

1. The measurement and comparison of comparable results.
2. The analysis and comparison of the conditions under which given results are secured — especially of the means and time employed in securing given results.
3. The consistent adoption and use of those means that justify themselves most fully by their results, abandoning those that fail so to justify themselves.

This conception, especially the second and third points, could have been interpreted as being similar to at least the first of Taylor's prin-

[6] Italics mine.

ciples which concerned the scientific analysis of a job, the selection of the best methods, and then the adoption of those methods. Certainly Spaulding's emphasis on the "analysis and comparison of conditions" which brought the best results, and then the "consistent adoption" of the most effective means, provided the basis for a high degree of similarity. This potential close similarity did not materialize, however, for he took the form and some of the superficial aspects of Taylor's system and neglected its substance. In this he was not alone, for, as Taylor himself pointed out, many of the self-styled efficiency experts, and even some time and motion study men, did not understand his system, or at least they did not apply it correctly.

Spaulding began the presentation of his work by stating that he knew of "no single adequate measure of the efficiency of a school either absolute or relative" and that he knew of no combination of measures whereby the "exact superiority of one school over another can be expressed in a single term." But, he said, there were "important products or results" which could be measured and, "the efficiency of schools in these respects can be definitely compared." When these "products or results" had been measured, the means used to achieve them would be studied and those that had produced the best results would be adopted. What were the kinds of "products" or "results" that could be measured? Spaulding stated,

I refer to such results as the percentage of children of each year of age in the school district that the school enrolls; the average number of day's attendance secured annually from each child; the average length of time required for each child to do a given definite unit of work; the percentage of children of each age who are allowed to complete their schooling, with the average educational equipment of each; the percentage of children who are inspired to continue their education in higher school; and the quality of the education that the school affords.

With the exception of the last point, these were the kind of results easily obtained and of limited value in ascertaining the educational work of a school. But the last point Spaulding listed, i.e., the quality of education the school affords, was of vital importance to any educational endeavor and indeed the basic criterion for determining the effectiveness of a school.

Admitting that the matter of quality was as important as it was difficult to measure, Spaulding described how the problem had been handled under scientific management at Newton. They had obtained "not a perfect nor a complete, but an exceedingly valuable comparative measure of the quality of education afforded by the several grammar schools." A chart which he claimed indicated the comparative success of students in the Newton schools showed that students from school number nine had done the best work and students from school number eleven the poorest, although the differences, even between the extremes, were not great. Converting the differences from the chart into percentages, Spaulding stated that school nine was superior to school eleven by 17 per cent.

The important question was, of course, how was this comparative "success" determined? What was his "exceedingly valuable measure of quality?" Spaulding stated succinctly, "It is unnecessary to explain in detail how these respective quality measures — represented graphically — of the work of the pupils of each grammar school are secured." Further than this he told his audience only that "this measure is found in qualitative success — that is the standing in the subject studied. . . ." Probably this standing was determined on the basis of grades, since, later in his speech, while discussing another aspect of the program, he said that grades were used in determining "average quality." He also used a quantitative basis — the number of "points passed or earned" — to determine quality, so it was possible that he used a combination of these factors to determine "qualitative success." In what elaboration he gave of his measure of quality, Spaulding justified glossing over the important question of the method by which he secured quality measurements of the work of pupils by saying, "Only comparative, not absolute value is claimed for them."

Then he discussed how these "quality measures" could be used: "of what practical use are they? They serve as a most powerful stimulus to analysis and study — study of the conditions and means, the expenditures of time, effort, and money, in the several schools that yield such varying results, to the end that every school may adopt those plans that are proving most effective." Spaulding gave an illustration of "some of the conditions involved" in the relative success of the Newton grammar schools.

The records show that in Number 9, although next to the smallest of all the grammar schools, with a total average membership in all eight grades of only 126, the per pupil cost for instruction averaged for a period of five years ending with 1911–1912, but 3½ per cent higher than in Number 11, although the latter was next to the largest of all the grammar schools, with an average membership of 817. Moreover, the value of the plants occupied by these two schools is inversely as the success of their respective products in high school: the plant Number 9 represents an investment of $131.00 per pupil, based on average membership, while that of Number Eleven represents an investment of $411.00 per pupil reckoned on the same basis.

This was *the* illustration Spaulding used for his analysis of *conditions.* If other studies were made to get at the factors responsible for the apparent differences in quality, he did not mention them. What seems significant are the conditions selected and the terminology used. The emphasis on per pupil cost and the reference to "school plant," "respective products," and "investment per pupil" is precisely the kind of analysis one would expect of a businessman, not an educator. With this statement the problem of the determination of the quality of education through scientific management was completed.

Spaulding abruptly shifted his attention to a consideration of the relative value of the various subjects being taught in the Newton high schools. He had given no indication earlier in his address that he intended to deal with this problem, and it was not listed as one of the kinds of results that could be measured or had been measured in the Newton schools. Nor did he, in making the presentation of his data on this curriculum problem, make any reference to scientific management, but it must be presumed that he was applying his conception of scientific management to this problem.

In his analysis of the curriculum he stated that the number of periods per week and the number of years spent on each subject gave no "adequate conception of the actual educational employment" of a high school student at a given time. Instead of following this procedure he worked out a "composite picture" of a mythical student in Newton's secondary schools showing that this average student spent one-tenth of 1 per cent of his week's time studying Greek, and 17 per cent studying English. His analysis revealed that the student spent the rest of his time proportionately as follows: mathematics, 11 per cent; commercial subjects, 10 per cent; French, 9 per cent; science, 9 per cent; Latin, 5 per cent; and less than 5 per cent each on machine shop, physical training, mechanical drawing, German, art, cabinet-making, printing, electricity, vocal music, and pattern-making.

This done he asked a basic question which turned out to be purely rhetorical since he made no effort to answer it. He asked whether the "Newton composite secondary-school pupil," whose educational photograph he had taken was adequately prepared to meet the demands of that society "which education should fit him to serve." He stated that his listeners could get some help in answering the question by studying his data, but he did not go into the matter further.

Then he turned to the perennial, always difficult problem of making decisions on the relative educational value of various subjects. This had always been, and probably always will be, crucial to education, but it had become especially difficult by this time because America had become a complex industrial nation in which knowledge was being accumulated and developed in many new fields at a rapid rate. The introduction of the elective system after 1865 had provided flexibility in educational programs, and had made possible the offering of new courses by enabling students to enroll in them. But the elective system had also complicated the problem, and it had forced educators to make some decisions on the matter of curriculum. Both the Committee of Ten and the Committee on College Entrance Requirements, each composed of leading American educators, grappled with this thorny problem. Their solution was to utilize a system of quantitative measures — points, credits, and units — and the notion of equivalents. Under this arrangement subjects which were on an approved list and which were studied for an equal length of time were equivalent and were to be accepted for graduation from secondary schools and for admission to college. Difficult as these problems of curriculum were, they had been eased somewhat because of the prevailing acceptance of the theory of mental discipline so that the decision could be made on the basis of whether a given subject did or did not develop the mind. However, when the psychological research on the transfer of training undermined this theory, the basis for the decision was changed. Since — in theory at least — any subject, properly taught was as effective as any other so far as the development of good intellectual habits was concerned, the problem shifted over to one of deciding which studies were of the greatest value socially and individually.

The net result was that before and after the publication of the transfer studies by Thorndike, educators had been engaged continually, and it seemed to Spaulding endlessly and futilely, in discussions over the question of which studies were of greatest value. So with the characteristic impatience of the practical man with the scholar, Spaulding told his audience of school administrators how the question could be and in fact was being settled. He began by saying that the "Academic discussion of educational values is as futile as it is fascinating. Which is more valuable, a course in Latin or a course in the machine shop? . . . there are, there can be, no permanent, no absolute and universal answers to such questions as these; but there are, and there must be, temporary, relative, and local assignments of value" and how were they being made? They were dollar values and they were being assigned every day by the school administrator. As he put it, "So while we educational practitioners have been waiting on the educational theorists for an evaluation of the various subjects of actual or possible school curricula, we have been determining for our own schools definitely and minutely the relative values of every such subject. And we have done this, for the most part, without knowing it! The school administrator simply cannot avoid assigning education values every time he determines the expenditure of a dollar."

He then went on to describe what relative value had been assigned to the various subjects taught in the Newton secondary schools. He found "that 5.9 pupil-recitations in Greek are of the same value as 23.8 pupil-recitations in French; that 12 pupil-recitations in science are equivalent in value to 19.2 pupil-recitations in English; and that it takes 41.7 pupil-recitations in vocal music to equal the value of 13.9 pupil-recitations in art." Undoubtedly Charles Eliot, Nicholas Murray Butler, William T. Harris, John Dewey, William Bagley, and many other educators who had wrestled with this difficult and important question would have been or were stunned by the simplicity and ease with which Spaulding disposed of the problem. They would have been even more stunned when they understood what these decisions meant in terms of the program of the school. After raising a question, the answer to which he apparently regarded as self-evident, he indicated how such value assignments might affect the curriculum as follows:

Thus confronted, do we feel like denying the equivalency of these values — we cannot deny our responsibility for fixing them as they are? This is a wholesome feeling, if it leads to a *wiser* assignment of values in future. *Greater wisdom* in these assignments will come, not by reference to any supposedly fixed and inherent values in these subjects themselves, but from a study of local conditions and needs. I know nothing about the absolute value of a recitation in Greek as compared with a recitation in French or in English. *I am convinced, however, by very concrete and quite local considerations, that when the obligations of the present year expire, we ought to purchase no more Greek instruction at the rate of 5.9 pupil-recitations for a dollar. The price must go down, or we shall invest in something else.*[7]

Spaulding's conception of scientific management obviously amounted to an analysis of the budget. By a study of *local considerations* he meant a study of the per-pupil costs and pupil-recitation costs. His scientific determination of *educational value* turned out to be a determination of *dollar value*. His decisions on what should be taught were made *not on educational, but on financial grounds*. This was not the first time nor was it to be the last. But this occasion was particularly unfortunate because it was presented to leading administrators from all over the nation by one of their leaders and because it clothed this business philosophy and practice with the mantle of science.

In his further application of scientific management, Spaulding turned to the problem of reducing expenditures and indicated his doubt that school administrators showed "any greater wisdom than

[7] Italics mine.

the average housewife in the disposition of our always limited school budgets." The first thing for both the "housewife and the school administrator" to do was to obtain detailed knowledge of the disposition of the budget. In Newton, "Of every dollar expended, 0.3 of one cent goes for Greek, while 15.6 cents goes for English. We buy 0.4 of one cent's worth of instruction in vocal music while buying 12.1 cent's worth of instruction in mathematics." The term "unit cost" had been used by Taylor and was widely used in the field of scientific management. Now Spaulding took it up for education:

Comparison of the costs of the unit under different conditions is perhaps the best starting-point for a campaign to reduce unit costs or to improve the quality of units of service.

Every school system presents within itself abundant opportunity for the comparison of unit costs; the conditions under which these costs arise are at hand, subject to any kind and degree of analysis and study that may be necessary.

His "unit" was one pupil recitation, and his analysis of these "units" in the Newton high schools showed that there was variation in their costs. So Spaulding asked his audience:

Why is a pupil recitation in English costing 7.2 cents in the vocational school while it costs only 5 cents in the technical school? Is the "vocational" English 44 per cent superior to the "technical" English or 44 per cent more difficult to secure? Why are we paying 80% more in the vocational than in the technical school for the same unit of instruction in mathematics? Why does a pupil-recitation in science cost from 55 per cent to 67 per cent more in the Newton High than in either of the other schools?

He indicated that the reasons for these varying costs of the same subjects could be determined by a study of the conditions in the schools, and, once the reasons were obtained, changes could be made to secure "a maximum of service at a minimum of cost in every school and in every subject."

As evidence of how, and what, conditions could be studied, Spaulding presented the results of the investigation which he conducted at Newton to determine the cost of classroom instruction. The information he had gathered illustrated, he said, "the prime necessity of *penetrating analysis* as a means of revealing significant facts."[8] This analysis indicated that the factors which worked to reduce costs between 1903–4 and 1910–11 were, increases in the *number of recitations per week per instructor* and increases in the *number of pupils per recitation class*, while those which were working to increase cost were *increases in teacher salaries* and increases in the *number of rec-*

⁸ Italics mine.

itations per week per pupil. The conclusions to be drawn were obvious if the objective was to reduce costs: increase the number of classes per teacher and the class size, and cut the teacher's salaries and the number of recitations given so that fewer teachers would be needed.

Spaulding did not assume that his audience would grasp the significance of his figures but instead discussed at some length the way in which costs had been reduced at Newton. On the matter of increasing the teacher's load, he pointed out that "The increase of 1.7 recitations per week per teacher reduced the annual cost per pupil by $3.10; this was equivalent to a saving for the school of nearly $2,200.00, enough to pay for nearly 13,000 pupil-recitations in expensive Greek. Did the teachers or the efficiency of their work suffer on account of this increase of fifteen minutes per day in their classroom service? If so, by how much? These are educational questions that may be separated — but only temporarily — from their financial bearings." Spaulding did not explore the question he raised concerning the effect on the teacher of increasing the load. Instead he concentrated on the savings to be achieved through increasing class size. In all of these examples he translated the small per-pupil figures into the more impressive savings for the entire system. Thus, "the increase of 1.9 pupils per recitation class further reduced the annual per pupil cost by $3.24 — equivalent to a savings of over $2,200.00 for the school."

Spaulding made one other significant point in his speech. He claimed that the financial and the educational aspects of the administrator's job were inseparable and should be handled by the same person. For years superintendents in the larger cities had been concerned with this problem, and the educational literature, especially after 1890, contains many articles upon it. It is clear that in the larger systems the job of the superintendent had grown until it was impossible for one man to handle. The solution most often proposed was that of delegating the business functions of administration to one man and the educational functions to another. It was not thought that the two problems could be separated, although in some school systems it undoubtedly turned out this way. Rather, the view was that the superintendent needed to be familiar with the financial aspects of the school system, for the simple reason that educational decisions, policies, and programs had to be formulated within the limits of the money available. On the other hand, only a person who was thoroughly acquainted with the purpose and program of the school could decide how much money was needed. The aim was not to separate the two aspects of the job, but to make the one subordinate to the other (since the function of the school was to educate, not to operate as a successful business) and to relieve the superintendent of the less important, mechanical tasks (bookkeeping, ordering supplies, etc.) so that he could devote his time to the essential task — that of helping to establish conditions under which teachers could teach and students could learn.

Spaulding criticized this "prevalent effort" and recommended that the two functions be joined in one man:

There are two phases of every practical problem of school administration, even of the details of classroom procedure; these are the financial and the educational. They are inseparable; the frequent, I may say the prevalent, effort to distinguish the problems of the school into financial or business on the one hand, and educational on the other, results in two groups of problems barren of significance. Those school boards who insist on reserving to themselves, or committing to a special business manager, supposedly an expert, the business administration of a system of schools, while they impose on a superintendent, presumably an educational expert the so called professional administration of that same system of schools, and those superintendents who advocate this plan, or meekly acquiesce in it, give evidence of about as sound and comprehensive a grasp of the real problem of educational administration as the would-be manufacturer of shoes must have of that industry who would put his factory in charge of two independent experts, one of whom knew all about shoes as a finished product, and all about the processes of their manufacture, but knew little and was expected to know less about costs, while the other knew nothing about shoes, but was a past master of business and finance.

Spaulding's motivation in making this recommendation is not clear, but he may have been trying to justify his own concern with the business aspects of education. Certainly he was consciously or unconsciously pointing a way out of the wilderness for his fellow administrators. For if the superintendents followed his example and adopted his business and financial philosophy and practice in education, they would be in a much better position to defend themselves and their schools against the criticism of the business community. Furthermore, by emphasizing the business nature of the superintendency they could elevate their status and possibly even raise their salaries.

Increases in status and salary (and sometimes an enhancement in the reputation of the individual) did actually result in some cases from the application of business, efficiency methods to the schools. This was attested by a prominent educator in September, 1914, in the *American School Board Journal*:

Recently there has been a tendency to increase the salaries of school superintendents and supervisors in large cities, and considerable competition has arisen between cities to secure the services of men and women who have distinguished themselves for efficient administration. Recently a large western city sent out a committee to investigate personally the records of prominent superintendents. As a result a man was chosen who had distinguished himself most along the line of efficiency engineering and unit cost accounting in education. As time goes on such incidents will become frequent and a distinct profession of educational engineers — if such a word may be used for non-physical construction — will emerge.[9]

It may well be that the superintendent Dr. Brittain referred to, although not named, was Spaulding himself, for Spaulding had been appointed in May, 1914, to the superintendency of Minneapolis, Minnesota, under conditions agreeing with the above statement, at a salary of $8,000.00 a year, double the salary he had been paid at his appointment in Newton.[10] When it is realized that in the State of Massachusetts only Boston paid its Superintendent more than $4,000.00 it may be judged that the salary of $8,000.00 yearly, which Minneapolis offered him, was an exceedingly good one for a school superintendent.[11]

And Spaulding's star continued to rise, for three years later the *American School Board Journal* carried the following news item:

Press reports indicate that the Cleveland Board of Education has elected Dr. Frank E. Spaulding of Minneapolis as superintendent of schools for a term of four years. The election followed a nation wide search for the best available educator. . . . The result was that Dr. Spaulding was tendered the office for a term of four years at a salary of $12,000.00. Throughout the negotiations the members of the board exhibited perfect unanimity. They openly declared that they were seeking the strongest, scientific administrator who could be found, and that no extraneous consideration would influence their action.[12]

Other superintendents could deduce that successfully introducing so-called scientific methods into the schools could result not only in greater security but also in greater financial success. The only question raised by these actions was an educational one, that is, what effect would such a conception of the nature of the superintendency have upon the quality of the educational programs in the schools.

Aside from any question of financial advancement, it is not difficult to explain Spaulding's business approach to educational admin-

[9] Horace L. Brittain, "The Financial Relations of Boards of Education to Municipal Governments," XLIX, No. 3, 14.

[10] Frank Spaulding, *School Superintendent in Action in Five Cities* (Rindge, New Hampshire, 1955), p. 382. According to his own testimony Spaulding landed the Minneapolis job by cleverly convincing the school board that he was an efficient, business-like, cost-conscious administrator and this was exactly the kind of an educator they wanted. *Ibid.*, pp. 429–33.

[11] *Ibid.*, p. 222.

[12] "Dr. Spaulding to Cleveland," editorial, *American School Board Journal*, LIV, No. 2 (February, 1917), 61.

istration. For nine years prior to his speech before the Department of Superintendence, he had been forced to deal first, last, and always, with "one perennial issue: cost."[13] He was appointed to the superintendency of Newton, Massachusetts, in 1904, and accepted the job even though Newton had the reputation for being, as he put it, "the burial ground of Superintendents."[14] Newton was a prosperous suburb of Boston, and Spaulding records that "most of the leading people of Newton — those who set the standards — were owners, directors, and managers of large commercial and industrial establishments; there were bankers and brokers; there were lawyers and physicians. All were financiers. . . . They had the characteristics usually manifested by the successful and prosperous. . . . They were strongly conservative; they were progressive within limits; and for every expenditure they demanded full return in values which they appreciated." And these values which "Newtonians prized" were primarily attached to material things which could be "easily demonstrated and measured. . . ." As Spaulding carefully put it, their values "were by no means limited to material things but . . . they often seemed more willing to spend for tangibles than for intangibles."[15]

In such a community, at a time when the emphasis on efficiency and economy was increasing year by year, it is not surprising that Spaulding should report that "one issue, and only one, ran through the ten years of my Newton superintendency. That issue was the total cost of maintaining the school system."[16] The result was that he was "engaged in budget making throughout the year, every year."[17] And as "the cost issue grew more intense, the subject of education in relation to cost became the dominant theme of my annual reports."[18] Spaulding, far from resenting this pressure which forced him into a continuous educational cost-analysis, regarded it as fitting and proper and accepted his task as budgeter cheerfully. In commenting on the fact that his annual report was primarily concerned with costs, he said this was fortunate "for from the standpoint of costs, every aspect of a public educational program can be most effectively presented."[19] With this background, Spaulding's speech becomes more understandable, as does the fact that in the years ahead the annual

[13] Spaulding, *School Superintendent in Action*, p. 382.
[14] *Ibid.*, p. 223.
[15] *Ibid.*, p. 227.
[16] *Ibid.*, p. 382.
[17] *Ibid.*, p. 384.
[18] *Ibid.*, p. 393.
[19] *Ibid.*

reports of superintendents came more and more to resemble the reports of business corporations.

Management and the Worker in Education

The other major effort to apply scientific management to education coincided with Spaulding's and was made by Franklin Bobbitt, instructor in educational administration at the University of Chicago.[20] His work was published in 1913 as the Twelfth Yearbook of the National Society for the Study of Education, under the title *The Supervision of City Schools*. This society, which included in its membership most of the leaders in American education, exerted a great influence — chiefly through the publication of its yearbooks, which certainly were the most important annual professional publications in the field. This influence was increased by the fact that the annual meeting of the society (at which the new yearbook was discussed) was held in the same city and a day or so before the annual meeting of the Department of Superintendence.

Undoubtedly, Bobbitt had been selected to write the yearbook by the committee of the National Society because he had written an article on scientific management and education early in 1912,[21] in which he had connected the origin and development of the platoon school in Gary, Indiana, with scientific management and had described how scientific management principles had been applied in the Gary schools. His task in writing the yearbook was similar except that instead of dealing with the organization of the schools he applied Taylor's system to the "problem of educational management and supervision." [22]

In his introduction Bobbitt stated his purpose and justified the un-

[20] Bobbitt had received his bachelor's degree from Indiana University in 1901 and had served for some years as an instructor in a normal school in Manila. Returning to the United States, he enrolled at Clark University, taking his Ph.D. there in 1909. His doctoral thesis was a statistical study of the physical growth of several hundred Filipino children in which he measured their height, span of arms, sitting height, weight, vital capacity, and the grip strength of both hands. At this time he was a strong proponent of the eugenics movement which had taken hold in America after 1900. (See *Pedagogical Seminary*, XVI [September, 1909], 385–94.) In some ways his enthusiastic response to eugenics and to scientific management constitute a pattern. Both movements claimed to be based upon science, both seemed to offer rather clear cut, definite solutions to complex and difficult problems, and both were mechanistic in nature. Bobbitt not only accepted both doctrines or systems but actively advocated them. And in the case of scientific management he was not, as a professor at the University of Chicago, subject to the pressure from the business community that other schoolmen, such as Spaulding, had experienced.

[21] See pp. 130–34 for an account of this article.

[22] Franklin Bobbitt, *The Supervision of City Schools: Some General Principles of Management Applied to the Problems of City-School Systems*, "Twelfth Yearbook of the National Society for the Study of Education," Part I, (Bloomington, Ill., 1913), p. 7.

dertaking on the ground that in all co-operative endeavors, whether in the field of manufacturing, government, philanthropy, or education, the "fundamental tasks of management, direction, and supervision are always about the same." [23] Then Bobbitt indicated that he had studied Taylor's writing very carefully as he listed the essential tasks of management in all organizations, including the schools, as follows:

In any organization, the directive and supervisory members must clearly define the ends toward which the organization strives. They must co-ordinate the labors of all so as to attain those ends. They must find the best methods of work, and they must enforce the use of these methods on the part of the workers. They must determine the qualifications necessary for the workers and see that each rises to the standard qualifications, if it is possible; and when impossible, see that he is separated from the organization. This requires direct or indirect responsibility for the preliminary training of the workers before service and for keeping them up to standard qualifications during service. Directors and supervisors must keep the workers supplied with detailed instructions as to the work to be done, the standards to be reached, the methods to be employed, and the materials and appliances to be used. They must supply the workers with the necessary materials and appliances. They must place incentives before the worker in order to stimulate desirable effort. Whatever the nature or purpose of the organization, if it is an effective one, these are always the directive and supervisory tasks." [24]

Since this was so, it was possible, he said, to find inherent in every fully developed organization certain principles of management which had "universal applicability." These principles had been most highly developed and applied in business and industry, but governmental and educational institutions had lagged behind. He claimed, however, that these latter institutions were learning their lesson and were "busily making application of proven principles of good management to the special problems of their own field." So far as education was concerned, it was "rather backward" compared to industry, but this was understandable, he said, because our educational system was of "very recent growth" whereas the development of business organization began in the Middle Ages. Therefore it was natural that education should borrow from business.[25]

The substance of the work was divided into seven major sections, each with a statement of the principles to be followed. Thus the first major section was devoted to "standards" and two of his basic principles. They were:

[23] *Ibid.*
[24] *Ibid.*, pp. 7–8.
[25] *Ibid.*, pp. 8–9.

Principle I. — Definite qualitative and quantitative standards must be determined for the product.

Principle II. — Where the material that is acted upon by the labor processes passes through a number of progressive stages on its way from the raw material to the ultimate product, definite qualitative and quantitative standards must be determined for the product at each of these stages. [26]

Without definite standards for the product which the organization was to turn out, the work could not even be started. The steel plants if they were to manufacture rails had to have precise specifications for this product, and these standards were not determined by the steel mill but by those who ordered the rails. This principle was equally applicable to education, for, said Bobbitt, "education is a shaping process as much as the manufacture of steel rails." He admitted that the educational shaping was more complex and that it was complicated by the factor of growth. But he said the growth factor was also a problem in agriculture and yet standards had been applied with great success by farmers. In discussing the great variation in productivity among farmers who did and did not set standards, he attributed the success of a man in Wyoming who had raised two hundred bushels of potatoes to the acre to the fact that he had set a high standard for himself. "It was not," said Bobbitt, "superior soil or climate; it was having a high standard on the basis of which to adjust and control all the necessary processes."

In education it was the same. Some eighth grade classes, he said, did addition "at the rate of thirty-five combinations per minute" while another "not dissimilarly located will add at an average rate of one hundred and five combinations per minute." And he added that if these differences were true among pupils of "supposedly equal ability" in these simple matters, it was reasonable to expect much greater variation in "science, history and the humanities. . . ." Within the last decade educators "had come to see that it is possible to set up definite standards for the various educational products. The ability to add at a speed of 65 combinations per minute, with an accuracy of 94 per cent is as definite a specification as can be set up for any aspect of the work of the steel plant." [27]

But setting up standards was only the first step. Scales of measurement were necessary to determine "whether the product rises to standard." In most schools, he said, the teacher "if asked whether his eighth grade pupils could add at the rate of 65 combinations per minute with an accuracy of 94 per cent, could not answer the ques-

[26] *Ibid.*, p. 11.
[27] *Ibid.*, pp. 11–15.

tion; nor would he know how to go about finding out. He needs a measuring scale that will serve him in measuring his product as well as the scale of feet and inches serves in measuring the product of the steel plant." [28] Although it may seem to the reader that teachers with a watch and a knowledge of sixth grade arithmetic could measure this rather easily, Bobbitt assumed that they could not and so he devoted several pages to a description (complete with scales and charts) of the work that T. W. Stone and S. A. Courtis had done in creating scales for measuring simple arithmetical skills.

These scales were of great value to the teacher, he said, because "Having these definite tasks laid upon her, she can know at all times whether she is accomplishing the things expected of her or not. She can herself know whether she is a good teacher, a medium teacher, or a poor teacher." [29] And they were of great value to the supervisor since they enabled him to tell at a glance which teachers were strong and which ones were weak. A teacher who fell short of the standard was "unmistakably shown to be a weak teacher," and the supervisor would have "incontestable evidence of inefficiency against the weak teacher who cannot or refuses to improve." This knowledge would enable the management to "instantly overcome" one of the most troublesome problems in the schools — that of getting rid of inefficient teachers. [30]

There were practically no limits to the benefits to be achieved through the adoption of standards. Teachers would know instantly when students were failing. Principals would know when teachers were inefficient, and they could easily determine how their school compared with other schools, not in a vague, general way, but precisely and absolutely. And superintendents would benefit most of all for they, "by glancing over the number of units of results obtained by each teacher in each building in his city, especially when thrown into distribution tables and graphs, can locate instantly the strong, the mediocre, and the weak teachers. By noting the distribution by buildings, he can also see at a glance what building principals are doing a superior grade of work, what ones relatively poor work. Thus he is able to tell at once where his strong subordinates are and where his weak ones are. He can *know with certainty* the building principals and the teachers that are especially in need of help from the central office." [31]

With this system neither students, teachers, nor principals could

[28] *Ibid.*, p. 15.
[29] *Ibid.*, p. 23.
[30] *Ibid.*, pp. 27–28.
[31] *Ibid.*, p. 30. (Italics mine.)

offer lame excuses for inferior performance, for with everything so definitely recorded there would be no place to hide and responsibility could be fixed. Furthermore, this would be done (as Taylor claimed it would be done in the machine shop) without anyone feeling that he had been treated unfairly because all of this would not be done arbitrarily but scientifically. Finally, Bobbitt pointed out that the adoption of definite standards and the use of measurement scales which made it possible to report results in quantitative terms enabled schoolmen to improve their relations with the community since the results could be presented in "specific understandable terms." [32] Bobbitt was not motivated, as other educators were, to use scientific management as a means of defense, but it is significant that he indicated its value in this regard. Undoubtedly this did not diminish the attractiveness of the system to the administrators who read the Yearbook.

Having established that standards, and means for measuring them, were necessary and desirable, Bobbitt turned to the question of how they were to be determined. This should be done in education just as in industry. The standards and specifications for steel rails were set by the railroads, not by the steel plants, and the specifications for educational products should be set by the community, not by educators. "A school system," he said, "can no more find standards of performance within itself than a steel plant can find the proper height or weight per yard for steel rails from the activities within the plant." [33] And the specifications must be definite and exact. For example, in setting specifications for a house "every element in the building, exact to a fraction of an inch, must be exactly stated. Nothing less will serve." [34] The same principle applied to education, therefore "in the case of the instructions of our general society to its agent, the school, specifications must be equally definite." Thus he suggested that "the commercial world can best say what it needs in the case of its stenographers and accountants. A machine shop can best say what is needed in the workers that come to it. The plumbing trade contains the men who are best able to state the needs of those entering upon plumbing; and so on through the entire list." [35]

Bobbitt went beyond merely suggesting that the business and industrial world enter the schools and set up standards: he made it their civic duty. He stated that through such action the business world would be doing a "valuable service" for the schools — far

[32] *Ibid.*, pp. 31–32.
[33] *Ibid.*, p. 34.
[34] *Ibid.*, p. 35.
[35] *Ibid.*, p. 36.

more valuable than the "present method of complaining." And he implied that the businessmen were partly to blame for the inefficiency of education because "they have never told the schools exactly what they do want." [36]

The logical question that arose was what the role of the educator was to be. Bobbitt contended that he should not "stand idly by and passively wait" for the men of the practical world to make their needs known, but rather he should go to them and inform them of their role. The men of practical affairs were unaware of their responsibility for "definitely saying what they want." When laymen were convinced that they should provide the specifications for the products they needed and expected from the schools, and when "society has given to the school its ultimate standard in any particular case, it then is certainly the business of the educational and psychological experts to determine the time of beginning, the intensity of the work, and the standards to be attained in each of the successive stages." [37] This work, said Bobbitt, was highly technical in nature and could be done only by experts. In this sphere, the untrained layman could have no opinion and he had no right to interfere. In brief, the educators' function was not to determine what the schools were to do, but rather how they were to do what they were told. Doubtless many educators who had devoted years of study and thought to the aims and purposes of education were surprised to learn that they had misunderstood their function. They were to be mechanics, not philosophers.

In this discussion of the need for standards, Bobbitt had illustrated his points with examples from simple arithmetical skills, and he did this because Stone and Courtis had done work in this subject and their material was available. He extended the application of his main points to spelling, handwriting, and composition, for in each of these subjects scales had been created. Although he conceded that some aspects of composition were difficult to measure quantitatively and that there was room for improvement in the measuring instruments, he was satisfied with the progress that had been made. But so far he had dealt only with simple skill subjects. Could standards be established and scales be developed in areas such as history and literature, where some of the expected outcomes involved social and moral attitudes, judgment, and appreciation? Bobbitt took the view that this would be difficult but it could be done "for every desirable educational product whether tangible or intangible." It might take some time, and much preliminary work would have to be done, but, he said, "After our profession has scaled the lower heights, it will be

[36] *Ibid.*
[37] *Ibid.*, pp. 36–37.

time enough to prepare to scale the higher." However, no matter how difficult it would be "to set up quantitative standards in the more intangible fields" it had to be done, for, he said, "It will work harm to establish definite standards for only a portion of the tasks of education, leaving the rest to the traditional vagueness and uncertainty of aim. The remedy is to establish equally definite standards in every field of educational labor. There can be no other remedy." [38]

After settling the problem of establishing standards and developing measuring scales for all educational products, Bobbitt turned to the question of who should do the testing. It should be done, he said, by the "workers all along the line" but since it was "an accepted principle in the business world that the department which inspects the product must be wholly independent of the department which is responsible for securing the product," it would be necessary to have a special inspection department. However, because of the "greater probity" of educators over "corresponding workers in a business organization" the rule would not need to be applied as strictly. Yet, he pointed out that when salaries and promotions hinged on test results the temptation to cheat a little would be great; therefore it would be necessary to "reinforce this probity." This distrust Bobbitt extended even to the superintendent. He thought it possible that a man who wanted to make a favorable impression on his community might "manipulate results" in his favor. Since this was so, he believed that "those who set aside the school organization as their agent might very well have an inspectorial department for independent testing of the work of their institutional agent." [39]

In applying his system of scientific management in various industrial plants, Frederick Taylor had encountered opposition from some men in management who thought that the extensive records and the elaborate paper work would offset any gains made in increasing productivity. Taylor had answered these objections by citing figures which he claimed proved that great savings were achieved, even with the additional expense involved in detailed planning, record-keeping, and accounting. Bobbitt, perhaps taking advantage of Taylor's controversy, anticipated that this objection would be made to his "scientific direction and supervision." He conceded that under his system education would require "an even more elaborate system of accounting than is required by a factory or a railroad," but he pointed out that such records had been profitable in business and they were "an indispensible basis for efficient management, direction, and supervision." If a 10 per cent increase in expenditure had brought a 100 per

[38] *Ibid.*, pp. 42–44.
[39] *Ibid.*, pp. 45–46.

cent increase in profit to industry, he thought there was no reason why the increased expenditure for such services should not bring equally large returns to education.[40] Despite Bobbitt's defense, Superintendent Maxwell of New York City pointed out that if Bobbitt's recommendation were followed the bookkeeping required in his city "would exceed by many fold the bookkeeping required for the largest railroad corporation in the United States." If this work were done by the teachers, said Maxwell, they "would have no time and energy left for teaching." If it were done by clerks, they would have to be trained in statistical method.[41]

Bobbitt concluded his remarks on standards by stating that the development of such a system as he described "constitutes the most practical single task at present before the field of education." And he claimed that his ideas pointed the way to a level of "administrative efficiency as far above the present as scientific management in the business world is above the ordinary crude, empirical management." The greatest obstacle to the development of such a scheme was not the difficulty of the task nor the lack of technique, but a lack of co-operation among educators. Most schoolmen, he said, were "intellectualists," individualists who went their own way, and the result was a "low and primitive form of organization, direction, and management." It would be necessary in the future for educators to set social service above self-interest, and Bobbitt believed that there were many men in the profession who were ready to submerge themselves for society's benefit and that this was fortunate, for, as he put it, "the time is ripe." [42]

The second major section of the yearbook was devoted to what Bobbitt termed "Methods," which he began with his third principle, *"Scientific Management finds the methods of procedure which are most efficient for actual service under actual conditions, and secures their use on the part of the workers."* Thus the first two major sections of his work and his first three principles corresponded roughly to Taylor's first principle of developing the science of the job. Bobbitt informed his readers that the "secret of the startling transformations in industry that are at present being brought about by the much-heralded scientific management" was the taking over by management of the responsibility for deciding on the methods to be used in manufacture. It followed that this procedure had to be applied in education. Just as Taylor had said that the development of the science of

---

[40] *Ibid.*, pp. 46–48.

[41] William H. Maxwell, "On a Certain Arrogance in Educational Theorists," *Educational Review*, XLVII (February, 1914), 181.

[42] Bobbitt, *General Principles of Management*, pp. 49–50.

the job was too difficult for the worker in the machine shop, so Bobbitt took the position that "The burden of finding the best methods is too large and too complicated to be laid on the shoulders of the teachers." [43]

Bobbitt discounted the objection that the schools should not experiment on children by stating that actually they were being experimented on all the time. The trouble was that this experimentation was on a trial and error basis and not done systematically. He proposed that supervisors study the various methods that were being used, measure the results, select the best one, and put it into effect. And to show how this might be done he gave the following illustration:

Suppose among schools that give sixty minutes per week to drill in penmanship, it is found that one group of schools distributes the time into thirty-minute periods twice a week; another group of schools has twenty-minute periods three times a week; another group distributes the time into twelve-minute periods of drill five times a week; a fourth group distributes the time into six-minute periods ten times a week, or a short period twice each day. Now suppose each of these groups of schools to be measured in the first week of the school year by the Thorndike or the Ayres writing scale as to quality, and tested *by the stop-watch as to speed*. If they are then measured again at the end of the year in the same way, it is possible to determine which of the modes of distributing the sixty minutes of time for teaching the writing is the superior. [44]

The establishment of such scientific procedures was necessary, Bobbitt said, to take education out of the realm of opinion and put it on a more definite basis. Unless this were done, the supervisor was relatively helpless, for his opinion was not better than the teacher's opinion. Again the business world, he said, "shows us how to proceed more nearly than any illustration that I can take from the educational field." This time he cited the success of the Harriman railroad system in having a central office select the best methods of operation and then enforce their adoption throughout the system. In education the "expert staff in the central office of our large city system . . ." could perform the same service and increase the efficiency of instruction correspondingly. [45]

Bobbitt's next three steps dealt with the selection and training of teachers and corresponded to Taylor's second principle concerning the scientific selection and training of the workmen. To the first of these steps, "qualifications of teachers" he applied his fourth principle, "*standard qualifications must be determined for the workers.*"

[43] *Ibid.*, pp. 51–52.
[44] *Ibid.*, pp. 54–55. (Italics mine.)
[45] *Ibid.*, pp. 57–61.

Bobbitt cited Taylor's account of the "scientific" selection of the girls in the bicycle factory and indicated that, although the task would be more difficult in education, it had to be done. He pointed out that standards were already being applied to the academic aspects of teaching; now it was necessary to develop such criteria for the personality characteristics necessary for teachers.[46] To illustrate the progress that had already been made in this direction he included two rating sheets which were being used in the schools. One of these was developed by Professor Edward C. Elliott and entitled "A Tentative Scheme for the Measurement of Teaching Efficiency." Bobbitt approved of Elliott's rating sheet and thought it indicated "a practical belief in the possibility of drawing up definite plans and specifications which exhibit the elements and proportions of personality that are necessary for the fully equipped teacher." But he also thought that the instrument was not definite enough. His advice to the profession was to follow the best practices in industry, e.g. Taylor's work in the bicycle factory, where "Empirical vagueness and uncertainly gave place to absolute certainty." If and when this were done, he said, "we shall be able to place our workers with the same efficiency, justice, and certainty."[47]

In the second step of his treatment of the selection and training of teachers, Bobbitt dealt with the "preliminary training of teachers" and his fifth basic principle, *"the management must train its workers previous to service in the measure demanded by its standard qualifications, or it must set up entrance requirements of so specific and detailed a nature as to enforce upon training institutions the output of a supply of workers possessing the desirable qualifications in the degree necessary for entrance into service."*[48] This principle, he said, indicated one of the "major supervising functions" and also one that had been completely neglected. When teachers came out of the teacher training institutions poorly prepared the supervisors in the school systems had to spend more time bringing them up to standard. The way to proceed was to have the school systems inform the colleges as to what their specifications for new teachers were, for, as he put it, "They have the same right to say to colleges what product shall be sent to them as a transportation system has to say to a steel plant what kind of rails shall be sent to it. They are in a position to command." He suggested that these specifications should be drawn up by committees from the elementary and secondary schools. He realized that it would not be an easy task because supervisory offi-

[46] *Ibid.*, pp. 62–64.
[47] *Ibid.*, pp. 69–70.
[48] *Ibid.*, p. 74.

cials were not agreed on the "standard qualifications necessary for entering upon professional labor in the various departments, especially so in secondary education, where the need is greatest." Even where there was agreement, he complained that it was expressed in general terms which were not sufficiently specific and accurate for practical use. Despite the difficulty of the assignment, Bobbitt believed specific formulation of the details of the kind of qualities expected was necessary if the training institutions were to turn out the desired product.[49]

In the third step of his treatment of the selection and training of teachers, Bobbitt dealt with "training during service" and applied his sixth principle, *"the worker must be kept up to standard qualifications for his kind of work for his entire service."* The role of the supervisory staff in this connection was to see to it that teachers had an opportunity to "exercise" the many aspects of the standard teacher's personality, and to organize and control incentives (Taylor's bonus plan), so that teachers would take advantage of these opportunities for "personality exercise." This activity by the teacher was needed continuously, for without such exercise these personality traits would dwindle and decay, "leaving hollowness, feebleness, indifference, and disproportion."[50] The opportunities listed by Bobbitt included attending professional meetings, participating in the life of the community, visiting other schools, travel, etc. It was also necessary to see to it that teachers had the time and energy to take advantage of these opportunities, and he suggested that this could be done after definite standards and definite methods had been developed. With this professional assistance, he said, "it appears possible so to speed up the work that one teacher may be able to handle two shifts of pupils in academic subjects during a six-hour day with not more than two hours required for daily preparation. The teacher may then be told that the remaining four hours of the day not needed for sleep and meals may be used for the variety of necessary humanizing activities for keeping one's self up to standard."[51] Incentives could be provided through higher salaries, the development of a pervading scientific spirit, and through an emphasis upon the social service possible through teaching.

Finally Bobbitt devoted himself to the problem of getting teachers to understand and to carry out the instructions of the school administrators. He entitled this part of the work "Definiteness of Instructions." *"The worker must be kept supplied with detailed instructions*

[49] *Ibid.*, pp. 74–78.
[50] *Ibid.*, p. 79.
[51] *Ibid.*, p. 85.

as to the work to be done, the standards to be reached, the methods to be employed, and the appliances to be used." He described briefly the functions of the planning room and the system of functional foremanship which had been devised "by the well-known efficiency engineer, Mr. Frederick W. Taylor," and indicated that when the system had been given a fair trial under favorable conditions it had been "wondrously successful."[52] Although Bobbitt accepted the Taylor system in this respect, and approved the idea that management (through the planning room) should work out and decide on methods and standards, and in general develop the science of the job, he was reluctant to follow the Taylor system down to giving minute, detailed instructions to the worker. He believed with Taylor that efficiency depended on "centralization of authority and definite direction by the supervisors of all processes performed," but he also thought that some initiative should be left to the teachers.[53] Despite his enthusiastic endorsement of the Taylor system he had his doubts about this one aspect. As he said, "It is hard to see how this could do otherwise than mechanize the worker, destroy all powers of thought and initiative, and in the end undermine in large degree his working efficiency."[54]

His solution to the problem was to train the "workman," both prior to and during service, so that he would be "reasonably familiar with the controlling science in its general outlines as used by the planning room." If this were done, the instructions could be more general and the worker would have more flexibility in his work. Still, Bobbitt said, the results of the work of the planning department had to be "transmitted to the teachers so that there can never be any misunderstanding as to what is expected of a teacher in the way of results or in the matter of method. This means that instruction must be given as to everything that is to be done." As long as teachers used the standard methods and accomplished standard results, management would not need to interfere. If, however, the teacher could not or would not do this, the supervisory staff would have to step in, and the authority would be theirs to decide when they needed to interfere with the teacher.[55]

While he appeared to be giving the teacher more freedom than Schmidt had, Bobbitt made the limitation of this freedom quite clear:

Teachers cannot be permitted to follow caprice in method. When a method which is clearly superior to all other methods has been discovered, it alone can

[52] *Ibid.*, pp. 89–91.
[53] *Ibid.*, p. 89.
[54] *Ibid.*, p. 92.
[55] *Ibid.*, pp. 92–94.

be employed. To neglect this function and to excuse one's negligence by proclaiming the value of the freedom of the teacher was perhaps justifiable under our earlier empiricism, when the supervisors were merely promoted teachers and on the scientific side at least knew little more about standards and methods than the rank and file.[56]

He conceded that under his system "the teacher's freedom is necessarily narrowly limited," but he justified the limitation in the same way that Taylor did, by stating that the "limitations are those of law and not the limitations of personal arbitrary authority."[57]

The last short section in his analysis contained "Other Principles":

Principle VIII. — It is a function of the management to discover and to supply the tools and appliances that are the most effective for the work in hand.

Principle IX. — Responsibility must be definite and undivided in the case of each task to be performed in the total series of processes.

Principle X. — Incentives must be placed before the workers so as to stimulate the output on their part of the optimum product.

Principle XI. — In a productive organization, the management must determine the order and sequence of all of the various processes through which the raw material or the partially developed product shall pass, in order to bring about the greatest possible effectiveness and economy; and it must see that the raw material or partially finished product is actually passed on from process to process, from worker to worker, in the manner that is most effective and most economical.[58]

So the great panacea was applied to education. Spaulding's effort certainly provided a practical means for reducing education to financial terms and thereby enabled schoolmen to meet their economy-minded critics on their own ground. At the same time, by giving to the work of the administrator the appearance of scientific respectability, Spaulding not only contributed to an improved status for the administrator but also provided him with a professional rationalization for an overemphasis upon the financial aspects of education. Bobbitt's system, which had the merit of being very definite, presented an interpretation of education which men in business and industry could understand. It too, if applied, would enable schoolmen to defend themselves, in the first place by making their work seem scientific, and in the second place by relinquishing the responsibility for deciding on educational objectives and — to a great extent — for formulating the contents of the curriculum, and turning these functions over to business and industry. Following Bobbitt's plan, school-

[56] *Ibid.*, p. 95.
[57] *Ibid.*, p. 93.
[58] *Ibid.*, pp. 95–96.

men would become mechanics whose task would be to figure out ways and means of doing what they were told.

But if these proposals had advantages they also had disadvantages and these were *educational* in nature. Some of the unfortunate aspects of Spaulding's recommendations were discussed previously. The most unfortunate aspects of Bobbitt's system were his invitation to laymen, and especially businessmen, to interfere with the work of the schools; his oversimplified and mechanical conception of the nature of education and his almost complete lack of understanding of teaching as an art, which made it possible for him constantly to draw parallels between management and the worker in industry, and the administrator and the teacher in education; his building up of the authority of the administrator on the one hand while limiting the freedom of the teacher on the other; and his completely unrealistic conception of what would constitute a scientific basis for education.

On this last point, Bobbitt, like many of his contemporaries in education, was impatient with educational theory, which he regarded as mere opinion. Certainly his desire to establish a scientific basis for education was commendable, but his notion of achieving absolute *certainty* in an endeavor as complex as education was overly optimistic, to say the least. In this aim Bobbitt (although he demonstrated more insight than Spaulding) failed to understand, or at least did not take into account in his analysis, the difficult, painstaking nature of Taylor's scientific work.

That Bobbitt perceived the problem in narrow mechanistic terms is clear from the sources to which he turned for guidance in developing a scientific basis for teaching. Instead of looking to the psychologist, the social psychologist, and the sociologist, he cited the achievements of the Harriman railroad corporation. So, while he realized that teaching had to be based on something other than opinion, he gave no indication that he understood the nature or the complexity of the task. While Bobbitt did state that the scientific work in education would be more difficult than the industrial research, he did not indicate that the study of teaching method would require extensive training on the part of the experts in his educational planning room. Of course, the behavioral sciences were in an early stage of development in 1913, and the knowledge and research skills necessary to provide fairly reliable answers on a more profound level were not available. It is doubtful that even a man of Edward Thorndike's ability and research experience, with unlimited time and money, could have done on a truly scientific basis, what Bobbitt expected the supervisory staff in the public schools to do. And it goes without saying that these men had neither the training nor research skill of a Thorndike, nor the funds necessary for the scientific analysis of the classroom.

Perhaps in the end this oversimplification of the knowledge, skill, and time necessary even to begin building a solid foundation upon which the art of teaching would be based was more unfortunate than inviting laymen in to direct the schools, or pressing the management-worker parallel, or contributing to the authoritarian position of the administrator. Under the circumstances, it would have been difficult for Bobbitt to admit, even if he had been aware of it, that neither he (who had received his Ph.D. under G. Stanley Hall at Clark University) nor other educators were qualified to carry on the difficult research work that was necessary. He and his fellow educators had to strengthen, not weaken, themselves, and to concede that they were not "experts" would have further weakened their already insecure position. The tragedy was that educators were forced to assume too soon the role of experts and that in so doing they either turned their attention to cost accounting (Spaulding) or to the simple mechanical problems (Bobbitt). This pattern was followed by other administrators who, in their conception and application of scientific management, changed its original meaning. These men were not scientists who were interested in inquiring into the nature of the educational process. They were undoubtedly dedicated to and genuinely concerned about improving public education, but they were under continuous pressure to economize and to operate the schools in a businesslike way and this fact, added to their inability to carry out scientific research on more profound problems, led them to devote their attention to applying the scientific method to the financial and mechanical aspects of education.

Spaulding and Bobbitt, in dressing up simple problems with impressive scientific-appearing presentations while ignoring more profound considerations, and then making extravagant claims which could not be realized, helped to build up professional education for a great fall. Perhaps an awareness of the difficulty of the task and of the skill and training necessary for the research work would have made the situation more difficult for them in 1913, but it would have contributed more to the study of education in the long run. Whether this awareness, if coupled with a determined effort to educate the public to the need for painstaking, systematic — and expensive — research in education, would have resulted in the formulation of a real scientific basis for education is, of course, an open question.

Few educators saw the need, and neither the research skill nor the money was available.[59]

Under the circumstances, however, these facts were not important. Schoolmen were responding to criticism and the critics were not interested in genuine research. They wanted to reduce, or at least to prevent an increase in school taxes and they wanted to be assured that their schools were being operated efficiently, i.e. that they were getting the maximum return for their expenditure. So administrators either studied the advice of the "experts" and applied the efficiency procedures themselves or if the situation was critical they called in the efficiency expert to help them save their jobs.

[59] Ironically it was the *Saturday Evening Post*, in an editorial entitled "Poverty-Stricken Schools," written in October of 1913, which pointed out the complete lack of funds provided for the careful study of education. The schools, said the Editor, were "like the farmer who sees clearly that he can never make more than a bare living unless he fertilizes, buys efficient machinery and gets better-bred stock; yet he cannot for the life of him scrape up a spare dollar for lime, a sulky plow or a thoroughbred cow." As an example, the *Post* reported that Thomas Edison had demonstrated his moving picture machine to a group of educators, including John Dewey, who were much impressed but saddened. Dewey was reported to have remarked regretfully upon "the immense advantage a great commercial enterprise has over the greatest of our educational institutions in the matter of systematic experimenting with a new proposal before putting it into general practice," and to have asked "Where is there a school system having at its command a sum of money with which to investigate and perfect a scheme experimentally before putting it into general operation?" Then the editorial concluded with these insightful and pathetic words: "The Steel Trust, the oil companies, and a thousand and one business concerns do that very thing day in and day out as a matter of course — because they know it pays in the end. But the poor out-at-elbows public has not a dollar for experimental investigation in education." *Saturday Evening Post*, CLXXXVI, No. 15 (October 11, 1913), 26.

5

THE EDUCATIONAL EFFICIENCY
EXPERTS IN ACTION

In the years between 1911 and 1925 educational administrators responded in a variety of ways to the demands for more efficient operation of the schools. Before the mania ran its course various "efficiency" procedures were applied to classroom learning and to teachers, to the program of studies, to the organization of the schools, to administrative functions, and to entire school systems. Most of these actions before 1916 were connected in some way by educators to the magic words "scientific management." This was especially true when someone who could lay claim to the title "educational efficiency expert" had participated in what was done, or when the work could be traced to the recommendation of such a person e.g., Spaulding or Bobbitt.

There were two groups of educators who were generally accepted and even labeled by administrators as "educational efficiency experts" or "engineers." There were those men who worked full time in the efficiency bureaus which had been established in many of the large cities after 1911, and prominent professors of education who made their services available as consultants. Evidence that these so-called efficiency experts were quite numerous by 1914, and that they were not always whole-heartedly appreciated, is given by one irritated schoolman, veteran Superintendent J. M. Greenwood of Kansas City who told a general session of the N.E.A. that there were "so many efficiency engineers running hand cars through the schoolhouses in most large cities that the grade teachers can hardly turn around in their rooms without butting into two or three of them."[1]

A majority of administrators, however, held views quite the oppo-

[1] N.E.A. *Proceedings* (1914), p. 117.

site of Greenwood's. One of the leading, if not *the* leading, educational administrators in the period between 1915 and 1934 was Ellwood P. Cubberley, dean of the School of Education at Stanford.[2] His textbook, *Public School Administration*, published in 1916, was described by George S. Counts in 1927 as "the most widely read and influential book on school administration of our generation." [3] This influential educator acknowledged the existence and importance of the educational efficiency expert by devoting a full chapter of this book to an enthusiastic account of his work. The chapter, entitled "Efficiency Experts: Testing Results," provides additional evidence of a direct link between educational efficiency experts and the scientific management movement. In a footnote on the first page of the chapter Cubberley used a newspaper statement which made a direct connection between education and Taylor's experiments. The use to which this footnote was put by Cubberley also demonstrates again the pattern of criticism and response. He used it to provide documentation for his assertion that the efficiency expert movement in education was partly a result "of public demand for a more intelligent accounting by school officers for the money expended for public education." [4] The footnote, identified simply as an "Editorial in the *Springfield Republican* 1912," read as follows: "New York City spent last year nearly $35,000,000 for education, and hardly a dollar of it was spent for measuring results. Are educators supposed to be such experts that their methods cannot be improved? Lately we have had a striking demonstration of what experimental science can do by reducing the motions in laying brick and the fatigue in handling pig iron. It can hardly be pretended that scientific efficiency is of less consequence in the schools.'" By featuring this statement, Cubberley helped to ensure that the thousands of students who used

---

[2] For a brief account of Cubberley's early life and professional career see pp. 182–85.

[3] George S. Counts, *The Social Composition of Boards of Education* (Chicago, 1927), p. 84.

[4] Cubberley, *Public School Administration* (Boston), p. 325. The same point had been made by H. B. Wilson, superintendent of schools in Topeka, Kansas, and chairman of the influential Committee on the Economy of Time of the Department of Superintendence. Speaking before the National Council of Education in 1915, Wilson stated "the progressive evolution of society" had produced the efficiency engineer, and that at the time of his appearance, fortunately, enough progress had been made in the scientific study of education so that "the *education efficiency engineer* became a possibility and consequently very soon a reality." To explain the sudden appearance of the efficiency expert's counterpart in education he added "his advent was hastened somewhat by rampant public criticism of the schools, in part led and inspired by such leading educational journals as the *Delineator* and the *Ladies Home Journal*." N.E.A. *Proceedings*, pp. 604–6. There was very little criticism of the schools in the *Delineator*. Certainly it was not "rampant." He was, of course, correct on the *Ladies' Home Journal* but he should have named the *Saturday Evening Post* as the other journal.

his text would be exposed, at least indirectly, to the pressure to adopt "scientific efficiency" procedures in education. (Incidentally, one wonders whether Schmidt would have agreed that experimental science had "reduced his fatigue" in handling pig iron.)

Cubberley described the emergence of the educational efficiency experts as "one of the most significant movements in all of our education history" and he added (prophetically, as it turned out) that their work would "change the whole character of school administration."[5] The same enthusiasm was conveyed throughout the chapter and particularly in the final section — a section which showed clearly that Cubberley had leaned heavily on the ideas of Franklin Bobbitt:

The work described in this chapter is new work, and work of a type with which schoolmasters are as yet but little familiar, but it is work of great future importance, work which will professionalize teaching and supervision, and work destined to do much to increase the value of the public service rendered by our schools. By means of standards and units of the type now being evolved and tested out it is even now possible for a superintendent of schools to make a survey of his school system which will be indicative of its points of strength and weakness, and to learn from the results better methods and procedures. In time it will be possible for any school system to maintain a continuous survey of all of the different phases of its work, through tests made by its corps of efficiency experts, and to detect weak points in its work almost as soon as they appear.

Every manufacturing establishment that turns out a standard product or series of products of any kind maintains a force of efficiency experts to study methods of procedure and to measure and test the output of its works. Such men ultimately bring the manufacturing establishment large returns, by introducing improvements in processes and procedure, and in training the workmen to produce a larger and a better output. Our schools are, in a sense, factories in which the raw products (children) are to be shaped and fashioned into products to meet the various demands of life. The specifications for manufacturing come from the demands of twentieth-century civilization, and it is the business of the school to build its pupils according to the specifications laid down. This demands good tools, specialized machinery, continuous measurement of production to see if it is according to specifications, the elimination of waste in manufacture, and a large variety in the output.[6]

In the body of the chapter Cubberley presented what amounted to a condensed statement of Bobbitt's version of scientific management. The purpose of the new scientific movement, he said, was to create standards so that the efficiency of the work of the schools could be determined, demonstrated, and communicated to the public in "a

[5] Cubberley, *Public School Administration*, p. 325.
[6] *Ibid.*, pp. 337–38.

language which the community could easily understand." This would elevate the work of education from where it was, based upon guess-work and personal opinion, to "scientific accuracy." [7] As a result everyone would benefit. Pupils would be carefully examined and properly classified and they could chart their progress and see their deficiencies. Teachers would know "definitely" what was expected of them, since they would have "definite tasks laid down." As for principals and supervisors they could tell

almost at a glance whether pupils or rooms are making proper progress; when any group has made all desirable progress and should advance; whether instruction is directed to what are the weak points for the group; where teachers who need help are located, and in what particulars they need help; in what rooms the load and the teacher are not properly adjusted; and what teachers are so inefficient or indifferent or incapable of progress that they should be dropped from the service. For the purpose of vocational guidance of pupils such records will be of great value. The superintendent, too, can use the results to talk to his school board and to his community and can justify both the work and the expense of his schools.[8]

Cubberley conceded, as had Bobbitt, that this work would require extensive records, but he justified them in the same way that Taylor and Bobbitt had done by stating, "The lesson of the business world, from which we have much to learn in the matter of efficiency, is that detailed records more than pay for their cost, and that an accurate knowledge as to manufacturing processes is impossible without such records." [9]

The combination of the great prestige which Cubberley enjoyed as an "authority" in educational administration and the widespread use of his textbook meant that his enthusiastic endorsement of the educational efficiency expert certainly contributed to the spread of knowledge about these men and to an acceptance of them in the years after 1916. This meant, of course, that it was Bobbitt's version of scientific management which was being spread and his conception of the efficiency expert which was being accepted.

Cubberley went beyond the general endorsement to advise any young man who desired "to prepare for school administration in the future" to "thoroughly familiarize himself with the aims and methods of this new phase of administrative service." [10] He also urged the creation of efficiency bureaus in every city school department of any size. Such bureaus had already been established in Boston,

[7] *Ibid.*, pp. 326–27.
[8] *Ibid.*, pp. 333–34.
[9] *Ibid.*, p. 335.
[10] *Ibid.*, p. 326.

New York, New Orleans, Detroit, Kansas City, Rochester, and Oakland, and he indicated that they would grow in numbers and that there would be opportunities for men interested in becoming educational efficiency experts. "Such positions" he said, "are almost certain to multiply rapidly, and they will offer attractive careers to certain types of men." [11] Then he indicated the kind of work which would be available by describing the "lines of service" which he said were "already clearly defined" within the field:

Part of these lie along the line of business organization, part lie along the lines of special-type educational adjustments, and part lie in the field of experimental pedagogy. These lines include at least the following: To study all phases of the process of preparing pupils for life-careers, and for efficient community service; to study the needs of life and the industries, with a view to restating the specification for the manufacture of the educational output; to study means for increasing the rate of production, and for eliminating the large present waste in manufacturing; to test the product at different stages of manufacture, and to advise the workers as to the results of their labors; to test out different methods of procedure, and gradually to eliminate those which do not give good results; to study the costs of production, not so much to cut down costs as to be able to show how the efficiency of the plant may be increased by a proper adjustment or even an increase in expenditures; to supply the superintendent with concrete data with which he may deal more intelligently with his board, the public, and the teaching staff; and to organize material for publication in the annual printed report of the school department.[12]

In his account of the educational efficiency experts Cubberley stated quite accurately that their work fell into two major categories: one, the construction of tests and rating scales for measuring school efficiency and the other, school surveys. Some of these experts were able to work in both capacities by conducting surveys in which the tests and rating scales used were ones they themselves had constructed. However, most experts specialized in one or the other of these two categories.

Efficiency Measures for the Schools

Questions about the effectiveness of teaching had been raised, and attempts to measure the achievement of pupils had been made before 1900. Joseph M. Rice, a physician turned educator, had worked out tests in arithmetic and spelling, had administered them personally to thousands of children in schools in several of the larger cities, and had published the results of his findings in the

[11] *Ibid.*, p. 336.
[12] *Ibid.*, p. 336.

Forum between 1895 and 1903. Partly because his findings showed much of the work of the schools to be poor, partly because he was not exactly gentle in his criticisms, and partly, perhaps, because he was an outsider, Rice and his work were not well received by educators generally. An analysis of his work shows that he lacked a knowledge of even elementary statistics and that many of his conclusions could not be supported by his data. Neverthless, he is generally credited with being a pioneer in the field of educational measurement. After 1903 a few other investigators, and especially E. L. Thorndike and his students, began to develop instruments for measuring achievement in the skill subjects of the elementary school, and by 1910 several tests had been constructed and were being standardized.

Almost immediately after the country became acquainted with scientific management procedures, pressure began to apply them to the classroom. In July of 1911, for example, a month after Taylor's series of articles was completed in the *American Magazine*, a school board member from Allegheny, Pennsylvania told the N.E.A. that the two words which were "electrifying the industrial world — scientific management" contained a "message" for every teacher, and near the end of his speech he indicated that if teachers did not voluntarily take steps to increase their efficiency the business world would force them to do so.[13] As a result great energy was expended on using the available tests and on developing new tests or scales or rating sheets or anything else that would seem to provide tangible evidence of efficiency. As one superintendent writing in 1912 put it, "the results of a few well-planned tests would carry more weight with the business man and the parent than all the psychology in the world."[14]

In the process of actually attempting to measure efficiency within the schools, educators engaged in a wide variety of activities, but most of the attention was devoted to developing and utilizing "objective" achievement tests in the language arts and arithmetic and in developing scales for rating the efficiency of teachers.

By the end of 1913 several tests had been developed and were being used in the schools. The most prominent of these were the arithmetic test developed by S. A. Courtis, the handwriting scales by Thorndike and Ayres and the English scales by Thorndike and Hillegas. The *Elementary School Teacher* reported in December of 1913 that these tests were being given "wide currency" in the schools.[15]

[13] N.E.A. *Proceedings*, p. 723.
[14] Don C. Bliss, "The Standard Test Applied," *American School Board Journal*, XLIV (May, 1912), 12.
[15] Vol. XIV, pp. 145–46.

The work of developing and extending the use of tests was furthered by the important Committee on Tests and Standards of Efficiency in Schools and School Systems appointed by the National Council of the N.E.A. in 1911. The committee, headed by George D. Strayer, reported to the N.E.A. in 1913 and again in 1915 on the progress being made and in each instance urged that more tests and scales be developed. Strayer, expressing his views in speeches and articles, believed "if scientific measurement is to be accomplished, we must have units or scales of measurement which will enable us to make measurements which are verifiable by other observers. We may not hope to achieve progress except as such measuring sticks are available or may be derived." [16]

Much of the work of developing these tests was done by professors of education in the universities and by "educational efficiency experts" who worked full time in efficiency bureaus. By 1915 nine of these bureaus had been established in large cities and the development of the new "profession" of efficiency experts looked so promising that a National Society of Efficiency Men was formed at the Department of Superintendence meeting held in that year. [17]

The attempt to measure efficiency was not, however, limited to the efforts of a relatively few men in universities or in efficiency bureaus. On the contrary, educators from all over the country engaged in this activity by developing rating sheets or offering suggestions to the profession on ways and means of increasing efficiency. The result of their labor is evident in the numerous articles and books which appear in the professional literature as well as in speeches at professional meetings. In his presidential address to the Schoolmasters Association of New York and Vicinity in October of 1912, Theodore C. Mitchell spoke of the great savings made in industry through efficiency studies and then asked "Has the school made equal progress? Has the conduct of the recitation kept pace with modern needs?" His answer was that it had not and he suggested to his audience how the situation could be changed. He warned in advance that some of his suggestions might seem trivial, but he said, "bear in mind that four places of decimals are charged against many railroad engineers for coal, water, lubricating oil, and waste. Time and energy lost in a hundred ways rapidly mount up to vast accounts on the wrong side of the recitation ledger." [18]

[16] George D. Strayer, "Is Scientific Accuracy Possible in the Measurement of the Efficiency of Instruction," *Education*, XXXIV (December, 1913), 253.

[17] *Elementary School Journal*, XV (April, 1915), p. 394.

[18] "Loss of Efficiency in the Recitation," *Educational Review*, XLV (January, 1913), 8–10.

Mitchell suggested that time should not be wasted scolding pupils or lost while students borrowed pencils or paper. To avoid this latter waste teachers should have a well-stocked satchel and carry it from room to room in case it was needed. He recommended an elaborate system of bookkeeping for he said, "Only a teacher would think of trying to keep adequate records of a complex business in one little book that can be slipped into the pocket." In the recitation itself, "Use should be made of all the available time." No time should be wasted in calling the roll, and "Too often valuable time is lost where groups are sent to the blackboards and their several tasks assigned to each one by one, while all the rest wait their turn. As much as four minutes idle time is spent by some." [19] The ideal of "cultured ease in the classroom, of drawingroom quiet and refinement" had to go, he said, and

> It must give way to an ideal of timesaving through preparation for dealing expeditiously and variously with a variety of needs, to the end that maximum results may be attained under pressure of time and with economy of material. By better use of ground space, by better setting of machinery, by better placing of raw material, by the cutting down of labor motions, by producing harder and more lasting cutting tools — by these and other means the factories have increased their output, have lowered the cost of production, have met the demands of their very existence. In a word they have learned to "speed up," not only without placing fresh labor burdens on the workman but on the contrary, with beneficial results in the matter of energy expended and wages earned. And we teachers ought to do the same. We should be compelled to, were we, like members of other professions, as often under watchful, critical adult eyes — were our mistakes to carry as quickly as do theirs, the penalty of almost immediate retribution. We are curiously protected in inefficiency.[20]

Another educator, a superintendent from Portland, Oregon, noting in a speech before the Department of Superintendence in 1913 that "the proceedings of this Association for the last few years show clearly that educational leaders are trying to find some *meter* that can be fitted to our educational *pushcart*," reported that he had developed an observational chart by means of which teachers could mark the progress of pupils in forming habits.[21] Still another described how teaching efficiency could be increased through the use of pictures.[22]

These earnest and sometimes curious efforts continued through

[19] *Ibid.*, p. 15.
[20] *Ibid.*, pp. 27–28.
[21] N.E.A. *Proceedings*, p. 64. (Italics mine.)
[22] Horace G. Brown, "Efficiency in Teaching by Pictures," *Education*, XXXIV (November, 1913), pp. 171–76.

1916. In August of that year the *American School Board Journal* reported in a news item under the caption "Efficiency in the Classroom" an "interesting efficiency system involving the adoption of modern factory systems to the work of the classrooms. . . ." This system had been installed at Bay City, Michigan by the superintendent, and it consisted of hiring a group of substitute teachers who, working under the supervision of the superintendent, tested students extensively and kept records of their progress. The *Journal*, reporting that some fifty thousand examinations had been given, stated that the system made it possible for the superintendent to locate the strong and weak points in the schools and closed by pointing out to its readers that "The system is similar to that in use in factory and commercial establishments and offers a method of determining where the city's money is being invested to best advantage, and where the results are not commensurate with the expenditures." [23]

A major part of the effort to measure efficiency in the school consisted of the attempts to rate teachers. In the early years efforts were made to connect this work very closely with the procedures that Taylor had developed, but later this was not done and the actions were generally justified by reference to the business and industrial world's promotion of workers on the basis of merit. Joseph S. Taylor, district superintendent of schools in New York City, tried to adapt Taylor's ideas to the school and to draw the parallels between the worker and the teacher.

He asked the basic question of whether quantitative measurement could be applied to teaching ability. He then gave an accurate account of the basic principles of Frederick Taylor's system — the employer determining the science of the job, the task and bonus system etc. — and then drew his parallels in education.

One may easily trace an analogy between these fundamentals of the science of industrial management and the organization of a public school system. For example: (1) The state as employer must cooperate with the teacher as employee, for the latter does not always understand the science of education; (2) the state provides experts who supervise the teacher, and suggest the processes that are most efficacious and economical; (3) the task system obtains in the school as well as in the shop, each grade being a measured quantity of work to be accomplished in a given term; (4) every teacher who accomplishes the task receives a bonus, not in money, but in the form of a rating which may have money value; (5) those who are unable to do the work are eliminated, either through the device of a temporary license or of a temporary employment; (6) the differential rate is applied to the teacher, quantity and quality of service being considered in the rating; (7) the result ought to be a maximum output at a low relative cost, since every repeater costs as much as a new pupil; (8) the teacher thus receives better wages, but only after demonstrated fitness for high position; (9) hence we ought to have the most desirable combination of an educational system — relative cheapness of operation and high salaries.[24]

In his adaptation of scientific management, Joseph Taylor was too much of an educator to suggest applying Frederick Taylor's ideas in a mechanical way in the schools. For example, he stated that "after a teacher has become an artist and has learned to secure results in her own way, no principal or superintendent should come along with his petty prescriptions issued in mandatory fashion." [25] Yet he could not bring himself to accept the notion that successful teaching could not be measured, since this acceptance constituted a denial of the "possibility of an educational science." [26] So he worked out charts on which teachers were to be rated, and his attention to detail (e.g. teachers were rated on the time spent in passing and collecting papers) would have done justice to any efficiency engineer. And despite his words about the teacher as an artist, he stated that if her work was "inefficient" the supervisor had the right to say "take my way or find a better one." [27]

In March of 1913 the *American School Board Journal* reported that the educators in large cities were "almost without exception" working out "elaborate plans for rating the work of instructors." The editor complained that most smaller cities and villages had neglected this opportunity for increasing efficiency but some plans had been put into effect by "earnest and fearless superintendents." One such man, reported the *Journal*, was the Superintendent at Park City, Tennessee, who rated his teachers on a 100 per cent scale on the following points: "Influence upon students — in study, in life goals, in nobler ideals etc.; teaching ability — methods, professional progress, tact and skill, enthusiasm, adaptability etc.; discipline; scholarship — accuracy in things taught, preparation of lessons — promptness etc.; energy — snap, go, force in class work etc.; growth — improvement, professional zeal, etc.; results measured by preparation of pupils; relations with other teachers, principal, and ways of cooperating with all that goes on in school; care of books, property etc." [28]

In June of 1915 the education profession acknowledged the im-

    [23] Vol. LII, p. 54.
    [24] "Measurement of Educational Efficiency," *Educational Review*, XLIV (November, 1912), 350–51.
    [25] *Ibid.*, p. 363.
    [26] *Ibid.*, p. 353.
    [27] *Ibid.*, p. 359.
    [28] Vol. XLVI, p. 48.

portance it attached to the problem of measuring teachers' efficiency. In that month a yearbook devoted to the subject was published by the National Society for the Study of Education. The Yearbook was written by Arthur C. Boyce, an assistant in the Department of Education at the University of Chicago and therefore an associate of Franklin Bobbitt. Boyce sent out a questionnaire to educators in 350 cities of over 10,000 population and found that most of them were rating teachers in some way but that many of the schools used only "general impression" methods, while others used scales which were vague and indefinite and had methods of recording judgments (of supervisors) which were "frequently wasteful of time or inaccurate or uncontrolled or all three." [29] To correct this situation Boyce developed a rating scale (presented below) which was designed to overcome these weaknesses and to eliminate "arbitrary personal opinions" from the ratings.

Although the results of a trial run in which this scale was used on 424 teachers in 39 cities showed that it had weaknesses which were due, Boyce said, to differing standards of excellence in the minds of the rating officers and to differences in the ability of school officials to discriminate carefully between the various qualities listed on the scale, it was warmly received by administrators and adopted in many school systems. This was so partly because the scale was simple and easy to use and partly because it was backed by the prestige and authority of the National Society for the Study of Education. Also important was the support of the leading administrative periodical — the *American School Board Journal* — a periodical which reached school board members as well as schoolmen. The scale had been printed in this journal in March of 1915, three months before the publication of the yearbook, and the *Journal* continued to endorse Boyce's work editorially and to praise his ideas frequently in articles.[30] Thus in January, 1917, one superintendent in discussing the rating of teachers, described his work as the "clearest analysis of the whole subject." [31] Even when Boyce's scale was not adopted as such it was apparently used as a model; for many of the rating forms which appeared subsequently in the educational literature were remarkably similar to his.

Since most of the teacher-rating sheets had to be filled out by school principals it followed that means should be devised for measuring *their* efficiency. One of the many rating forms devised for

[29] *Methods for Measuring Teachers Efficiency* (Chicago, 1915), p. 77.
[30] Vol. L, p. 10.
[31] Mary D. Bradford, "How the Superintendent Judges the Value of a Teacher," *American School Board Journal*, LIV (January, 1917), 69.

EFFICIENCY RECORD

Teacher   *Miss M.*   City   *VIII–S*   Grade taught   *8*
      Experience   *20*   years. Salary   *$72.50*   per month.
Highest academic training   *Two years in High School.*
Extent of professional training   *One year in Normal School.*

Detailed Rating	Very Poor	Poor	Medium	Good	Excellent

I. Personal
Equipment —

1. General appearance
2. Health
3. Voice
4. Intellectual capacity
5. Initiative and self-reliance
6. Adaptability and resourcefulness
7. Accuracy
8. Industry
9. Enthusiam and Optimism
10. Integrity and sincerity
11. Self-control
12. Promptness
13. Tact
14. Sense of justice

II. Social and
Professional
Equipment —

15. Academic preparation
16. Professional preparation
17. Grasp of subject-matter
18. Understanding of children
19. Interest in the life of the school
20. Interest in the life of the community
21. Ability to meet and interest patrons
22. Interest in lives of pupils
23. Co-operation and loyalty
24. Professional interest and growth

III. School
Management —

25. Daily preparation
26. Use of English
27. Care of light, heat, and ventilation
28. Neatness of room
29. Care of routine
30. Discipline (governing skill)

IV. Technique of
Teaching —

31. Definiteness and clearness of aim
32. Skill in habit formation
33. Skill in stimulating thought
34. Skill in teaching how to study
35. Skill in questioning
36. Choice in questioning
36. Choice of subject-matter
37. Organization of subject-matter
38. Skill and care in assignment
39. Skill in motivating work
40. Attention to individual needs
41. Attention and response of the class
42. Growth of pupils in subject matter

V. Results —

43. General development of pupils
44. Stimulation of community
45. Moral influence

this purpose was drawn up by the superintendent of schools in Everett, Washington, and printed in the *American School Board Journal* in July, 1917.[32] Teachers were to rate their principal on the following items:

I. *Personal Equipment*
   1. General Appearance
   2. Health
   3. Initiative
   4. Enterprise
   5. Capacity for leadership
   6. Accuracy
   7. Industry
   8. Enthusiasm
   9. Integrity and sincerity
   10. Self-control
   11. Promptness
   12. Tact
   13. Sense of Justice
II. *Social and Professional Equipment*
   14. Academic Preparation
   15. Professional Preparation
   16. Understanding of children
   17. Interest in life of school
   18. Interest in life of community
   19. Ability to interest patrons in school
   20. Interest in lives of pupils
   21. Co-operation and loyalty
   22. Professional interest and growth
   23. Use of English
III. *Management*
   24. Care of light, heat and ventilation
   25. Neatness of buildings and grounds
   26. Care of routine
   27. Handling of discipline
   28. Management of play and athletics
   29. Definiteness and clearness of aim
IV. *Technique of Supervision*
   30. Follow-up work in supervision
   31. Helpfulness to teachers in supervision
   32. Helpfulness to teachers in discipline
   33. Value of teacher's meetings
   34. Value of visits to rooms

[32] Vol. LV, p. 79. About the same time an educator from New York proposed to clock and standardize the work of the principal to make sure he was not being overpaid. He concluded his proposal by suggesting that "those who oppose the scheme most loudly should be selected for closest investigation." Felix Arnold, "The Unit of Supervision, Cost and Efficiency," *School and Society*, II, 1–11.

35. Moral influence
36. Spirit and tone of school

As might have been expected in the efficiency mania of the time, efforts were made to measure the efficiency of all other individuals in the schools including superintendents, students, and even janitors. One suggestion to check the efficiency of superintendents came from Superintendent William Vance of Delaware, Ohio, in a round-table discussion at the Department of Superintendence meeting in 1914. His recommendation was that the administrator determine his efficiency through "self-analysis," and he listed the qualities which he said all would agree "must characterize the equipment and output of any efficient man . . ." and certainly the "successful superintendent." One of these "fundamental qualities" was that the superintendent be a "man of affairs" and, said Vance, "By this I mean not only that he should know the details of the school plant and equipment, from pens and ink to plumbing fixtures and vacuum cleaners, but that he should be an expert in warming, ventilating, school seating, decorating, and landscape gardening. . . . In cities of less than 25,000 he is frequently the purchasing agent of the board of education, and hence he must be a compendium of school and office supplies. Catalogues, samples, and pricelists comprehensively filed are at his finger tips. He familiarizes himself with the quality of the manufactured output of the various houses. He inspects the school grounds, basement, furnace and engine rooms, toilets — the entire realm of which the janitor is king, and even ventures a suggestion or a correction, if need be, to that potentate." [33]   In prefacing this statement Vance had said: "In these days of scales and standards or norms, when there is a burning desire to reduce everything in the pedagogical universe to the fraction of something else, and then to hold it up to public view as a percentage, or a graph, or a segmented line, or a sectored circle, or groups thereof, one device seems to have escaped the inventive diabolism of the experts, namely, a contrivance whereby the superintendent of schools may take his own measure, quickly, accurately, privately. But how is he to do this himself? How can he anticipate the inquisitorial methods of some Holy Office of a Survey?" [34]

Other educators added to these contributions by Superintendent Vance. One administrator from the Brooklyn schools, noting in March of 1915 that the age was one of "weighing and counting," believed that it was time that such terms of "accurate description and

[33] N.E.A. *Proceedings* (1914), pp. 280–81.
[34] *Ibid.*, pp. 279–80.

efficiency be applied to the superintendent." To achieve this goal he had drawn up a chart through which the administrator could measure his own efficiency.[35]

Less attention was given to developing scales for rating the efficiency of students than was given to teachers, but they were not neglected completely, and from time to time forms which were being used were reproduced in the professional journals so that educators all over the nation could benefit from the creative efforts of a talented few. One such form, by the superintendent of schools in Blackfoot, Idaho, was printed in the May, 1915, issue of the *American School Board Journal* as follows:

STUDENT EFFICIENCY TEST [36]

Place after each item the per cent which is a fair estimate of your personal attainment in the particular line and add the total. This will be your per cent of efficiency as a student.

1. Do you take joy in your school work? 5%. . . .
2. Can you finish your lessons in two hours' home study? 2% . . .
3. Do you have a regular schedule of study? 4% . . .
4. When you are mentally tired, do you take physical exercise in the open air? 3%. . . .
5. Do you have a place for home study apart from the family? 4%. . . .
6. Do you get all of your lessons each day? 4%. . . .
7. Do you sleep with at least one window open? 2%. . . .
8. Do you study by a good light from behind or over your left shoulder? 3%. . . .
9. Do you get enough sleep to awaken of your own accord at a regular hour? 3%. . .
10. Do you read newspapers? 3%. . . .
11. Do you read magazines? 2%. . . .
12. Do you read good books? 3%. . . .
13. Do you enter into discussions of local interest in civic and state affairs? 3%. . . .
14. Do you keep up a correspondence with some sympathetic friend or relative? 2%. . . .
15. Have you a bank account? 6%. . . .
16. Do you "loaf on the streets"? 2%. . . .
17. Do you earn some money each month, other than that from your own family? 2%. . . .
18. Have you one special friend of your own sex? 3%. . . .
19. Do you attend and enjoy church? 3%. . . .
20. Do you attend and enjoy musicals and lectures? 3%. . . .

[35] Frederic L. Luqueer, "Self Accounting in Supervision," *Educational Review*, XLIX, 460–68.

[36] Vol. L, p. 50.

21. Do you take part in some wholesome exercise (Outdoor) ? 5%. . . .
22. Do you make it a rule to do a kindness toward someone each day? 5%. . . .
23. Do you help with the common duties of the home? 5%. . . .
24. Do you enjoy going to places with your parents? 3%. . . .
25. Do you contribute, by your work, to the maintenance of the home? 6% . . .
26. Do you find your home a place of pleasure and enjoyment for yourself when none but the family are present? 3%. . . .
27. Do you give your best efforts to study when at study and play when at play? 3%. . . .
28. Are you proud of your report card as representing the best that you are capable of doing? 5%. . . .
29. Do you study the manners of other people, imitating the good and avoiding the bad that you see about you? 3%. . . .
30. Have you a good 'HOBBY'? 3%. . . .

Total Efficiency ———

Name ———

Four years later a teacher from Salem, New Hampshire sent the editor of the *Journal of Education* a copy of a "High School Student's Efficiency Score" which, she said, was a modified version of a scale she had seen in another educational journal. Some of the items on which students were scored were: "According to your age and height is your weight up to standard?" "Do you read at least one standard book a month?" "Is your language always clean?" "Do you keep an expense account?" "A bank account?" [37]

Finally administrators carried the effort to measure and demonstrate the efficiency of the schools to its logical conclusion by creating and using rating scales for janitors. In May of 1917 the *American School Board Journal* printed a copy of a rating card which was being used in Rockford, Illinois. The duties of the janitor were listed and points assigned so that his efficiency could be rated on a one-hundred point scale. [38]

By the end of 1918 the campaign to introduce efficiency measures into the schools had been successfully consummated and evidence that this was so was provided by an educator from Pittsburgh. "Any teacher" he said, "who has attended an educational meeting in recent years has heard discussions of Educational Measurements. Scales and tests and standards are numerous. Surveys and investigations and comparisons are being made in almost every school." [39] By

[37] Vol. XC (October, 1919), p. 376.
[38] Vol. LIV, p. 60.
[39] Arthur G. Skeeles, "The Educational Yard Stick," *Journal of Education*, LXXXIX (January 23, 1919), 93.

1920 rating scales for teachers were being used extensively but there was also widespread dissatisfaction with their use. As one educator put it, teachers had accepted the ratings "meekly but resentfully" for many years.[40] Yet, except in cities such as New York and Chicago, where teachers had strength through organization in teachers' unions, they had little choice but to accept the rating system. And despite the dissatisfaction, leading administrators defended its use. For example, William McAndrew, superintendent of schools in Brooklyn and later (1924) in Chicago, justified teacher ratings by stating that "Every principal is responsible for a good-sized pay roll. If he doesn't follow up the work of those he is put to supervise he is not doing his duty as a financial manager. If he doesn't keep an account of his appraisal of work he's likely, I think, to be a poor business man. If he does, I don't see any objection to his summarizing it as A, B, C, D." [41]

Although some educators undoubtedly believed that the education of children would be improved through the introduction of the various efficiency measures, the primary motivation for their adoption by administrators was self-defense. This comes out in some of the material presented above and it was stated specifically by leading educators from time to time. Thus Edward Elliott, professor of education at the University of Wisconsin and one of the leading efficiency experts in education, in his report in 1913 to the National Council of the N.E.A. as a member of the Committee on Tests and Standards of Efficiency in Schools and School Systems stated, "The ultimate problem of this Committee . . . is that of creating a new kind of confidence on the part of the public in the work of the public schools. This confidence constitutes the capital with which the efficient school system must develop its dividends and activities." [42] And he went on to say that the efficiency measures which were undertaken had to be reported simply and understandably and in a language businessmen would understand. Evidence that this same motivation applied to the efforts to measure the efficiency of teachers was provided by a superintendent of schools from Beaver Falls, Pennsylvania, who stated before the Department of Superintendence of the N.E.A. in 1915, "The desire to apply sound business principles has prompted the administrative authorities of most large cities and many small ones to adopt some form of the merit system of promot-

[40] Alexander Fichlander, "Teachers Ratings," *Journal of Education*, XCI (February, 1920), 243.
[41] *Ibid.*
[42] N.E.A. *Proceedings*, p. 398.

ing teachers and fixing their salaries."[43] Even educators who were bitterly critical of the movement, such as James L. McConaughy, professor of education and English at Dartmouth and later President of Wesleyan University, provided evidence that the motive was to ward off criticism by seeming to demonstrate efficiency. McConaughy began an article written in March of 1918 and entitled "The Worship of the Yardstick" by stating, "This is an age of efficiency. In the eyes of the public no indictment of a school can be more severe than to say it is inefficient."[44]

The School Survey

The other major activity engaged in by educators in which they identified themselves and were identified by others as efficiency experts or engineers, was in the work of surveying school systems. The procedure generally followed was to call in an outside "expert" or experts who studied the schools and made a report to the board of education. These men were usually professors of education from the leading universities and most often specialists in administration, but frequently a prominent superintendent (e.g. Spaulding) was engaged, and occasionally men from the educational foundations such as Carnegie directed or participated in surveys. The length of time spent upon these investigations varied from one week to a year or more, but most of them (at least of a single school system) were completed in less than a month. Some surveys were conducted by one or two men while on others a team of five or six educators was employed. In the years between 1911 and 1925 hundreds of surveys of schools were made — so many, in fact, that it seems there was hardly a state or local school system in America which was not surveyed. One educator, describing the situation in 1919, wrote that it was "quite the fashion for the schools to be 'surveyed' and many hundreds of systems have been through the operation." And he added sarcastically that the result of this work was contained in volumes of "findings" which he said laymen "cannot interpret and which no one with the least grain of sense would attempt to read. . . ."[45]

The growth in numbers of the surveys paralleled the growth of the strength of the efficiency movement and the accompanying criticism of the schools in the years after 1911. As early as February, 1912, superintendents were briefed at their annual meeting by one

[43] N.E.A. *Proceedings* (1915), p. 473–74. Proof that this was so was provided in January, 1915, by the editor of the *American School Board Journal*. He reported "the growing necessity of efficiency tests in school departments is reflected in every annual report issued from the larger cities of the country." Vol. L, p. 27.

[44] *Educational Review*, LV, 191–92.

[45] "An Unintentional Survey," *Journal of Education*, XC (July 3, 1919), 8.

of their leaders on the situation regarding surveys and were given some advice on how to proceed. The speaker, Calvin N. Kendall, Commissioner of Education in New Jersey, told his audience that the investigation of school systems by commissioners or committees was being pushed to answer two basic questions: "What return is the community getting from its investment in the schools? How can the investment be made to yield greater returns?" Kendall reported that only a few investigations had been made so far, but he said that signs were not wanting that such inquiries would increase greatly. He spoke of the great concern for efficiency which was sweeping the country and the increasing criticism of the schools and he warned that "In this practical age there is sure to be a search for tangible results of educational processes." Kendall, aware that administrators were growing anxious and fearful concerning these investigations, tried to reassure them. It was possible, he said, that the results of the surveys could be helpful to schoolmen and he cited the Baltimore survey as an example of a case in which the facts indicated that more money needed to be spent on the schools. Then he provided some advice for administrators on how to proceed — advice which was repeated frequently in the years that followed. The superintendent, he said, could take the initiative in arranging for a survey. By doing this he could beat his critics to the punch, for, as he put it, "Obviously it is much the wiser course for him to take the initiative than to have it taken by hostile influences in the community." [46]

Year after year these themes presented by Kendall were repeated by educators. In 1913 the superintendent of schools in Boise, Idaho, Charles S. Meek, reported enthusiastically to the National Council of the N.E.A. on the results of a one-week survey made of the Boise schools by Edward Elliott, Charles Judd, and George Strayer. He quoted the president of the Boise school board as saying (after he had read the survey report) that he was glad to see that education had "at last reached such a stage of development that it is indeed a profession. The report . . . will certainly compare favorably with expert reports made by engineers etc." This statment must have been like sweet music to administrators who had been subjected to severe criticism the previous year. And it certainly contributed to the popularity of the school survey, for here was a means whereby they could apparently achieve professional status and defend themselves at the same time. On this latter point Meek had more reassuring words to say: "The comparisons these men made with other cities, as on expenditures, have placed us in an entirely defensible position

[46] N.E.A. *Proceedings*, pp. 376–80.

before the taxpayers and will convince even the most critical that we are not spending too much money, and that the results that we are getting are certainly commensurate with the expenditures made." [47]

By 1914 the school survey had become so important that the Committee on Tests and Standards of Efficiency in Schools and School Systems reported at length to the N.E.A. on the purpose, nature, and conduct of school surveys. George Strayer, chairman of the committee, said that obviously any consideration of the study of efficiency in the schools had to include "some treatment of that form of inquiry now so commonly advocated by the critics of public education. . . ." The critics of education had succeeded in forcing many investigations and evidently these were causing administrators to be apprehensive, for Strayer labored to effect a change in the name and in the spirit of these inquiries. He urged educators to use the term "survey" for these inquiries instead of the word "investigations." The latter term he said had an "invidious connotation" which implied seeking proof of *inefficiency*, of putting the schools on trial. On the other hand the "survey" was positive in nature and was concerned with constructive criticism.[48] Clearly Strayer had no difficulty getting schoolmen to accept this view; the problem was to get a critical public to do so.

At the same meeting Superintendent Meek of Boise gave another speech on the school survey and provided additional evidence of the need for and the usefulness of the new means of defense. He reminded his colleagues that the public schools were being "assailed today more vigorously, even viciously, than ever before," and he quoted a statement from a recent report of the National Manufacturers Association which charged that the schools were so "hopelessly, wickedly inefficient and damaging as to call for instant and tremendous consideration and readjustment." Then, speaking of the public, Meek told his audience of educators, "They want to know that no part of the vast sums they each year pay for the support of public education is wasted, but that all of it is wisely and economically expended; that all of it is yielding for their children the greatest possible return in terms of educational units." His recommendation was based on his own experience in Boise — arrange for a survey of the schools by outside experts, and he described its function as follows: *"As a protection to competent school administrators, as an effective device to convince the public that the enormous sums the schools are each year exacting are being wisely and economically*

[47] N.E.A. *Proceedings* (1913), p. 398.
[48] N.E.A. *Proceedings* (1914), p. 302.

expended and are yielding commensurate returns in educational units, and as a means of educating the patrons to an appreciation of the newer phases and modern trend of education, the work of a school-inquiry committee is invaluable." [49] It was necessary to bring in *outside* efficiency experts, he said, because they would have no interest in the local situation whereas local schoolmen might not render a decision against themselves. Testimony such as this from men who had survived a crisis contributed to the spread of the survey movement and to the demand for the services of the educational efficiency engineer.

In the years between 1912 and 1916 school administrators were told repeatedly by leading educators that the survey was an excellent device to use in defense against hostile critics. They were also told that it was a valuable instrument for obtaining more money for the schools. Bobbitt described how this could be done in an article published in the fall of 1914, and the message was repeated frequently.[50] By 1915 superintendents heard testimony at their annual meeting from one of their prominent members, James Van Sickle of Springfield, Massachusetts, that the survey was doing the job. He reported that "the most conspicuous immediate result of surveys, and one which seems to have been attained in nine of the ten about which I have made inquiry, is the very decided help given in securing adequate appropriations to the support of the schools." [51] Under the circumstances administrators could have been forgiven for inviting in the visiting firemen.

The school surveys were initiated either by groups in the community or by schoolmen, and sometimes by a combination of the two. The giant Cleveland survey conducted in 1915 was brought about partly as a result of the activity of the Cleveland Engineering Society. This group had charged, in the fall of 1912, that according to their standards the Cleveland schools were operating at less than 50 per cent efficiency.[52] The *American School Board Journal* provided evidence of the impetus for the San Francisco survey (as well as giving other interesting aspects of the situation regarding surveys) in the following news item in its May, 1915, edition. "Upon the suggestion of the school board and the superintendent, the Chamber of Commerce has appointed a committee to undertake a thorough and complete survey of the city schools to increase the efficiency of the system and to reduce the cost of operation. In the conduct of the

[49] *Ibid.*, pp. 310–13. (Italics mine.)
[50] John Franklin Bobbitt, "The School Survey," *Elementary School Journal*, XV, 41–54.
[51] N.E.A. *Proceedings*, p. 382.
[52] *Elementary School Teacher*, XIII (October, 1912), 59.

survey, the school authorities will assist in every way possible and experts of national reputation will be in direct charge." [53] In the state of California as a whole, surveys were stimulated by the Taxpayers' Association of California which in May, 1917, established a special Bureau of Educational Investigation. The director of the bureau described its work in a statement which was reprinted in the *Elementary School Journal*: "The Taxpayers' Association of California exists for the purpose of eliminating waste and promoting greater efficiency in the administration of public affairs. As a part of its operating program it will attempt to show the business men and taxpayers of California how they can get better educational results for the money spent. Educational leaders for many years have been demanding changes for the better, but either have achieved no results or else have had to be satisfied with so many compromises that it is generally admitted that the highest efficiency is not being obtained even with the large amount of money now being spent. The direct object of the new bureau will be to show the men who pay the bills that the principles of good school administration are fundamentally related to the cash drawer and the pocketbook. . . . If the Bureau of Educational Investigation selects any city or county as a base of operations, it will be because a beginning must be made somewhere. It is hoped that the Association and its Bureau will have the hearty co-operation of public officials throughout the state." [54] The *Journal* reported also that the association had secured the services of Ellwood P. Cubberley as a "consulting expert."

In the extensive and controversial survey of the New York City schools the inquiry was initiated in 1911 by the financial authorities, the Board of Estimate. [55] In St. Louis, a survey was organized by the Board of Education, apparently without outside pressure, in order to persuade the citizens that more money was needed for the schools. [56]

The nature of the surveys was determined partly by the individuals who initiated them and partly by the "experts" who actually made the studies. Clearly the dominant motivating force in most instances was economic, not educational. What was wanted was a decrease or at least no increase in taxes. Since this was so, the financial aspects of the operation of the schools were very prominent in most survey reports, as anyone who can stand the boredom of reading them will discover. On the other hand, the outlooks and competence

[53] Vol. L, p. 51.

[54] Vol. XVII (May, 1917), pp. 623–24.

[55] *Elementary School Teacher*, XII (September, 1911), 42.

[56] *Survey of the St. Louis Public Schools* (Board of Education, St. Louis, Missouri, 1917), p. 1.

of the surveyors influenced the nature of the survey. When Charles Judd was director, as in the St. Louis survey cited above, the emphasis was upon instructional problems, although the financial and organizational aspect could not be neglected. When Bobbitt, Spaulding, Ayres, Cubberley, Strayer, or N. Engelhardt were involved, they emphasized the financial, legal, or organizational side even when they were dealing with instructional or curricular problems. And the survey reports by these men were filled with business and industrial terminology, and parallels were drawn frequently between these areas and education. For example, Bobbitt in his report on his Denver survey (1916) included a point-by-point analysis of the relation between school management and the management of a business corporation.[57]

There were other reasons for the emphasis on the financial and mechanical aspects of education in these surveys. Generally funds were limited and time was short and so a thorough study was impossible. Also, the *Plans for Organizing School Surveys*, published as the Thirteenth Yearbook of the National Society for the Study of Education in 1914, stressed the financial and mechanical. Even the section on the child was limited largely to enrolment and promotion statistics. The same thing was true of the section on teachers. Consider, for example, the section under the heading "The Work of the Teacher," which included the following items to be checked in the survey:

1. Number of pupils per teacher.
2. Number of classes per teacher.
3. Number of preparations per teacher.
4. Total amount of time per week teacher is required to spend on school work.
   a) During school hours.
   b) Outside of school hours.
5. Degree to which teachers are consulted concerning —
   a) General school policies.
   b) Making of course of study.
   c) Selection of supplementary material.
   d) Change of textbooks.[58]

Probably, too, the connection of the school survey and the educational engineer with the efficiency engineer in industry, and especially with the Taylor system, contributed to its financial and mathematical emphasis. It will be remembered that scientific management was

---

[57] *Elementary School Journal*, XVII (December, 1916), 223.
[58] P. 31.

perceived by the American press largely in terms of the financial saving its application made possible. That the school survey with its experts was patterned after the industrial scientific management system was indicated by Cubberley as well as by other educators.[59] One educator, Jesse B. Sears, gave explicit testimony on this point. Sears, who was a pupil and colleague of Cubberley at Stanford, had participated in many surveys and through his acquaintance with Cubberley was thoroughly familiar with the development of the movement. In his book, *The School Survey*, published in 1925 (to which Cubberley wrote an introduction), Sears gave the following explanation of the origin and spread of the survey, showing its connection with industrial scientific management:

> *With a critical public opinion demanding economy and efficiency*, and with a new conception of education growing rapidly into a science of education, we had both the motive and the means by which the survey movement could take form. Under these circumstances it was not strange that the *public should take readily to the survey idea. People were already familiar with the work of the efficiency engineer and the accounting expert in business and industry*. Naturally, then, when boards of education called upon *educational experts* to help point the way out of difficulties, the idea was promptly understood and sanctioned by the public, and the *school survey movement had begun.*[60]

The purpose and nature of the school survey have been considered. Its effects on American education are more difficult to determine. Undoubtedly it contributed to the adoption by the schools of standardized tests and teacher-rating procedures. More important, however, was the effect it had on the nature of educational administration. After all, the men who made the surveys were recognized "authorities" and if they emphasized the financial and mechanical aspects, why should an ordinary superintendent, or board member, or citizen question that these were the important elements of education. Were not these men experts? And was not this work scientific? Equally important was the fact that the published reports of the school surveys were used as texts or at least as basic documents in the newly formed (and rapidly expanding) courses in educational administration in the universities, where they contributed toward a business and mechanical conception of school administration among newcomers in the field.

[59] E.g. in October, 1914, Howard T. Lewis of the University of Idaho, writing on the school survey in rural areas, gave an account of the increased efficiency gained by Frederick W. Taylor in industry and then stated: "So ought it be in education." *Educational Review*, XLVIII, 270.

[60] Jesse Sears, *The School Survey* (Boston, 1925), pp. 3–4. (Italics mine.)

There were other unfortunate effects of the surveys. In many instances and especially when a hostile group had initiated the survey the experts tended to be extremely critical and when these criticisms were exploited by the newspapers some poor schoolman was in for trouble.[61] In some instances superintendents fought back and the result was a hot controversy which certainly disrupted the educational work of the schools. Such a situation resulted in New York City, where the Board of Estimates hired experts, Professors Hanus of Harvard and McMurry of Teachers College, among others, to investigate the schools. The findings, published in several volumes, were critical and many New York schoolmen, including Superintendent William Maxwell, thought unjustly so. Maxwell accused McMurry of making sweeping conclusions based on inadequate evidence, and other educational leaders in New York described the survey as "setting third rate men at the task of inspecting and estimating what first rate men were doing." [62] As the controversy raged in the press and in the educational journals some telling criticisms were made of the experts, including the most basic of them all: *What special competence did these men have? What was the basis of their claim to expertness? What right did they have to pass judgment on the schools?*

Although similar situations undoubtedly developed on other occasions as a result of a survey, the evidence indicates that generally they were helpful to school administrators in their efforts to defend themselves. Regardless of the long-range effects, they helped schoolmen meet the demands of an economy-minded, business society. As a

[61] This situation developed in Cleveland in 1915. *Elementary School Journal*, XVI, (January, 1916), 220.

[62] "Good and Bad in New York Schools," *Educational Review*, XLVII (January, 1914), 67–68. Some evidence of the consequences of a survey made of the University of Wisconsin in 1913 will show what could ensue from a survey by so-called "efficiency experts." This survey was directed by William H. Allen, whose qualifications were certainly questionable but who nevertheless made surveys and even went into the business of selling pamphlets on how to survey a college, etc. Testimony on the effect of Allen's work on the university was presented by Jerome Bumpus, later President of Tufts College: "Three or four years ago, when the 'lost motions' of the brick layer were being capitalized and 'Success Magazines' were going into the hands of receivers, certain efficiency experts were assigned to 'speed up' the University of Wisconsin, that held at that time the foremost position among publicly-supported educational institutions. The men assigned as efficiency experts began with the business side of college administration; they were not college men, but accountants, men ignorant of college purposes. . . . The injury that the University of Wisconsin has suffered since the inquisitorial methods of so-called efficiency experts invaded the educational side of the institution is irreparable. For over a year an educational staff costing the state a million and a half has had its attention and its energies diverted from its legitimate work and centered upon the formulation of protests against unwarranted interference, unfair misrepresentation, and against the ruthless destruction of long-established educational ideals." "Efficiency in the University," *Education*, XXXV, No. 10 (June, 1915), 663–64.

superintendent from Boston put it "Even an investigation, as bad as some of them are, may have this advantage — that the conclusions, if any are made, will be so confusing that the business man cannot understand them; and it will therefore be a valuable asset in our defense of the public schools." [63] The tragedy, however, was not only that surveys helped orient the nature of the "profession" of school administration in its formative years toward the business and mechanical aspects of education, but also that many intelligent educators were forced to spend their time on trivial matters. To be sure, much of the work done was valuable and the millions of facts gathered were useful and could have been even more useful if they had been put to educational and not to financial purposes. In the end, the American people got what they deserved for forcing their educators to spend their time on accounting rather than on the education of children.

The Unavailing Dissent

Enough evidence has been presented thus far to indicate the strength of the efficiency movement and of the business philosophy in America in the second decade of this century. American society was saturated with the business-industrial ideology and, as I have shown, American public education did little but respond to the dominant forces. But some evidence has been given of the existence of dissenting opinions by educators. More of this dissent will be included in subsequent chapters but it seems appropriate to present at least a brief account here of the nature, the sources, and the effectiveness of this opposition to the various phases of the efficiency movement.

I have chosen to describe this dissent as unavailing because, although voices were raised in protest against each of the various efficiency procedures which were introduced into education as well as against the inappropriate application of the business philosophy generally, in the total picture the dissenters were such a small minority that their voices were barely audible, and they were unable to stem the tide. Occasional victories were won, such as that against the platoon school in New York, but even in this instance success was due to the fact that the educational issues became involved in political controversy.[64] What opposition there was among teachers was limited to a few large cities where strong teachers' unions or professional associations existed. This was to be expected because teachers generally worked without tenure and were at the mercy of

---

[63] Stratton D. Brooks, *School Review*, XX (May, 1912), 318.

[64] Cf. pp. 136–41.

the school boards and of the administrators. Teachers as a group were quite timid, partly because of their insecure position, and partly because, as Dewey pointed out, "in the main the most docile among the young are the ones who become teachers when they are adults. Consequently they still listen docilely to the voice of authority." [65]

The loudest voice of protest among teachers was raised by the *American Teacher* which became the official journal of the American Federation of Teachers, a teacher's union affiliated with the A. F. of L. As early as 1912 this journal carried an article by a teacher from New York who charged that the schools had become commercialized.

By this I do not mean that the management of the schools is motivated by an itch for profit, as is implied, for example, when we speak of the professions of law and medicine having become commercialized. I mean merely that our educators have yielded to the temper of their surroundings, which are distinctly commercial. The organization and the methods of the schools have taken on the form of those commercial enterprises that distinguish our economic life. We have yielded to the arrogance of 'big business men' and have accepted their criteria of efficiency at their own valuation, without question. We have consented to measure the results of educational efforts in terms of price and product — the terms that prevail in the factory and the department store. But education, since it deals in the first place with organisms, and in the second place with individualities, is not analogous to a standardizable manufacturing process. Education must measure its efficiency not in terms of so many promotions per dollars of expenditure, nor even in terms of so many student-hours per dollar of salary; it must measure its efficiency in terms of increased humanism, increased power to do, increased capacity to appreciate.[66]

The editors of the *American Teacher* continued their opposition through the years and printed the following statement in bold letters on the title page of the March, 1916 issue:

If efficiency means the demoralization of the school system;
    dollars saved and human materials squandered;
    discontent, drudgery and disillusion —
We'll have none of it!
If efficiency denotes low finance, bickering and neglect;
    exploitation, suspicion and inhumanity;
    larger classes, smaller pay and diminished joy —
We'll have none of it!

[65] John Dewey, "Education as Engineering," *New Republic*, XXXII, No. 407 (September 20, 1922), 91.
[66] Benjamin C. Gruenberg, "Some Economic Obstacles to Educational Progress," *American Teacher*, I (September, 1912), 90.

We'll espouse and exalt humane efficiency — efficiency that spells felicity, loyalty, participation and right conduct. Give us honorable efficiency and we shall rally to the civic cause.

There were only a few administrators who objected to the efficiency measures being introduced into the schools and they were the older men such as William E. Maxwell of New York and J. M. Greenwood of Kansas City. These men accepted the notion that schools should be efficient but questioned the definition of efficiency that was being used and the means of measuring it. Maxwell, for example, doubted whether "time-wasting, energy-destroying statistical research" could determine the efficiency of a school system or could give new information to the experienced teacher. He believed the standard of efficiency could be set as a considered, philosophical definition of an efficient school in terms of what it should do for its students in life. But he asserted the real test of what the school had done could come only in the adult life of the student, for, he reminded those who had referred to the child graduate as the "ultimate product" of the school, only the adult in actual life could be termed the "ultimate product." As for the value of tests on immediate ability in school subjects, he was apparently somewhat scornful, for he said:

When I read that, in one of the older eastern cities, after shedding lakes of ink and using up untold reams of paper and consuming the time of unnumbered teachers in administering and scoring the Courtis standard tests in addition, subtraction, multiplication, and division, the learned director reached the conclusion that "29 per cent of the pupils in the eighth grade could exchange places with a like number of pupils in the fourth grade, without changing, in the slightest, the arithmetical ability in the fundamental operation of either class as a class," I am inclined to exclaim:

My dear sir, what did you expect? That all the children in a grade would show equal ability in adding, subtracting, multiplying and dividing? Any teacher of experience could have told you that they would not. You should have known it yourself. One flash of Horace Mann's insight would be worth a thousand miles of your statistics.[67]

He went on to say:

these new doctrines usually run a regular course and that course involves three stages. In the first stage, everything hitherto done in the schools is wrong; in the second stage, if the new theory receives any popular support, everything will be well; the new subject or the new method is a panacea that will cure all educational ills; in the third stage, the practical teachers have divested the new theory of its superfluous trappings, have swept away the preposter-

[67] *Elementary School Journal*, XVII (December, 1916), 223.

ous claims of its advocates, and have discovered and used whatever small kernel of truth it contains or conceals. . . . Our friends of the standard-test-scale-statistical theory . . . are still in the second stage of reform accomplishment — the stage in which they proclaim their theory as a panacea for all educational ills.

Maxwell believed, however, that the standard-test-scale-statistical plan of testing efficiency should not be absolutely rejected because it could not realize a "tenth part" of the claims of "Professor Bobbitt," its "most elaborate exponent," for he hoped that such tests might become an improved form of the old state examination and, as such, could help restore "that thoroughness of teaching and that accuracy of scholarship which, to no small extent, vanished with the old examinations." [68] But, he said, if the tests turned teachers into bookkeepers, the tests too, would vanish.

An amusing sidelight of this same talk was the barb Maxwell aimed in the direction of Bobbitt and his university colleagues.

Our good friends, the statistical professors of education, would do well to try their theories on the work of their college and university colleagues before applying them to the common schools. The college or university student is more nearly an ultimate product than is a sixth-year child. How would it do to determine the efficiency of college teaching by grading the Juniors according to their ability to solve six problems in the differential calculus in twelve minutes, to estimate the English compositions of Seniors on a scale graduated from the style of William H. Allen, of New York, up to the style of Charles W. Eliot, of Harvard? Imagination pales before the attempt to picture the howls of horror raised by the ordinarily peaceful and placid professors.[69]

This satirical picture actually came into being, for when the efficiency experts did invade higher education, there was vigorous dissent by professors.

Occasionally, questions about the efficiency measures being used were asked by statisticians themselves, men who could not have been suspected of hostility toward genuinely scientific attempts to measure the results of education. The doubts these men raised were concerned with the qualifications and accuracy of those who used the statistical tools, and with the use to which they were put. Edward M. Hartwell, Secretary of the Statistics Department of the Boston schools made some comments which were representative of the reservations of the conscientious expert in statistics:

[68] *Ibid.*, p. 401.
[69] *Ibid.*, p. 398.

Doubtless the scientific admeasurement of measurable quantities may be made to yield valuable criteria of the efficiency of certain methods and procedures pertaining to school life and administration. But the measurements must be made by patient and skillful measurers, who can be depended on to winnow and classify their results and not jump to conclusions. . . . But I must confess that the glowing accounts of the rapid spread, in the last few years, of comprehensive statistical investigations of schools and scholars does not elate me overmuch. Supposedly professional statisticians not infrequently do such queer things that the prospect of a possibly too-rapid multiplication of amateur school statisticians is not inspiring.

When I hear that state-wide investigations of schools or school children have been completed in a year, I cannot forbear wondering how many of the investigators were experts, where they came from, how much money they spent, and what they really accomplished. . . . My plea is that we should discriminate in our investigation and consideration of educational matters between methods and criteria that are applicable to living mechanisms and their activities and those which pertain to the realm of the inventor, the engineer, and the manufacturer.[70]

This was similar to the attitude Richard C. McLaurin, president of Massachusetts Institute of Technology, had shown in 1910 when he said, "Now . . . its [science's] merits are loudly proclaimed on every hand, and its importance is emphasized, with tiresome repetition, by college presidents and others, often, indeed, by men who have little real knowledge of its methods and little real sympathy with its progress."[71]

The most insightful criticisms, however, of the efficiency devices were made by two outstanding educators, William C. Bagley and John Dewey. Both men opposed the inappropriate application of business and industrial values and procedures to the schools and both criticized the oversimplified and superficial activity being engaged in, often in the name of science. Bagley believed that the scientific movement held great promise for education but warned educators not to expect miracles. "If the history of our art teaches us anything," he said "it is that nostrums, panaceas, and universal cure-alls in education are snares and delusions. In a field of activity so intricate and so highly complicated as ours, it is both easy and disastrous to lose the perspective. To keep this clear perspective must be our constant struggle. We must give up the notion of solving all of our problems in a day, and settle down to patient, painstaking, sober, and systematic investigation."[72] And Dewey wrote and spoke repeatedly on the same theme. He pointed out that "would-be pio-

[70] *School Review*, XX (May, 1912), 314–17.
[71] "Science and Education," *Ibid.*, XVIII, 319.
[72] N.E.A. *Proceedings* (1912), p. 639.

neers in the educational field need an extensive and severe intellectual equipment." And while approving the testing movement he criticized the use that was being made of the tests. They should be used, he said, for diagnostic purposes, to provide a better understanding of children, and not as a convenient means of classifying and standardizing students. He charged that much of the "scientific" work being done was not really scientific in the sense of inquiry into processes, but merely the same old education "masquerading in the terminology of science." The change, he said, had made little difference "except for advertising purposes." [73]

So the dissenting voices were raised — strong, intelligent, prophetic voices — but, as it turned out, voices lost in the wilderness.

[73] John Dewey, *loc. cit.*, p. 90.

6

THE "FACTORY SYSTEM" IN EDUCATION—THE PLATOON SCHOOL

As a part of their total effort to demonstrate efficiency between 1911 and 1925 administrators worked to attain greater efficiency and economy through a more intensive and extensive use of the school "plant." Complete and intensive use of plant facilities had not been stressed by Frederick Taylor, but it was a logical application of his gospel of efficiency. In any case it was certainly to be expected that, among all the other questions, questions would be raised concerning the use of the school buildings. And so educators were put under pressure to demonstrate that they were not allowing part of the expensive "plant" to stand idle. Sometimes the activity used for such a demonstration was labeled as an application of scientific management, but more often it was not. This was true primarily because the major efforts for full plant use were made after 1915, and by this time there had been some disenchantment with the Taylor system. The very great concern for efficiency remained, however, and this was to be achieved by the application of various procedures roughly classified as "modern business methods."

Better utilization of the school buildings, like many other administrative developments between 1911 and 1925, had been discussed earlier but did not develop into a major concern until after 1911. As early as 1903 Charles Eliot, president of Harvard University, urged school administrators to make more extensive use of the educational facilities and in so urging used the industrial analogy. Speaking before the Department of Superintendence of the N.E.A. on the topic "The Full Utilization of a Public School Plant," Eliot told his audience that schoolhouses were in use for only six hours a day for one-half the days in the year, and he said, "It is obvious at a glance that so partial a use of an industrial plant would never be thought possible. No productive industry could be successfully carried on with so incomplete a use of an expensive plant." [1] He suggested that the schools be kept open in summer and in the evening, and that the schoolhouse be conceived of as an educational center for the community. He realized that his recommendations would involve a larger expenditure of funds, but he said, what he wished to urge was, "the full utilization of a public school plant is the only true economy; that the present inadequate use of schoolhouses is wasteful precisely in proportion to the costliness of the grounds and buildings, and that reform in this respect means a larger and better yield, physically, mentally, and morally, from the public schools, and therefore a significant addition to the health and wealth of the nation and to the public happiness." [2]

This theme had been presented before and it was repeated from time to time in the years that followed. Superintendent Maxwell of New York, for example, favored the idea and inquired into the possibility of applying it in the New York schools. The difficulty was that despite its educational value, such a plan cost more money and so Maxwell had to abandon the scheme, as did others who favored its adoption. The truth was that the school-factory analogy was unsound, which was clearly demonstrated in this instance. Operating industrial plants at capacity meant increased production and greater profit. Operating schools in this way undoubtedly increased the educational "production," but this production was difficult to see or measure. What could be seen, of course, was increased costs. Even Frederick Taylor had difficulty convincing industrialists that some expenditures (e.g. for research), which did not produce an immediate return, were desirable. Of course, in a relatively short time his methods usually produced greater profit. In education this could not be done and it was clear that proposals which increased expenditures would be difficult to defend on the ground of "true economy."

The truth of this fact was illustrated some years later when educators, applying the industrial analogy again, urged the establishment of the twelve-month school. The superintendent of schools in the state of Indiana, for example, had suggested in 1912 that schools be operated on a twelve-month basis. But the *Elementary School Journal* reported that interviews obtained with the leading businessmen of at least one city, Richmond, Indiana, indicated that the great majority

[1] N.E.A. *Proceedings* (1903), p. 241.
[2] *Ibid.*, p. 247.

of them were opposed to the plan because it meant "additional expense and the consequent raising of the tax rate." The editor of the
Journal commented that "this type of objection is likely to interfere
with vacation schools for some time, but if the advantages can be
clearly set forth by those who have had experience in such schools,
the financial difficulties will eventually disappear."[3] In the years that
followed some educators continued their efforts in behalf of the
twelve-month school, apparently with some success, but the "advantages" they set forth were financial ones.[4]

However, despite the impressive financial arguments which were
given, the record shows that the effort to achieve full utilization of
the school facilities through the year-round school was not permanently successful. The increased cost was the most important reason for this failure but it is possible that the children of America,
who would have been the unwilling victims of this scheme, played
a role in getting their parents to protest. And there were groups such
as the National Child Labor Committee who opposed the twelve-
month school. The committee, for example, criticized the Chicago
school superintendent who had urged the continuous use of the school
plant:

> If we, personally, were a Chicago child faced with the prospect of attend-
> ing school the whole year round — no matter if it would give us a Ph.D. at
> the age of sixteen — we would immediately call a strike. We urge education
> as the greatest blessing of childhood, it is true; but we also urge recreation
> and the development of an appreciation and utilization of lesiure as a prime
> necessity for a healthy childhood.
>
> It is true that children in the congested districts of large cities find it
> difficult to obtain such recreation in a satisfactory way. Therefore, we would
> suggest that if Chicago's superintendent of schools is so concerned with that
> terrifying problem of "continuous use of the school plant," he should devote
> his ingenuity to devising ways in which school buildings in crowded districts
> might be used for play purposes in the summer.[5]

The Gary Plan and Scientific Management

While the proposals for the establishment of the twelve-month
school were unsuccessful, another plan which fully utilized the school
building during the regular school year *and saved money* flourished
in the age of efficiency. This plan was originated by William A. Wirt
while he was superintendent of schools in Bluffton, Indiana, and he
introduced it into the schools of Gary, Indiana, when he became su-

[3] Vol. XII (September, 1912), pp. 3–4.
[4] Cf. *Elementary School Journal*, XVI (June, 1916), 520, and *School Review*, XXIV
(August, 1916), 477–78.
[5] *School Review*, XXXIII (November, 1925), 645–46.

perintendent there in 1908. Wirt had been a student of Dewey's at Chicago and was impressed with the value of enriching the regular academic program by connecting it with nature study, art, music, and industrial education. Wirt's innovation was to introduce an organizational scheme which would offer children the benefit of these special studies and still be economical. This would be done through a departmentalized system in which the students moved from room to room. The plan was arranged so that all of the rooms, either home rooms or special rooms, were in constant use. For example, while one group was in its home room receiving instruction in reading, writing, and arithmetic, another group was in the music room, another in the shop, another on the playground, etc. When the bell rang, the students would shift to their next class. Generally, children had two ninety-minute periods or three hours a day in the basic subjects, and six thirty minute periods in special subjects the other three hours of the school day. Obviously to function effectively this scheme required a high degree of administrative planning and precision timing in the moving of children. This was particularly true if the schools were large, as they were at Gary, where some of them included all twelve grades and eventually had as many as 3,000 students.[6]

Wirt called his system a "work-study-play school" but it has commonly been referred to as the "Gary Plan" and was later described as a "platoon" school. The use of the term "platoon school" has been credited to one of the leading efficiency experts in education, Leonard Ayres, but it was popularized by S. C. Hartwell, superintendent of schools at Kalamazoo and later St. Paul, in his book, *Overcrowded Schools and the Platoon Plan.*[7] Although at times minor distinctions were drawn between the Gary Plan and the platoon school, for the most part the terms were used interchangeably and Case, in his study, describes Wirt as the father of the platoon school in America and Hartwell as the first pioneer following Wirt.[8] In any case in the years after 1911, and especially after 1915, when the full impact of the efficiency-economy drive was being felt, the plan was widely discussed and strongly recommended, especially in the administrative journals. The movement continued to grow and by 1925 the platoon plan was being applied in 632 schools in 126 cities. In this same year a national platoon school association was formed. This group, whose officers were all school administrators, held annual conferences and in January, 1927, began the publication of a journal, the *Platoon*

[6] Roscoe David Case, *The Platoon School in America* (Stanford, Calif., 1931), p. 21.

[7] *Ibid.*, p. 9. Hartwell's book published in 1916 was one of the reports of the Cleveland survey.

[8] *Ibid.*, p. 23.

School.[9] By 1929 the plan (or variations of it) was being used in 1,068 schools in 202 cities — schools with an estimated enrolment of 730,000 pupils.[10]

The reasons for the success and extensive growth of the platoon school are not difficult to determine. Most important was the financial saving which was possible through its use; of importance also was the argument that the plan provided an enriched educational program for children. Clearly this combination was hard to beat. The Gary School plan also was presented by some educators as being an example of the application of scientific management to education. This claim gave it the halo effect of that magic name, identifying its users with the ultimate in efficiency. Its success was also due to the fact that it provided an answer to the problem of the shortage of classrooms — a problem which resulted from the increasing school population and one which was particularly acute after World War I. Finally, the platoon school was pictured as requiring exceptional administrative ability. As Cubberley put it, "The Gary plan calls for good organization, along lines which school men are not commonly either familiar with or capable of; large executive capacity, imagination, and clear insight into community needs. . . ."[11] Consequently its adoption not only enabled administrators to economize and defend themselves against the charge of inefficiency, it also enabled them to prove their administrative ability at the same time.

The connection between the Gary plan and scientific management was made in the *American School Board Journal* in February, 1911, just three months after the railroad hearings and at a time when the newspapers and journals were featuring the new panacea. The *Journal* printed a statement by Superintendent Wirt under the title "Scientific Management of School Plants." Significantly, the statement began with the economic advantages of the plan. The readers were told that it was possible to "Reduce the first cost of your school plants and the actual per pupil cost of school maintenance . . ." and do this while adding "manual training, nature study, music, drawing, playground and gymnasium equipment and specially trained teachers for each of these departments." Wirt then explained how his "improved school machine" operated and how the number of pupils in one of his eight-room schools had been doubled. In the last paragraph Wirt was quoted as saying "The salaries of special supervisors are saved, since the special subjects are taught by specially trained teachers," and the statement ended with his assertion that "The per

[9] *Ibid.*, pp. 268–71.
[10] *Ibid.*, p. 30.
[11] Ellwood P. Cubberley, *Public School Administration* (Boston, 1916), p. 318.

capita cost for fuel, light, janitor service, and plant investment is practically reduced one half." [12]

The first extensive, systematic effort to present the Gary plan as a manifestation of the principles of scientific management in the schools was made by John Franklin Bobbitt in an article published in February, 1912, entitled "The Elimination of Waste in Education." According to Bobbitt, the schoolmen in Gary had had two alternatives in attempting to solve the educational problems of the new, rapidly growing, industrial center that had been created by the United States Steel Corporation. One was to "build inferior buildings, omit playgrounds, school gardens, laboratories, workrooms, and assembly halls, to employ cheap teachers, to increase the size of classes, to cut down the yearly term to eight months, or to accommodate two shifts of children in the same building each day by doing half time work." The other alternative was to "create a thoroughly modern school plant, equipped with every modern necessity; then to operate it according to recently developed principles of scientific management, so as to get a maximum of service from a school plant and teaching staff of minimum size." [13]

He said that most cities suffering from a shortage of funds had used the first alternative but Gary was being built by engineers and business managers who were familiar with the principles of scientific management in the steel industry. Therefore "when the educational engineer appeared and showed how it was possible to introduce similar principles of management into the operation of the school plant, his words fell upon understanding ears; and Gary, contrary to the usual plan, adopted the latter alternative." Despite Bobbitt's statement, the idea of connecting the platoon school with scientific management and, in fact, of conceiving of the new plan as the result of the application of the new system of industrial management, does not appear to have been Wirt's. For within the same month that Bobbitt's article appeared, Wirt described his plan before the Department of Superintendence in St. Louis and did not even mention scientific management, much less indicate that his system was a result of its application. [14] In fact, Wirt might have been disavowing the connection because he began his speech by stating that his plan was not new or revolutionary and that he wanted to have nothing to do with what he termed "an undigested educational philosophy."

Bobbitt in his article presented his version of the principles of

[12] Vol. XLII, p. 2.
[13] John Franklin Bobbitt, "The Elimination of Waste in Education," *Elementary School Journal*, XII, 260.
[14] N.E.A. *Proceedings* (1912), pp. 492-95.

scientific management and then described how each had been applied in the Gary schools. The principles were stated as follows:

A first principle of scientific management is to use all the plant all the time.

A second principle of scientific management is to reduce the number of workers to a minimum by keeping each at the maximum of his working efficiency.

A third principle of efficient management is to eliminate waste.

A fourth principle of general scientific management is: Work up the raw material into that finished product for which it is best adapted.

Bobbitt began his analysis by showing how the ordinary school violated his first principle of complete utilization of the plant. The ordinary school, he said, consisted of a number of classrooms plus wide corridors, an assembly room, a gymnasium, shops, laboratories, and playgrounds. When all the classrooms were in operation the other "facilities of the plant would be lying idle." When the other facilities were being used the classrooms were "lying idle." The result was that only half of the plant was being used at any given time and thus a fully equipped school was "operated during school hours at about 50 per cent of efficiency." In this situation, according to Bobbitt, "the task of the educational engineer at Gary was to formulate a plan of operating his plant during school hours at 100 per cent efficiency."

He then described the Gary organizational scheme in which the children were platooned so that while half of them were occupying the regular classrooms, the other half were in the special activity areas. Through careful scheduling the children were moved from place to place and all of the "school plant" was in constant use. The school was in session six hours a day and during the half day devoted to regular classroom work the teacher was to divide the work between recitation and study. As Bobbitt stated it, "This gives her an opportunity to train pupils in methods of study, to supervise their study, and to give individual help to those in need of it. During these study periods she is expected to do all the paper work that falls to her for the day, so when her six hours' schoolroom service is ended, her day's work is done." It would appear that under this arrangement the students would have very little time for the regular work that was supposed to be taught in the half day spent on the "regular studies," which Bobbitt said consisted of "arithmetic, history, geography, and the formal language studies of reading, writing, spelling, and composition." Furthermore, with forty or more students in a class it would appear that the teacher would have had a difficult time giving individual instruction much less get her "paper work" done. No mention was made of the time that was necessary for preparation, and the statement that with the completion of formal class work the teacher's work was done implied that preparation outside the school was not considered necessary. This, of course, was not the first time nor the last that the work of the teacher was conceived of as being limited to the actual time spent in class. This misconception, which still persists in our own time, was and is one of the most harmful outcomes of the confusion of the school with the factory and of the teacher with the worker whose work is finished when the whistle blows.

Even though under this system 100 per cent efficiency had been achieved in the utilization of the school plant, Bobbitt stated that "still the educational engineer is not yet satisfied with the percentage of efficiency attained. The six-hour day is not enough. The plant might well be operated continuously from eight o'clock in the morning until six o'clock in the evening." He indicated that a start had been made at Gary in this direction. The playgrounds, manned by teachers, were open an hour before school in the morning, during the noon hour, and for "an hour or two — after school." This plan, he said, was soon to be extended to the laboratories and shops. Still the educational scientific manager was not satisfied and the fact that "an expensive plant should lie idle during all of Saturday and Sunday" was "a further thorn in the flesh of the clear-sighted educational engineer. . . . Scientific management demands that the school buildings be in use on Saturdays and Sundays." He pointed out that some progress had been made since the schools were open for seven hours on Saturdays, and he reported that teachers were paid extra wages for their voluntary work on these days. But *still* the efficiency expert was not satisfied for, according to Bobbitt, "there is a further loss of efficiency in the use of the plant by closing the building the two months of summer. This alone is a loss of some 16 per cent, no small item in the calculations of the efficiency engineer." Unfortunately nothing could be done about this waste for although the twelve-month school had seemed a desirable feature of scientific management the "antiquated legal machinery of the state" forbade such an arrangement.

The second of Bobbitt's principles of scientific management — that of reducing the number of workers to a minimum by keeping each at the maximum of his efficiency — was achieved by having specialized teachers. The regular classroom teachers would teach only the regular subjects but to many groups of children, while the special teachers would teach their special subjects to these groups which rotated through their classes. In this way no special supervisors were needed. He stated that the objections to the departmental plan of organization, which were raised particularly against the use of the plan in the elementary school, were overcome by having each class intact so that even though pupils were moved from place to place on a precision time schedule throughout the day they remained in the same group.

In describing how his third principle — that of eliminating waste — was applied at Gary, Bobbitt centered his attention on the loss in efficiency due to retardation, poor health, and "the pernicious effects of the vicious street and alley influences." He cited Ayres' study (described in chapter i) to prove that there was waste involved in retardation and said that Gary attempted to solve the problem by providing Saturday classes, and by juggling schedules to allow a pupil to omit some special classes and double up in others. Waste due to ill-health and lowered vitality was treated by providing extra outdoor play until the child was able to resume regular work. The evils of the street and alleys and the resultant "waste" were counteracted by extending the school day and making the school a recreation center. Bobbitt indicated that the Gary schools were, in fact, utilizing their facilities extensively for recreational purposes by showing that the Gary school facilities were used much more extensively than Chicago's parks.

By the fourth principle — that of working up the raw material into the finished product for which it was best adapted — Bobbitt meant adjusting each individual's program to fit his abilities. Thus, if a student happened to be of the "motor type of mind," he would concentrate more on the manual activities with a minimum of work in the academic studies.

Despite Bobbitt's article and a speech by Wirt on his system before the Department of Superintendence in February, 1912, significantly entitled *The Utilization of the School Plant*, the Gary plan was not widely discussed in the journals or adopted by many schools before 1914. After that time, however, the plan spread rapidly and whereas only three cities had adopted it by the end of 1913, between 1914 and 1920 it was adopted in 37 cities in 14 states and involved 136 schools.[15]

There were several reasons for the rapid growth of the plan after 1914. It will be recalled that the crest of the wave of criticism against the schools was reached late in 1912. A time lag occurred because the plan required building, curriculum, and personnel changes which could not be effected in a few days or weeks. Important, also, was the fact that while the pressure for economy grew stronger, the rapid increase in enrolment due to the growth of population and to the improved attendance legislation and enforcement procedures added to the cost of education, especially in terms of the additional buildings

[15] Case, *Platoon School*, p. 26.

and classrooms which were necessary. These two factors alone would have been enough to explain the rapid growth of the platoon school, but it was also aided by the strong favorable public support given it by some leading educators and by the influential *American School Board Journal* in the years after 1914.

Early in 1914 the Bureau of Education of the Department of the Interior published a report on the Gary schools which was a strong endorsement of Wirt's system and which, because of the professional prestige of the bureau and of the author of the report, undoubtedly contributed to the growth of the platoon school. The author was W. P. Burris, dean of the College for Teachers at the University of Cincinnati. Burris described the departmentalized, room-shifting, organizational pattern at Gary and lauded both its economic and educational features. He stated that the year round use of the school plant was one of Wirt's cardinal principles and was regarded by him as "good business economy." [16] He included a copy of a statement which had been submitted to the Gary school board which indicated that the shops were nearly all self-supporting and some were a source of income to the school.[17] He also devoted one section of the report to "Getting More for the Money" and at the end of his report presented statistics on the cost of education at Gary and at three nearby communities. These figures showed that the costs at Gary were low whereas the enrolment of pupils per teacher was considerably higher.[18] His only question about the plan was the length of school day which he said "appears to be excessively long. For the lower grades it is from 8:45 to 11:45 in the forenoon, and from 1 to 5 in the afternoon, making a total of seven hours; for the upper grades and high school it is from 8:30 to 12 in the forenoon, and from 1:15 to 5 in the afternoon, making a total of seven hours and a quarter. Nor is this all. Teachers are required to be on duty at 8 o'clock in the morning to assist pupils in work or play. The regular classroom teachers may depart at 4 in the afternoon; all others must remain till 5." [19] In addition to this crushing load which was, as Bobbitt had pointed out, no heavier than any other factory worker's, teachers were "called upon" for Saturday and evening work. However, they were paid "$1 per hour for the extra service" and the system was arranged so that each teacher would not be required to work more than two evenings per week.[20]

[16] *The Public School System of Gary, Indiana*, U.S. Bureau of Education, Bulletin No. 18 (Washington, D.C., 1914), p. 10.

[17] *Ibid.*, p. 18.

[18] *Ibid.*, p. 49.

[19] *Ibid.*, p. 16.

[20] *Ibid.*, pp. 16–17.

Some of the luster was taken off Burris' report when in 1915 the Gary school board ordered a retrenchment in some of the educational work but continued to platoon the schools during the regular school year. An editorial comment by the *American School Board Journal* on the action indicates what was eliminated and also throws light on the educational climate in 1915:

Some satisfaction has been derived by certain opponents of Superintendent W. A. Wirt and his plans for the wider use of the school plant, in the news that the Gary schools closed a month earlier, that they have discontinued summer sessions and that the board has sold the school farm, because of lack of funds. The conclusion has been drawn that Mr. Wirt has been extravagant and that his ideas have plunged the Gary schools into debt. . . .

The economics which the board is introducing are no reflection upon Mr. Wirt or his methods. Rather, they are an indication that Gary is no longer a boom town, but a sober community which has adopted safe and efficient financial methods. That Mr. Wirt should accede quietly to the wishes of the board is another evidence of his desire to work for the best interests of the children and the whole community of Gary.[21]

The New York Story

Two of the most interesting events in the history of the platoon school in America occurred in New York City. One was the introduction of the Gary plan into the elementary schools, and the other was the consideration of the possibility of introducing a variation of it into the secondary schools. Both of these efforts (but especially the former) became the subject of bitter controversy and when the dust had cleared neither was retained in the schools.

In September, 1915, in the same month the Gary school board had ordered Wirt to retrench and economize, it was announced that he had been hired to serve as an advisor to the school boards of Troy, New York and New York City to help them instal his system into those cities. For these services the *American School Board Journal* proudly announced that he would receive $10,000 per year for two years from New York City and $2,500 on the same basis at Troy. These salaries plus his $6,000 per year from Gary made his annual income $18,000.[22] Some of the schools in New York City were converted immediately and after they had been in operation for four months were evaluated and compared with the traditional schools. The results showed that the schools using the Gary plan made less academic progress than the traditional schools. As a result Superintendent Maxwell, in his annual report issued in April of 1916, said he felt

[21] Vol. LI (September, 1915), p. 26.
[22] *Ibid.*, p. 39.

the experiment should be discontinued, and he charged that the whole scheme was planned by the Board of Estimate to justify cutting the budget on the basis of economics expected from the Gary plan.[23] Despite Superintendent Maxwell's views, in March, 1916, $150,000 was appropriated for the full development of the Gary plan in Public School 45 in the Bronx.[24]

In the summer of 1916 Mayor John Mitchel of New York, in his welcoming address to the National Education Association, told the assembled educators that Wirt had been hired and that experimentation was being carried out in "from eight to twelve schools." After the data on these experiments had been gathered the Board of Education would decide, he said, on how far the plan could be extended and to what extent it would help "solve the most difficult financial problem we face, namely, that of providing a sufficient school plant in buildings to give a seat to every child in the city of New York." [25] Nine months later, in March of 1917, Joseph S. Taylor, a district superintendent in New York, and one of the strongest advocates of the Gary plan, wrote an account of its introduction and operation in the New York schools and judged it a success.[26] Apparently Taylor, and others who believed as he did, convinced the Board of Education, for in September of 1917 that group made a budget request of $5,000,000 to enable it to extend the Gary plan to the entire school system.[27]

Opposition to Wirt and his system had been manifested in New York almost immediately after the announcement of his appointment. The charge was made that politicians were attempting to market the Gary plan as a "system of economics" rather than as a "system of education." [28] But the controversy which went on, both within the schools and in the press between September of 1915 and September of 1917, was only a prelude to the real battle over the platoon school. For in September and October 1917 it became one of the central issues in the election campaign for the office of mayor of the city of New York. The incumbent, John Mitchel, supported the plan while the other candidate, Judge John F. Hylan, opposed it. Hylan accused Mitchel's administration of real estate scandals in which money which should have been spent for school buildings had instead provided "enormous profits for private individuals" and he charged that "in

[23] *School and Society*, III, 628–29.
[24] *American School Board Journal*, LII (March, 1916), 44.
[25] N.E.A. *Proceedings* (1916), p. 32.
[26] *School and Society*, V, 301–7.
[27] *School and Society*, VI, 291.
[28] *Ibid.*, II (October, 1915), 528–30.

the futile attempt to make a financial showing to the taxpayers and offset the money wasted in the purchase of useless real estate the present administration has sought to economize on the schools. They have instituted a system which is called the Gary system, the result of which has been to greatly reduce fundamental education and place an added physical strain upon the child." [29] One commentator believed that John Mitchel encountered especially stiff opposition from parents of students in "Garyized" schools but whether he did or not, he lost the election. [30] The new mayor appointed a new school board and the result was that the Gary plan was discontinued. [31]

The other aspect of the New York story involved an attempt to achieve economy and efficiency by introducing double and triple sessions into the secondary schools. It will be recalled that under the leadership of William T. Morrey the High School Teachers Association of New York City conducted a series of studies on ways and means of applying the principles of scientific management to high school problems. Morrey, who was president of the association and principal of the Commercial High School, had launched the program by inviting Harrington Emerson, a consulting engineer and an associate of Frederick Taylor, to speak to the association. [32] One of the results of Emerson's appearance and the subsequent attempt to apply his ideas was a consideration of the possibility of introducing shifts into the secondary schools of New York City. Apparently the plan had been introduced into at least one school and had become a controversial subject within the association, for the meeting of March 7, 1914, was devoted to a discussion of the merits of the plan. At this meeting the topic under consideration was "The Efficiency of Factory Methods in Education as Exemplified in the Double and Triple Sessions of Our Large High Schools." [33]

In the discussion, speaker after speaker arose to criticize the double and triple session. Dr. Larkins, principal of the Manual Training High School, stated that "You can put more checkers on the board but it spoils the game." Dr. Tildsley, principal of the DeWitt Clinton School, said there was no saving of money, the mortality rate in terms of failures was higher, and the life of the school was demoralized. He said that even under the regular arrangement students had had too

[29] Quoted in the *Elementary School Journal*, XVIII (October, 1917), 89, from the *New York Tribune*, September 8, 1917.

[30] *School and Society*, VI (October, 1917), 503.

[31] *American School Board Journal*, LV (December, 1917), 48.

[32] Cf., pp. 55–58.

[33] *Efficiency in High Schools, Studies, 1911–1914, in the Application of the Principles of Scientific Management to High School Problems*, Bulletin No. 44 (May 2, 1914) of the High School Teachers Association of New York, pp. 190–94.

little contact with teachers and in the double sessions program students had to be moved in and out so quickly that there was even less time for personal contact between students and teachers. The plan, therefore, was a step in the wrong direction. Principal Rollins of Bushwick High said that the extra sessions required additional funds for cleaning and maintenance which offset their gains. Furthermore, he said, there were more student failures under the new system. Since these students had to be taught again, this was added expense. Dr. Denbigh, principal of the Morris High School, in a speech that was printed in the Brooklyn *Daily Eagle*, stated that all of the principals in the association except one were opposed to what he called "factory education." After pointing out that under this arrangement students had no study periods, he concluded by saying that the extra sessions were actually more wasteful since they were a detriment to work and character "at the most critical period of habit formation." He was in agreement with Dr. Sullivan of the Boys High School that double and triple sessions only deceived the public into believing there was financial saving.

After the principals had spoken in opposition some of the teachers continued the attack. John Avent of Morris High spoke on "The Waste of Triple Sessions" and then criticized the Board of Education for its mechanical business-like views by stating that "to 'count em' whether pupils, or instructors, or personal influence, is indeed the only test of educational practice that makes an impression on the guardians of the budget." Avent was followed by Benjamin Gruenberg of the Commercial High School, who read a prepared statement which he entitled "Factory Efficiency in Education." He began by noting that one of the major forces which had brought the New York educators to seek the establishment of the maximum use of the school plant was the "idea of one hundred per cent efficiency." This idea had to be resisted, he said, because "If our schooling is to be more than school-keeping, we must consider something more than units and hours. We must make no concession to the economic fallacy." He then spoke on the difference between a factory and a school and the difficulties encountered when methods which were applicable and successful in one institution were applied in the other. The success and efficiency of the factory methods, he said, were based on the manufacture of a uniform, standardized product. In achieving this end, material and process could be perfected, and once perfected, standardized, and used over and over again. This situation did not exist in education and therefore factory methods could not be used. He noted that money could be saved by enlarging classes, but he said, "we no longer look to en-

larged classes as a legitimate means of saving money. Yet we do
seriously consider the closer congestion of the school as a sound solution of the problem." He opposed this "closer congestion" for two
reasons. The first was that having school rooms used successively by
several teachers made individualization of the rooms impossible. He
conceded that certain types of rooms might be standardized, e.g., laboratories and shops, but others, and especially the home rooms should
not be so arranged. With the double sessions and increased congestion
the home-like atmosphere which he thought desirable was impossible.
In fact, he said, students did not even have a place to keep their books
and had to carry them about throughout the school day. His second
reason was similar to Dr. Tildsley's, that personal contact between
student and teacher, difficult at best under the regular arrangements,
was impossible with the double and triple sessions. As he put it, under
the new system "it is touch and go, in the most literal sense."

Then Gruenberg presented a point that had been made earlier by
President McLaurin of Massachusetts Institute of Technology in criti-
cizing the Cooke report for the Carnegie Foundation,[34] and a point
that was to be made again by others in the years that followed. He
took the position that the efficiency of an object or an institution could
be judged only in terms of its function and not on the basis of whether
it was in constant use. He mentioned McLaurin's example of the
utilization of life belts to illustrate this meaning and then went on to
use two examples of his own. He pointed out that "It has been estimated that in this country there is invested in tooth-brushes the sum
of $1,432,678.15; yet these articles are used only a few minutes each
per day. No one advocates an increase in the use-efficiency of tooth-
brushes. The best example of high use-efficiency of an article of
common use was that furnished by certain southern cotton mills that
shocked us all a few years ago, when we read that the beds in which
the child workers slept never got cold. One shift of workers turned in
as soon as the sleepers were turned out. There was no time lost. And
yet we were shocked." He concluded his paper by conceding that the
demand for a greater use of the schools was legitimate. But he believed this wider usage should be realized through evening classes
and by opening the schools for use by the community and not by
"following the method of the steel-trust." He admitted also that
because of the building shortage in New York it might be necessary to
overcrowd classes or even to use double or triple sessions. But, he
said, "We must not forget that these are emergency measures, and we
must not let anyone suppose for an instant that these schemes solve

[34] Morris L. Cooke, *Academic and Industrial Efficiency* (New York, 1910).

the fundamental problems of adequate housing, and we must not ourselves accept them as such solution."

After the discussion was completed the High School Teachers Association of New York City passed a resolution, with only two dissenting votes, placing itself on record as being strongly opposed to the double and triple session plan and appointing a committee of three principals to present their case to the Board of Education.

A Question of Motive

Despite the setback in New York the platoon school idea spread rapidly after 1915, and it is clear that this was due to the combination of its features. Its advocates could and did claim that it provided an enriched educational program for the children *and* saved the taxpayers money. Clearly any plan with these assets would have had an appeal for a business society in an age of efficiency. But it is also clear that the economy feature was the *primary* factor in its appeal. Other schemes which utilized the school facilities more fully but which cost more money were quickly abandoned.

In the early stages of its development advocates of the plan openly emphasized its contributions to efficiency and economy in education. The statements of the editor of the *American School Board Journal* and the article by Bobbitt in this connection have been discussed. In both instances the Gary plan was linked to scientific management — the very embodiment of efficiency. And Bobbitt not only entitled his article "The Elimination of Waste in Education" but also listed the complete utilization of the school plant as his first principle of scientific management. But this emphasis upon the economic aspect was not limited to outsiders. Wirt himself, in describing his system to the administrators assembled at the Department of Superintendence meeting in St. Louis in February, 1912, used the title "The Utilization of the School Plant." And in the speech itself Wirt described the financial savings which were possible through complete plant utilization and the elimination of extra teachers, *before* he presented his views on the educational advantages.[35]

As the Gary plan began to be adopted as an economy measure, and especially when Wirt was brought to New York, opposition began to appear. When this happened defenders of the plan responded by claiming that they had been misunderstood. Thus Bobbitt, in an editorial in the *Elementary School Journal*, printed excerpts from Wirt's report to the New York Board of Education, in which Wirt stated that he was "not especially interested in running school systems cheaply."

[35] N.E.A. *Proceedings*, pp. 492–95.

Yet Bobbitt had to admit that the economy motive was responsible for Wirt's invitation to apply his system in New York. "There can be little doubt," he said, "that one of the strong motives which impelled Mayor Mitchel and the other city officials when they brought Superintendent Wirt to New York was the hope that sweeping economies might be made possible in the school budget. The rumor had reached New York, as it has every city, that at Gary twice or three times as many children can be put into a school as is now commonly done." [36]

For this misconception (if indeed it was a misconception) Wirt had to assume some of the responsibility, as did other educators. For example David Snedden, Commissioner of Education in Massachusetts, delivering a speech before the Department of Superintendence in Cincinnati in February, 1915, listed the unique features of the Gary system at the very beginning of his talk entitled "The Pros and Cons of the Gary System," and placed utilization of the school at the top of the list of pros. Speaking of the plan, he said "It permits such use of school buildings that substantially twice as many children can be accommodated in the ordinary type of school building as is usually the case." [37] Like Wirt, Snedden, in his analysis, did not overemphasize the economic advantages, but he followed the Gary superintendent in the order in which he presented the various advantages of the plan. In the same month the *American School Board Journal* carried an article in which the author described the adaptation of the Gary plan at Swarthmore, Pennsylvania. In discussing the merits of the plan he said that "Chief among the advantages of the new plan over the old, I would put: First, *financial economy*. (a) In teaching force, under the old plan we would need thirteen teachers to do for eight grades what we are now doing with ten teachers. As our salaries run, this means a saving of $2,000 or over per year." [38]

In 1916 and 1917 a great deal of attention was given in the professional journals to the Gary plan, the platoon school, and the general problem of achieving maximum utilization of the school "plant," especially in the leading administrative journal — the *American School Board Journal*. Their endorsement of the platoon plan was so enthusiastic and so consistent that virtually every issue in those two years contained articles, editorials, or news items on the subject. Invariably these accounts emphasized financial saving. For example, in June, 1917, the *Journal* carried the following news item:

[36] *Elementary School Journal*, XVI (November, 1915), 108.

[37] N.E.A. *Proceedings*, p. 363.

[38] B. H. Wallace, "The Adaptation of the Gary Plan at Swarthmore, Pennsylvania," L (February, 1915), 32.

Supt. Charles E. Chadsey of Detroit, Mich., has asked the common council for an appropriation of $180,000 with which to make an experiment of the Gary plan of organization. The money will be spent for additions containing an auditorium in each of the three schools which have not such facilities. The estimated saving to the city is about $5,000,000 in fifteen years.[39]

Two months later another item appeared:

A shift system intended to lengthen the school day and to provide for increased accommodations is proposed by Supt. F. E. Spaulding of Cleveland. The plan which was carried out at Minneapolis, where Dr. Spaulding formerly was located, resulted in an increase of the capacity of the average school from 25 to 50 per cent.[40]

In the years after 1918 the platoon plan continued to spread rapidly, the peak year being 1925, when 158 schools were converted or established in 28 cities. By 1929 there were over 1,000 schools operating under the platoon plan in 202 cities in 41 states. Among the large cities which adopted the plan were Detroit, Pittsburgh, Birmingham, Dallas, Newark, Portland, Akron, Seattle, Salt Lake City, and Tulsa. Apparently the Detroit school system adopted the plan most extensively and it did so for the same reason that New York had adopted the plan a few years earlier. As Deputy Superintendent Charles L. Spain of Detroit (who wrote a book on the subject in 1924) described it, the city in 1919 was faced with a financial crisis in education and turned to the platoon school organization as a way out.[41]

Events in Chicago in the twenties give additional evidence on the question of who favored the plan, administrators or teachers. Late in 1923 a commission appointed by the Board of Education, after visiting cities in which the platooon plan was being used, including Rochester, Pittsburgh, Gary, Akron, and Detroit, recommended the adoption of the plan in Chicago. In the first paragraph of the report the commission stated that "it cuts down the amount of building space required and in a large school system results in important savings in expenditures for both buildings and equipment."[42] The commission stated that by adopting the platoon plan the school housing capacity would be increased from 30 to 35 per cent and that as a result of such increase in building utilization the school district of Chicago would save one million dollars a year. One member of the group opposed the plan because she believed the system was too mechanical.[43]

[39] Vol. LIV, p. 64.
[40] Vol. LV, p. 46.
[41] Charles L. Spain, *The Platoon School* (New York, 1924), p. 47.
[42] *Proceedings of the Board of Education* (Chicago, 1923–24), p. 1453.
[43] *Ibid.*, pp. 1457–58.

At the same time the Chicago Teachers' Federation appointed a committee of nine to study the platoon schools in Detroit. This group, after completing its investigation, recommended that the system not be adopted in Chicago. The federation then notified the Board of Education that it was opposed to the platoon plan in a letter to that body dated June 25, 1924. In addition to this action, the Elementary Teachers' General Council protested against the plan to adopt the platoon school system at its meeting in March of 1924 and notified the Board of Education of its opposition in a formal letter on June 23, 1924.[44] Despite this opposition, the superintendent of schools, William McAndrew, who had taken office in February of 1924, recommended to the board on July 9, 1924, that the system be adopted in Chicago. Some insight into McAndrew's views on this matter and, incidentally, their similarity to Bobbitt's scientific management philosophy of education, can be gained from a statement from his Annual Report in 1926. He wrote that "Chicago has a school plant valued at $120,000,000.00. This plant is in large part idle during the summer months. No industrial concern would voluntarily keep its plant idle for two months a year." [45]

Other educators, writing in the twenties, after the platoon school had been in existence for more than a decade, concurred in the opinion that economy was the primary factor in the appeal of the plan. For example, Charles L. Robbins of the University of Iowa, writing in 1924 on developments in elementary education from 1900 to 1924, stated that it was the mechanical aspect of the plan — that of having two schools in one building — that had "attracted the most attention and has led to much discussion and imitation." [46] And George Counts, writing in 1930 after the platoon school had reached its peak and started to decline, stated that "undoubtedly the feature of the scheme which has appealed to those practical men who control public education in America is its provision for an efficient use of school resources." [47]

The primacy of the economic motive was denied, however, by some of the supporters of the platooon school. In 1931, for example, Roscoe David Case, former superintendent and instructor in education at the University of Denver, published evidence which purported to show that the economic factor was "really after all a secondary considera-

[44] *Ibid.*, p. 1451.

[45] *Annual Report of the Superintendent of Schools* (Chicago, 1926), p. 62.

[46] "Elementary Education" in I. L. Kandel (ed.), *Twenty-Five Years of American Education* (New York, 1924), p. 237.

[47] George S. Counts, *The American Road to Culture* (New York, 1930), p. 145.

tion. . . ." [48] The evidence consisted of the results of a questionnaire which had been sent to schoolmen who had adopted the platoon school. They were asked whether they had done so (a) for financial reasons; (b) to relieve congestion; (c) to secure a better program for children; or (d) to keep teachers satisfied and make them happy. As might have been expected from such a questionnaire, 65 per cent of the respondents indicated that their reason had been to secure a better program for children. These results were accepted at face value and were presented by Case as having settled the matter. Similar techniques were used to show that teachers, parents, and children preferred the platoon school over the regular school. Questionnaires were apparently sent to the superintendents of school systems which had adopted the plan asking them whether teachers, parents, and pupils approved the system. Thus, superintendents were asked, "About what percentage of your patrons like the platoon plan?" [49] The predictable answers were then used as proof that these groups strongly favored the plan.

As these facts might indicate, Case's study was a strong endorsement of the platoon plan and one in which its inadequacies were either conveniently overlooked or deliberately omitted. No mention was made, for example, of the extensive investigation of the academic work in the Gary schools made by Stuart A. Courtis in 1919. As a result of his study Courtis concluded that

the product of classroom teaching of the fundamentals is, at Gary, poor in quality and inadequate in amount; it approximates in character the product of the poorer conventional schools, and reveals in no particular the slightest indication that it has been affected either favorably or unfavorably by the enriched curriculum, or other special features of the Gary schools. The progress from grade to grade is relatively small, the final levels of achievement reached are comparatively low, and the differences between the results of simple and complex tests in any one subject increase progressively. The entire investigation reveals many and consistent evidences of careless work, imperfectly developed habits, and marked lack of achievement.[50]

Nor did Case make any mention of the bitter opposition of teachers to the platoon schools in New York and Chicago. In fact, no mention was even made that the plan had been introduced in these cities.

Despite the strongly optimistic picture drawn by Case, the platoon school declined steadily after 1930 and few, if any, such schools are to be found in American education today. The opposition of teachers

[48] *The Platoon School in America* (Stanford, Calif., 1931), p. 13.

[49] *Ibid.*, p. 255.

[50] Stuart A. Courtis, *The Gary Public Schools — Measurement of Classroom Products* (New York, 1919), p. 384.

to the plan had grown stronger in the twenties and in 1924 reached a national audience through an article in the *New Republic* by Margaret Haley, veteran Chicago teacher and representative of the American Federation of Teachers, who had fought authoritarianism and mechanical procedures in education since the turn of the century. In her charge that the platoon school was a scheme for lowering the cost of education, she described it as a

plan of organization of the elementary school by which from ten per cent to seventy per cent more children are enrolled than there are seats for in class rooms. This is done by 'dumping' the ten per cent to seventy per cent on the playground and into the auditorium or basement, and by keeping all the children rotating from room to room, teacher to teacher, so that the same ten per cent to seventy per cent may not be kept waiting longer than thirty consecutive minutes to get into class rooms. Even the six-year-old children have six or seven teachers a day, and as many as twelve or thirteen in some cities. Teachers handle as many as four hundred different pupils a day, and a thousand in a week.[51]

The author then quoted from a letter written by a mother who had withdrawn her child from the Detroit schools. She described the long lines of marching children which "looked to me like nothing so much as the lines of uncompleted Ford cars in the factory, moving always on, with a screw put in or a burr tightened as they pass — standardized, mechanical, pitiful." Miss Haley ended her article by stating that the platoon school was "the factory system carried into the public school, which needs only the closing-time whistle to make complete its identification with the great industrial plants!"

A decade later leaders in administration were attacking the system. Among them was Worth McClure, superintendent of schools in Seattle, Washington. Writing in the influential Department of Superintendence yearbook, McClure described the platoon school as a "mechanical contrivance" and urged administrators to conceive of a school as a garden where individual personalities would be nourished under guidance and not as a place "where they are run through the mill."[52] So, just as some of the harshness was taken from the Taylor system in industry, some was removed on human grounds from the school. Still, the movement for the "complete utilization of the school plant" left its permanent mark on education and many an American will recall, probably without nostalgia, trying to study history or mathematics as he occupied one of the potentially vacant chairs in the rear of an English classroom in which the students were reading *Silas Marner* aloud. Unacquainted as he probably was with the details of the history of American education, he sat there blissfully unaware that even though he could not concentrate on history or mathematics, by merely occupying a seat he was making his own small contribution to the elimination of waste in America.

7

INSTRUCTION FOLLOWS ACCOUNTING

In the total story of the response by the educators to society's criticism and pressure in the first two decades of the twentieth century, perhaps the most important and, in consequences, the most far-reaching aspect was the change that occurred in the nature of the superintendency. Because of the nature of their position in the schools and of their vulnerability to public opinion and pressure, it was the superintendents who interpreted and applied scientific management, as well as other business methods, to education. One result was that by 1925 the position had more of the characteristics of a managerial job in business or industry than it did of an educational one in the schools. This was reflected both in the superintendents' work and in the nature of the work in administration being offered in the universities.

The transition of the superintendent of schools from an educator to a business manager, although most rapid between 1911 and 1918, was already going on at the turn of the century. At that time many educational administrators were quite conservative and tended to identify themselves with business leaders.[1] The strengthening of these tendencies paralleled the year-by-year ascendency of the businessmen to a position of dominance in American society. Temporarily deterred by the criticism of the muckrakers, the business groups recovered their prestige after 1909 and, assisted by the sensational debut of the efficiency expert and the subsequent miracles expected through the application of efficiency principles, and by the equally impressive achievements of the Ford Motor Company, they moved steadily to the peak of their power and influence in the twenties. Interestingly, although these great successes were in the main based upon advances in

[1] See Merle Curti, *The Social Ideas of American Educators* (New York, 1935), chap. vi, "The School and the Triumph of Business Enterprise, 1860–1914."

technology, in the educational literature at least, credit was generally given to businessmen and to "modern business methods."

Another factor which contributed to the tendency of administrators to think in business terms was the sheer size and magnitude of the school systems, especially in the large cities, which made the organizational and administrative aspects of the educational work seem — on a superficial basis, at least — comparable to those aspects of large industry which, it was claimed, were being handled so efficiently by businessmen. In these huge systems there was no question but that the administrative detail work was considerable. It was also certain that the financial aspects of the superintendents' job, involving as it did large sums of money, required that careful attention be given to expenditures.

In addition to the increasing difficulty and complexity of the administration of the large school systems, administrators had to contend with the interference of school boards in the administrative and often in the educational functions of the school. These had resulted in a general feeling of discontent and, frequently, in outspoken criticism by educators of the administration of the schools. Typical of such criticism was the statement by Andrew S. Draper, president of the University of Illinois, and later commissioner of education in New York: "It must be said that there has been much dissatisfaction with the way school affairs have been managed in the larger cities. . . . There have been many and serious complaints of the misuse of funds, of neglect of property, of the appointment of unfit teachers, and of general incapacity, or worse, on the part of the boards. . . . It would not be true to say that the business of the schools has suffered as seriously as municipal business, but it certainly has been managed badly enough." [2] To correct this condition Draper recommended that the school board be reduced in size, be appointed rather than elected, and be removed from partisan or municipal politics, and that it limit itself to legislative, as opposed to executive, functions. He also advocated the separation of the administration into two independent departments, one to manage the business interests and the other to supervise instruction.

There is no question that at the turn of the century new and large problems existed in educational administration — problems that to some extent at least, were comparable to other problems of municipal government at that time. And during the Progressive era the solution to these problems paralleled the solution to other problems of city

[2] Nicholas Murray Butler (ed.), *Education in the United States* (Albany, New York, 1900), p. 13.

government, which, as shown in chapter i, frequently entailed introducing businesslike procedures and often businessmen themselves into government. Thus, as the years passed, the school boards were reduced in size and were increasingly dominated by businessmen. By 1917, Professor Scott Nearing found in a study of the composition of school boards in 104 large cities that, of the total of 967 board members, 433 were businessmen, 333 were professional men, 87 were workers, and many of the remainder were either retired businessmen or the wives of businessmen.[3]

Many school administrators believed, and frequently asserted, that manufacturers, merchants, and bankers made the best school board members. This viewpoint was presented in an important book on educational administration in 1904 by William Estabrook Chancellor, superintendent of schools in Paterson, New Jersey. At the top of his list of those who were best qualified Chancellor placed manufacturers. "These men," he said, were "accustomed to dealing with large bodies of men and with important business interests." Second on his list were merchants, contractors, bankers, and "other men of large affairs." These men were qualified, he said, because "a board of education controls a business and deals with the business side of education." Among those whom Chancellor thought did *not* make good board members were inexperienced young men, unsuccessful men, politicians, newspaper men, men in subordinate business positions, and women.[4]

The same view was expressed by Superintendent L. N. Hines, speaking before the National Education Association in 1911 on the subject "The Ideal School Board from the Superintendent's Point of View." Hines believed that board membership "should be confined to wide-awake, sane, progressive, business and professional men who have business ideas. . . ."And he stated that a superintendent who had such a board could "count himself fortunate above all things." On the other hand, he said there was no room for cranks or extremists, women were not fitted to deal with the problems, and "politicians of a low sort, saloon-keepers, and kindred spirits have no place on school boards."[5]

These ideas were reinforced and spread throughout educational administration in 1916 by Ellwood P. Cubberley in his widely used textbook, *Public School Administration.* His words are interesting not only because they show a heavy borrowing from Chancellor and Hines, but also because they are not so much a statement of fact as

[3] *School and Society,* VI (1917), 297.

[4] William Estabrook Chancellor, *Our Schools: Their Administration and Supervision* (rev. ed.; Boston, 1915), pp. 12–13.

[5] N.E.A. *Proceedings* (1911), pp. 994–1001.

they are a projection of things as Cubberley would have liked them to be. Concerning the individuals who made the best school board members he wrote:

Men who are successful in the handling of large business undertakings — manufacturers, merchants, bankers, contractors, and professional men of large practice — would perhaps come first. Such men are accustomed to handling business rapidly; are usually wide awake, sane, and progressive; are not afraid to spend money intelligently; are in the habit of depending upon experts for advice, and for the execution of administrative details; and have the tact and perseverance necessary to get the most efficient service out of everybody from superintendent down.

Those who did not make good board members were: "Inexperienced young men, unsuccessful men, old men who have retired from business, politicians, saloon-keepers, uneducated or relatively ignorant men, men in minor business positions, and women. . . ."[6]

The evidence indicates that these educators got what they wanted and school board positions were occupied largely by businessmen. As a result, administrators did achieve more job security, but they had to behave and operate the school in a businesslike way to do so.

In addition to the influence of businessmen on school boards, and to the continuous pressure for efficiency and economy from the popular journals, outside businessmen and educators themselves prodded administrators into conceiving of education as a business enterprise. Thus a school board member from Huron, Ohio, wrote in October, 1911, that "a board of education is only a board of directors; the taxpayers, the stockholders. The superintendent is a sales manager; the teachers salesmen."[7] In 1915 a businessman speaking before the Department of Superintendence of the N.E.A. told his audience, "It is proper to say that the schools are like factories turning out graduates, which, in turn, became employees of the business houses and may be considered the raw material of business."[8]

[6] Ellwood P. Cubberley, *Public School Administration* (Boston, 1916), pp. 124–25.

[7] John H. McCormick, "What Is a Teacher Worth," *American School Board Journal*, XLIII, 30.

[8] N.E.A. *Proceedings* (1915), p. 319. At the same time that laymen were expressing these conceptions of education as a business, and drawing analogies between business and education, the same ideas were also being voiced by educators and particularly by administrators. For example, early in 1911 J. L. Upton, master of the Willard School in Quincy, Massachusetts, wrote that in order to make every child intellectually, socially, morally, and industrially efficient it would be necessary to "place education on a business basis, and maintain it on a business basis. We must run it on sound business principles just as we would any other business enterprise. The public has put its money in this business, elected a board, and they in turn, have chosen a superintendent or business manager to carry on the business. . . . If the business yields a product which is the best that can be made from the given material, it is a successful business; otherwise it is not." "The Problem of Public Education," *Education*, XXXI, 397.

Although educational discussion and educational writing, particularly that pertaining to administration, was saturated by business and industrial terminology and analogies, indicating that many administrators used them, perhaps the individual who did the most to contribute to the conception of education as a business and of the school as a factory was Cubberley. This was not because he believed more deeply in this conception or carried it further than many others, but because his writing was so widely read in the profession. His *Public School Administration*, while showing that the author had a deep concern for and dedication to public education, is filled with business-industrial analogies. For example, at one point he wrote,

Our schools are, in a sense, factories in which the raw products (children) are to be shaped and fashioned into products to meet the various demands of life. The specifications for manufacturing come from the demands of the twentieth-century civilization, and it is the business of the school to build its pupils to the specifications laid down. This demands good tools, specialized machinery, continuous measurement of production to see if it is according to specifications, the elimination of waste in manufacture, and a large variety in the output.[9]

This same theme with similar language was repeated in his history of American education, a book which was originally published in 1919 and which sold some 100,000 copies by 1941.[10]

That educators did more than just talk about efficiency and scientific management was shown by the account of some of their activities which was presented in chapters v and vi. Similarly, they did more than just talk about using modern business methods in the schools — they actually used them. And in the process, educational administrators, by devoting more of their time and energy to the financial aspects of education and less to the instructional aspects, moved closer to the business-managerial role and away from the educational role. It is true that Andrew Draper had recommended that the business and instructional functions of administration be separated, and through the years, especially before 1911, the same view was taken by many others. But Spaulding had taken a strong stand to the effect that the two functions could not be separated and the efficiency climate helped to strengthen his position. Of course, only the largest cities felt they could afford to hire a separate business manager and, as Strayer pointed out in 1913, in the great majority of school systems superin-

[9] Ellwood P. Cubberley, *Public School Administration* (Boston, 1916), p. 338.

[10] Ellwood P. Cubberley, *Public Education in the United States* (Boston, 1919), pp. 378–79. Statistics on the sale of Cubberley's books appear in a biography by Jesse B. Sears and Adin D. Henderson, *Cubberley of Stanford and His Contribution to American Education* (Stanford, Calif., 1957), p. 119.

tendents had to perform both functions, with conditions forcing them to give increasing attention to their business role.[11] Even in the largest systems, superintendents had to spend an increasing amount of time on business matters, and even interpret or translate educational activity into business terms in order to survive.

The varied actions taken by administrators for this purpose are best described as educational cost accounting. It includes their attention to records and reports, to the standardization of supplies and equipment, to an analysis of the cost of instruction, and to the financial problems connected with retardation and elimination that came to be known as child accounting. In each instance, their efforts were largely responses to criticism and constituted an attempt to show in very concrete, factual, financial ways that they were operating the schools efficiently. It is true that even without the stimulus of public criticism in the form of demands for demonstrations of efficiency and economy that more attention would have been given to these problems. But the amount of attention actually given to these matters by administrators and, more important, the way in which they were treated, was a direct result of the strength and nature of the demands being made upon them.

Demonstrating Efficiency through Records and Reports

Schoolmen had been criticized for not keeping adequate records and for not providing adequate reports as early as 1909 by Leonard Ayres in his study on retardation in the schools. In his book Ayres had told educators that large corporations regarded their records of the manufacturing process as their most valuable asset.

If the directors of large corporations have found through experience that it pays to know what happened to a stove or a shoe in the process of manufacture, who worked on it, how long it took to complete it, and, if it is in any way deficient, at whose door the responsibility lies, is it not much more the duty of those in charge of training citizens to be able to find out what happened in the course of the education given, when the child entered, how long he spent in each grade, where he progressed slowly and where rapidly, and, if he left school before completing the course, when and why? [12]

He claimed that despite "the hundreds of thousands of trained workers in education and *the millions of treasure freely spent each year*" that education was still based on "opinion, guess work, and eloquence." [13]

---

[11] George D. Strayer and Edward L. Thorndike, *Educational Administration* (New York, 1913), p. 270.

[12] Leonard Ayres, *Laggards in Our Schools* (Philadelphia, 1909), p. 217.

[13] *Ibid.*, p. 219. (Italics mine.)

Even before Taylor's debut and the efficiency drive, there were indications that Ayres's work had had a great impact as superintendents began to urge their colleagues to eliminate the waste caused by retardation and elimination by keeping better records and acting upon the data collected thereby.[14] Then in February, 1911, shortly after the railroad hearings, the Department of Superintendence heard a preliminary report from its Committee on Uniform Records and Reports. The administrators were told that school statistics and records were unreliable and of little value and that because of "new problems which have arisen in the last few years and new standards of efficiency which have been raised" better records and reports were essential. The most important of the new problems, the committee reported, was "one of educational waste," and it was largely responsible for the widespread criticism. To meet the "public criticism" schoolmen should engage in a campaign to enlighten the public, and the superintendents were told how to wage the battle:

In such a campaign mere assertion, personal opinion, personal bias have little weight. The public only takes seriously those presentations of school needs and conditions which are based upon carefully collected and well-interpreted facts. Only by the use of such data, set forth by means of tables, colored circles, curves, black-line graphs, or other graphic representations, can the people be made acquainted with the whole work of the school, be made to realize where the school breaks down, be brought to understand the necessity of certain adjustments within the school, be brought to appreciate the propriety of expending such large sums of public money on education.[15]

As the criticism of the schools mounted through 1911 and 1912, administrators were threatened and urged to make haste in giving more attention to records and reports and they continued to receive such advice as that from the Committee on Uniform Records and Reports. For example, at the annual meeting of the Department of Superintendence held in St. Louis in February, 1912, George H. Chatfield devoted part of his speech to the problem of adequate records. He told his audience:

There is in all well-conducted businesses strict accountability for raw material, labor, machine energy, overhead expense, completed product and residue. Inspection, supervision, records, at all stages of the process; inventories, balance sheets, detailed periodic reports, mark the intimate connection between facts and income. The absolute dependence of effective administration upon complete and well ordered information is clearly recognized.[16]

[14] William H. Elson and Frank P. Bachman, "School Records: Their Defects and Improvement," *Educational Review*, XXXIX (March, 1910), 217–26.

[15] N.E.A. *Proceedings* (1911), pp. 271–302.

[16] N.E.A. *Proceedings* (1912), p. 388.

Chatfield cited the example of large corporations which devoted great energy to keeping a record of their business, and climaxed his account by pointing out that the New York Central Railroad spent four times as much on records and reports as the New York City schools. Since the efficiency of the schools was being questioned as never before and since the tide of criticism was swelling not lessening, he advised the school superintendent to follow the example of business in the matter of records. "How else," he said, "may he justify himself on the purely quantitative side when the businessman complains of his product. . . ." [17]

Administrators responded quickly to the demands for records and in May, 1912, Ayres reported that, whereas in 1909 the number of cities having systems of individual record cards for keeping the school histories of their children was only 29, by 1912 "a uniform system for this purpose" had been adopted by 216. "Those cities," said Ayres approvingly, "intend to judge processes by results." And they responded even more quickly in adopting more elaborate, detailed, and uniform accounting records. Ayres stated that between May, 1911 (when Taylor's last article appeared in the *American Magazine*), and May, 1912, the number of school systems using such records increased from 15 to 418.[18] Commenting on this tremendous increase, George Strayer pointed out that it meant an "increased addition to the business aspect of school administration." [19]

Strayer also testified in 1913 that the increased attention to records and reports as well as other aspects of educational cost accounting resulted from public pressure. He wrote:

> The development of adequate school records and significant school reports may be traced on the one hand to the growth of the profession of education, and on the other to the demand which the public is now making for complete information concerning public enterprises. . . .[20]

> During the past five years there has been much discussion concerning the efficiency of those charged with the control of various city departments, budget exhibits and surveys. Our schools have come in for their share of these investigations. There has developed a demand for adequate records and reports, for the standardization of supplies and for definite units of cost for various education activities.[21]

The reasons for the energetic demand for uniform accounting records are not hard to find. With this system, as Ayres pointed out, school

---

[17] *Ibid.*, p. 389.
[18] Leonard Ayres, "Measuring Educational Processes through Educational Results," *School Review*, XX, 302.
[19] Strayer and Thorndike, *Educational Administration*, p. 258.
[20] *Ibid.*, p. 250.
[21] *Ibid.*, p. 270.

systems could be compared for their relative cost efficiency.[22] Obviously, leaders in the community and school board members would want a system that would enable them to compare their schools with those of other communities. As for the superintendents, they probably had no real choice in the matter but undoubtedly welcomed the system, as they welcomed the school survey, as a means of proving their operating efficiency, or, if they were found to be relatively inefficient, as a means of knowing exactly what to do to make their system compare favorably with the most efficient. With this arrangement, however, each system had to be brought in line with the most efficient — efficient, that is, in terms of costs. Thus if one school superintendent eliminated the teaching of Greek, or increased the size of his classes, or increased the load of his teachers and reduced expenditures thereby, other superintendents would be under pressure to do the same.

When educators spoke of "reports" in these years, they generally had in mind the annual report of the superintendent to the board of education. Unlike the situation regarding records, administrators were urged to produce annual reports, not because business firms did so but rather because they were useful in defense. At the same time they were given considerable advice by leading administrators on what the proper form and content of a good report should be. And, in this advising, these leaders emphasized some of the central aspects of the problems they faced and provided ample evidence not only that school administration had moved toward a business manager's job but also why it had done so.

The motive for preparing annual reports was to justify expenditures and to educate the public in case additional funds were needed. No less an authority than Ellwood Cubberley stated in his widely used text on administration that in dealing with the public the report could "be made to form a most effective bulwark in support of continued requests for larger funds." But not just any report would do — it had to be the right kind. What kind was the right kind? Certainly not those that had been published in the past, in which an educator such as William Torrey Harris had discussed the philosophical aspects of education with his constituents and assumed they would understand what he was saying. In the age of efficiency in a business society such reports were too theoretical — too filled with opinion. As one writer put it "Of the text of the superintendent's report one thing should be said emphatically: It must embody facts, not theories, or it is useless." Why? Because, he said, "Achievement, not intangible theory, approves itself to the taxpayers and wins their confidence in future

[22] Leonard Ayres, "Measuring Educational Processes through Educational Results," loc. cit., p. 302.

measures."[23] And schoolmen were told by a member of the State Board of Education in Massachusetts, that one of the two functions of a report was "to give the people of the community a clear idea of what the schools are costing, how they are organized and where the money goes." The same person advised administrators to utilize the methods employed by advertising experts.[24]

When educators were specific about what constituted an excellent modern report, they most often used Frank Spaulding's Newton reports as illustrations. His annual report for 1912 was especially recommended by leading administrators. This report, which emphasized detailed financial data and featured extensive use of graphs and charts, contained most of the material Spaulding presented to the Department of Superintendence in February of 1913 in his address on the application of the principles of scientific management in education. The 1912 report was lauded in an educational journal in September, 1913, by Franklin Bobbitt. In this report, said Bobbitt,

he [Spaulding] not only holds to the high standard set by his reports for several years past, but here surpasses his own previous best work in many ways. So far as it goes — and as compared with the usual report it goes a very long way — it is a model of what a school report should be. It is a publicity message from the superintendent of the city schools to his constituency which shows simply, accurately, and clearly just what the schools are attempting, where the emphases are being placed, where the moneys are being expended, where economies are being attempted, and the plans that are being made for the future.

The report presents certain questions in terms that the layman can understand; it answers those that the superintendent is expected to answer, and presents the facts needed by the layman for answering the questions asked of him. Some of the questions are: What are the Newton schools trying to do? With what success? Do you approve of their policy? Is it carried out economically? Is it administered efficiently? Can we afford to continue it? Can we afford not to continue it?[25]

More significant was the fact that these reports were praised by Cubberley in his administration text, since this book was used in administration courses. Cubberley told his readers, presumably thousands of school administrators, that it was only because of Spaulding's excellent reports which "showed in detail where every additional dollar went," that the citizens of Newton "rather willingly" supported their schools as well as they did.[26]

[23] Willard Doten, "The Annual Report," *American School Board Journal*, LII (May, 1916), 13–14.

[24] *Ibid.*, LIII (September, 1916), 29.

[25] *Elementary School Teacher*, XIV, 41–42.

[26] Ellwood P. Cubberley, *Public School Administration*, p. 427.

Another strong commendation for Spaulding's reports was given by C. N. Kendall, commissioner of education in New Jersey, in the *American School Board Journal* in August of 1915. Kendall, in featuring Spaulding's last report at Newton in his article, "What Should Go into a City Superintendent's Report?" not only approved the contents of this report, but also indicated the criteria by which a superintendent's report was judged in the age of efficiency:

Much of this report is an answer to the question, "In which of the twenty-three suggested ways may the expenses of the Newton schools be reduced?" Those of you who have read it recall that he suggests economies varying all the way from reducing the salary of the superintendent of schools to saving money on the kindergartens. With the exception of the proposition to reduce the superintendent's salary, which he does not oppose, each suggestion is discussed with a good deal of detail. No complaining taxpayer, after reading this keen, detailed and even adroit analysis of school expenses, could look upon those expenses in precisely the same way as he did before.[27]

Spaulding's reports were used as a model because they met the needs of the time; his success was proof that this was so. Not only had he maintained himself successfully for years at Newton, a city he himself labeled "the burial ground of superintendents," but he had been promoted in 1914 to Minneapolis and in 1917 to Cleveland, where he received a salary of $12,000 a year at a time when most superintendents were making about $2,000 and the average teacher's salary was about $750 per year. There is, of course, no means of measuring precisely Spaulding's influence upon other superintendents and upon educational administration, but it is certain that it was considerable, for he not only provided a formula for survival to an insecure group but also (at $12,000 a year) a formula for success in a business society which measured success in material terms. With such influential educators as Kendall, Bobbitt, and Cubberley praising his reporting methods, and directly or indirectly calling attention to his success, we cannot doubt it was partly through his influence that the annual reports of superintendents bore an increasing resemblance to the reports of corporations.

Educational Cost Accounting

A second major kind of activity engaged in by administrators and one which illustrated the extent of the infiltration of business values into education was the application of cost analysis and accounting to the work of the schools. In these efforts the objective was to determine the costs of instruction and to establish a "standard" cost for the purpose of cutting costs and of demonstrating efficiency. For the

[27] Vol. LI, p. 9.

most part the cost accounting was directed toward the high schools because they were more expensive, especially in the junior and senior years, than the elementary schools.

That a detailed financial cost accounting of the instructional work of the public schools would have been demanded by an economy-minded society seems natural enough. What was surprising was the eager way some administrators embraced and fostered the notion that educators were servants of the taxpayers and not only had to acquiesce meekly but also had to attempt to meet enthusiastically the demands made upon them by the public. One such administrator was William McAndrew, principal of the Washington Irving High School in New York City. In November, 1911, McAndrew wrote a statement on "Success in School" which was published in the *School Review*. Educators were told that the schools suffered from the lack of competition among teachers as well as from the reluctance of schoolmen to accept the business criteria. "We are accustomed," said McAndrew, "to regard ourselves as above business and incapable of measurement by dollars and cents, yet the past ten years have made it more clear that one of the best things that can happen to us is the realization that education is public business and that a dollar-and-cents measurement is inevitable. It is the duty of the principal to give to the city returns for this investment." [28]

But the real leaders in educational cost accounting were the two men who had led the movement to apply scientific management to education — Frank E. Spaulding and Franklin Bobbitt. It will be recalled that Spaulding's application of Taylor's system resulted in a cost analysis. His contribution had been the introduction of the dollar as the criterion for judging the relative value of the various school subjects. Characteristically, he had abandoned the attempt to attain a social-philosophical judgment in favor of a concrete, practical, financial one. He didn't know, he said, whether music was more valuable than Greek, but Greek was more expensive and so from a financial standpoint it was less valuable. Bobbitt, concerned about developing standards and impressed with Spaulding's work, turned his talent to applying Spaulding's standard — the financial standard — to the work of the secondary schools. Spaulding's advice was followed, and a number of studies were made of the cost of instruction. One of these was a study of nineteen high schools in the Chicago area in 1913 and in 1914 by Robert Charles Harris, who was a student of Bobbitt's. An account of the work was published in the *School Review* (of which Bobbitt was an editor) in June, 1914. Harris collected his data by

[28] Vol. XIX, p. 593.

means of a questionnaire and used the "cost per year-minute" as the basic unit since, he said, it was a much "fairer unit than the cost per pupil, because it takes into account the time that is distributed to each pupil." [29] His procedure was to determine the cost per pupil and divide this by the year-minutes of each teacher (a teacher with 5 weekly periods of 40 minutes each during the school year had 200 year-minutes) which gave him the cost per year-minute. His findings, which were presented in tables and charts, showed great differences in the cost of instruction among the high schools. After presenting his findings Harris made recommendations which would enable the schools with high year-minute costs to economize. For example, he indicated what changes he would make in one of the high schools which was paying "329 per cent above the average for Foreign Language." "Suppose the salary remains the same, $1,460. Let the teacher have five periods per day instead of 3.5. Let the size of the class be 25 instead of 12.8. Let the term be 40 weeks instead of 34. Then we shall have: salary, $1,460; number of pupils per teacher, 125; teaching time of teacher, 200 year-minutes. From these figures the cost-per-year-minutes is 5.84 cents as compared with 27.31 cents in the present case. The average for all the schools in Foreign Language is 6.37."

Harris had other recommendations for reorganizing the work of the schools. One of these was "in such subjects as History and Civics, English, Science, Manual Training, and Domestic Science, pupils of different years can be instructed in one class. Here again the saving is above one-half." And he had a plan to standardize the cost regardless of the size of the class. Under his arrangement "a class of 10 pupils ought not to be entitled to more than 20 minutes of recitation, if the standard for the size of the class is 25 pupils and the length of the recitation period is 40 minutes. Another plan is to have such a small class recite every other day, covering double work for the one recitation. Either of these plans would reduce the cost per year-minute for that subject approximately one half." In addition Harris worked out an equation for "cost efficiency" which provided a standard formula for the amount of time and the number of pupils a teacher should instruct per day.

At about the same time that Harris' study was published, an article written by a leading educator appeared in the *American School Board Journal* supporting Spaulding's educational cost accounting. The educator was W. S. Deffenbaugh, chief of the Division of School Administration in the U.S. Bureau of Education. He stated that before administration could be efficient such problems as "what instruction

[29] "Comparative Cost of Instruction in High Schools," XXII, 373–76.

to buy; how much and in what subjects; how many daily recitations a high school should conduct; and how many hours a high school pupil should carry" had to be solved. He pointed out that in a high school with 600 students, $3,000 a year could be saved by increasing the class size from 25 to 30 students because three fewer teachers would be needed, and he cited Spaulding's work at Newton in which $4,000 per year had been saved by reducing the recitations. Then he asked "what would be the educational loss if a high school teacher instructs six classes a day instead of five? What will be the financial gain?" Significantly, he did not discuss what the educational loss would be but he did point out the financial gain. Before educational administration could be efficient, he warned, "each superintendent must make a study of the problems I have just mentioned." [30]

The following year, 1915, Bobbitt made his contribution to cost accounting by publishing the results of a study he had made of costs in twenty-five high schools in seven states. His purpose was to "present a *method* of finding standards of practice and comparing individual schools with such standards." [31] He began his analysis with a lengthy statement in which he indicated how the problem was being handled effectively in industrial management:

Accurate cost-accounting lies at the foundations of all successful business management. In railroad administration, for example, it is known that under normal conditions locomotive repair-cost should average about six cents per mile-run; lubricating oils should cost about eighteen cents per hundred miles for passenger locomotives, and about twenty-five cents for freight locomotives; and so on for each item involved in the entire management. With these cost-standards at hand, derived from wide general practice, if a railroad manager finds at the end of the year that locomotive repairs average fifteen cents per mile run, then it is quite evident upon the surface that somthing is wrong somewhere. . . .

The same procedure could be applied to education if "standard unit-costs" were developed for the various school expenditures. If, he argued, educators knew

. . . that satisfactory instruction in high school English can be had for fifty dollars per thousand student-hours, and that this price represented the norm of practice, then those responsible for high-school management have a standard of judgment that can be used for measuring the efficiency of their practices. If instruction in this subject is costing them $75 per 1,000 student-hours, and they are aiming at results of only the usual sort, it is evident that they are wasting money, and that administrative adjustments need to be made.

[30] "Efficient Administration in Small City Schools," XLVIII (May, 1914), 15–16.
[31] John Franklin Bobbitt, "High-School Costs," *School Review*, XXIII (October, 1915), 505–34.

In his study the cost unit was the student hour (the instruction of one student for sixty minutes) and he determined the "cost per 1,000 student-hours" in mathematics, Latin, English, history, science, modern languages, commercial studies, household occupations, shop work, agriculture, music, and normal training. With each subject at each school he figured the cost per 1,000 student hours, and then the median cost among the twenty-five schools. Then he used the cost of the seventh most expensive school as one end of the scale and the cost of the seventh least expensive as the other to form what he called a "zone of safety."

He presented this explanation of his system, which indicated how his standard costs had been derived:

Fifty-nine dollars paid in Rockford is the median price paid for algebra and geometry. There is no reason to think that the results obtained in Rockford are in any degree inferior to those obtained in the dozen cities paying a higher price. Fifty-nine dollars for mathematics represents the consensus of practice and is a *safe* standard of judgment for high schools.

Such a standard of practice is too rigid for universal application. The diversity represented by the middle half of the cities is probably normal. The standard of practice should probably be so formulated as to permit the flexibility of practice found in this middle 50 per cent of the cities. We can say, therefore, that between $52 and $74 is a safe standard price for high-school mathematics. This is what we call the "zone of safety."

The same procedure was followed with regard to Latin instruction. He found that the cost ranged from $244 per 1,000 student hours in Maple Lake, Minnesota, to $46 in Greensburg, Indiana; his median was $71 in Dekalb, Illinois; while his zone of safety was from $92 to $54. This was 20 percent higher than the "price" for mathematics and this bothered him. The difference in price, he said, could not be "due to the greater value of the subject, to any diminished supply of the commodity, or to higher salaries paid to the teachers. It is simply due to administrative maladjustments in the teaching-hours per week." As a result he departed from his statistical procedure and gave his readers some insight into the thinking of the educational business manager, as well as a lesson in market place psychology:

It is interesting to observe the highly extravagant price paid by certain villages that really can least afford such wastefulness. Maple Lake is probably getting no more results for each 1,000 student-hours than is Dekalb at one-third the cost or Rockford at one-fifth the cost. Practical men, before buying wheat, or cotton, or railroad stocks, examine into market conditions and pay something in the neighborhood of current market prices. These figures appear to indicate that the same practical school-board members, when they are investing the people's money in a supposedly necessary community commodity, are, certain of them, paying prices very greatly in excess of current market prices as represented by the standards of practice in those cities that lie within the "zone of safety." It probably is sufficiently extravagant to pay even the price of $90 for its Latin, when the median city is getting it done for $71. When the same city is getting its mathematics for $59 and its English for $51, it is more than probable that the upper limit of our middle zone in this case represents wasteful extravagance; and that it is the lower portion of the middle zone that more nearly represents safety.

In order to standardize the costs Bobbitt advocated increasing the size of classes which were below average and reducing those which were above average, and the same procedure was suggested with regard to the working hours of teachers and to teachers' salaries. When this had been done, the administrators would have a basis for judging (as the railroad manager had) whether his enterprise was being operated efficiently. And by using this system of cost accounting continuously he would have a means "of diagnosing the situation and locating irregularities of management."

By the end of 1915 administrators were thoroughly acquainted with the merits of and the methods involved in educational cost accounting. But, evidently, it was not being applied rapidly enough, for in the years that followed schoolmen continued to be urged and warned to adopt it. One administrator noted that "efficiency surveys are spreading from business enterprises into the business of high school management," and he complained that no regional cost standards were available which could be used to compare and judge the efficiency of individual high schools after they had been surveyed. He warned schoolmen that since the high school was "a great public financial enterprise" that more attention had to be given to the "financial details involved in the operation of the high school plant." If they did not do this, he said, "the day of reckoning" would come. If they were "alert" and did standardize their financial management according to efficiency measures, "they would have little fear of a retrenchment stampede." [32]

As if in response to this urging a cost analysis was made by a high school principal in Kansas City, Missouri, and a detailed account of the findings was published in the *American School Board Journal* in December, 1917.[33] He began his report with a series of questions which indicated his debt to Spaulding and Bobbitt:

[32] William E. Andrews, "A Study in High School Cost of Production," *American School Board Journal*, LIII (September, 1916), 12.

[33] A. H. Monsees, "A Study of the Cost of High School Instruction in Kansas City," LV, 21-22.

Is there a reasonable degree of uniformity in conditions of economic importance among the high schools of the Kansas City school system? How much
is being invested in the high-priced subjects? In the light of a thorough investigation of the cost of the different subjects can all of the practices or policies
of the past be continued with wisdom in the future? Such questions as these
prompted this investigation, which was made in co-operation with the Department of Administration of Schools of the University of Missouri and the
Bureau of Research and Efficiency of the Kansas City Schools. It is presented
here in the hope that it will prove suggestive for similar studies of high school
costs in cities and towns. . . . The purpose of this study is to answer these
questions: How do the subjects of the different schools vary in cost? What
are the causes of the variations in cost?

He found, of course, that there were differences in cost in the various
subjects in the four Kansas City high schools. He also found that these
variations were due to differences in teacher salaries, class size, and
average daily attendance. As in the case of Spaulding's report of his
investigation into the causes of difference in costs, it would seem that
the answers would have been self-evident before the study was begun.
But undoubtedly the cost analysis made an impressive appearance and
it indicated that schoolmen were working at being efficient in a businesslike way.

In his study the author investigated the cost of the various high
school subjects in much the same way that Bobbitt had, but in addition
he compared the cost of "solids" (subjects requiring preparation outside of school) and non-solids (subjects which did not require outside
preparation). After presenting his data on this comparison, he raised
a series of questions in the Spaulding-Bobbitt manner as follows:

In connection with the above observations the following questions are to
the point: (1) Was instruction in solids worth $9.00 at Manual Training when
only $5.00 was paid for the same at Westport? (2) Was instruction in non-
solids worth $6.00 at Lincoln when only $4.00 was paid for the same at
Manual Training? (3) How much money should be invested in non-solids
as compared with solids when the average cost for non-solids is $16.00 as
compared with a cost of $7.00 for solids for an equal credit to the student?
In other words, are non-solid credits worth $2\frac{2}{7}$ times as much as solid credits?

By 1918 educational cost accounting was well established in American education, as was Spaulding's financial criterion for deciding on
the relative value of the various school subjects. Occasionally a question was raised about these procedures, especially about eliminating
such subjects as Latin or advanced courses in modern language or
science, but the answer was generally similar to that provided by
Spaulding in 1913: they had no data on the relative value of various

subjects and the financial answer was provided. If there was not sufficient demand to bring the price down to approximate the norm they
would invest in something else.[34]

The Educational Balance Sheet and Child Accounting

It will be recalled that Ayres brought the problem of retardation
and elimination to the attention of the country through his book *Laggards in Our Schools*. The report was significant because it accused
educators of gross waste in handling public funds and this accusation
was more effective because Ayres claimed his study to be (and it had
the outward appearance of being) "scientific." In the years that followed, Ayres continued to investigate and to publish his findings on
the problem under the impressive auspices of the Russell Sage Foundation. At the same time other educators joined in the work, contributing numerous articles and speeches that kept the problem before the
profession and an efficiency-conscious public. Most often these men
presented the problem in terms of economy and efficiency with the
result that school systems were judged wasteful and inefficient on the
basis of the number of children who dropped out before completing
the eighth grade or were "retarded," without regard to the social or
economic or educational factors responsible for the situation.

A few months after Ayres's book appeared, the superintendent of
schools in Cleveland, William Elson, together with one of his assistants, wrote an article in which they repeated Ayres's demand for better
records and reports, and his criteria for efficiency. Educators were
told that the school system was "most efficient" which had "the
smallest per cent of withdrawals." [35] The following year, through an
unfavorable comparison with industrial management, administrators
were criticized by another educator for allowing drop-outs. They were
told that the number of drop-outs was "a sheer loss of an astoundingly
large per cent of the raw material during the process of production,
any private manufacturing industry that should, because of operating
methods lose or cast aside from its unfinished product one-tenth of
what is lost through the maladministration of our school system would
be forced into voluntary or involuntary bankruptcy in an incredibly
short time — and it ought so to be." [36]

In the spring of 1911 under the sponsorship of the Russell Sage

[34] For example, see the article by Harry G. Wheat on the "Costs of Instruction in the
High Schools of West Virginia," *School Review*, XXVI (June, 1918), 449–50.

[35] William H. Elson and Frank P. Bachman, "School Records: Their Defects and Improvement," *Educational Review*, XXXIX (March, 1910), 222, 224.

[36] Calvin O. Davis, "Reorganization of Secondary Education," *Educational Review*,
XLII (October, 1911), 272–73.

Foundation, Ayres conducted another major study of retardation and elimination, involving 206,495 children in elementary schools. He received the co-operation of superintendents from twenty-nine cities. In January, 1912, when public demands for economy were growing stronger, an account of the study written by Ayres was published in the *American School Board Journal* with the significant title "The Money Cost of Repetition Versus the Money Saving through Acceleration."[37] Ayres stated that many studies of retardation and elimination had been made in the "past few years," but he said these studies were open to criticism because, while they computed the cost to the school of the repeaters, they did not take account of the "children who make rapid progress and thus counterbalance part of this added expense." He presented his solution for the problem and indicated how the educational balance sheet would operate: "Now it is evident that if the number of years lost by slow children in a school system were equalled by the number of years gained by those making rapid progress, the money expenditure would be just the same as though every child were regularly promoted every year."

According to Ayres the results of the study showed that while there were a few cities where the years lost by slow pupils were "nearly counterbalanced by those gained by the rapid ones" most were out of balance and in some cities the number of years lost was "from twenty to thirty times as great as the number gained." This indicated, he said, that most school programs were adjusted to the bright child rather than the average pupil. A well-adjusted school system would be one in which the number of double promotions balanced the number of failures so that from a financial standpoint the books would be in balance. Ayres cited Danville, Illinois, as a school system that was poorly adjusted in this respect and he pointed out that this cost the citizens $20,660. For all the cities he found that the "maladjustment" involved "an increase in school expense amounting to about 11 per cent" and the "annual money cost to the taxpayers" was about $45,543.

Undoubtedly the quick and easy manner by which such an efficiency test could be applied, plus the substantial saving which it was possible to achieve made Ayres's system seem attractive enough to superintendents and school board members. As if these factors were not sufficient, the editor of the *American School Board Journal* threw his weight behind the plans by endorsing the reports and suggesting that they would be "well worth the study of every school board member."[38] In addition to this he had requested superintendents to distribute copies

[37] Vol. XLIV, p. 13.
[38] Vol. XLIV (February, 1912), p. 30.

of the article to their board members. In response to this request, a superintendent indicated the inadequacy of Ayres's work and also what harm an irresponsible "expert" could do to a schoolman, especially when he was already under a heavy fire of criticism of the same irresponsible sort.

EDITOR SCHOOL BOARD JOURNAL:

You have requested me to distribute to our board of education a few sample copies of your excellent Journal in the thought that this particular issue will be of special interest to the members, since it contains Dr. Leonard Ayres' discussion of Age-Progress. *Let me say to you that just now in our city the discussion referred to is incendiary stuff. It feeds most inopportunely the fire of unfair criticism.* Consider the table of comparison of the twenty-nine cities.

No one has any moral right to spread before the country figures that in each individual case need explanation. Without such explanation the figures are worthless. We note the fact that a majority of our own schools would stand well in this "Age-Progress" list; but when one or two schools include large numbers of children born in foreign parts, or in the southern states, or have been handicapped in other ways, and are seven or eight years over age, the situation is very different. *Scores of our citizens are now saying: "What! our city so low as that in a list of twenty-nine! What sort of schools have we?"* The remark in the last paragraph of the report, namely, that this list does not determine which schools are the best, is seldom noted by those who do most of the talking. Such publication is especially obnoxious in a community that is already for various other reasons getting its full share of criticism.

Furthermore let me say: The figures in the tables referred to were not worked out on a common basis and are therefore unreliable for any purpose. I have inquired of at least eight of the cities included in the list and do not care to spend my time in further investigation. One-half of these cities have so reported the ages as to make approximately five-sixths of all their pupils one year younger or one year less in school than they would be if the method used in the other four cities, and also in our own city, had been followed! The work was not properly supervised. *Why was not investigation made before rushing into print? And all this is supposed to be the work of an expert!*

An "age-progress" study may be made serviceable for one thing. It may show to each separate system and to each separate school how best to fit the work to the needs of the pupils. Any comparative list of school systems is useless for this purpose. As I have said above, without ample explanation such a list is inherently vicious.

Permit me to say in closing that this letter is in no sense a reflection upon your valuable Journal, which I shall take pleasure in recommending to our board of education.

SUPERINTENDENT.[39]

[39] Vol. XLIV (March, 1912), p. 51. (Italics mine.)

Unfortunately for American education this criticism did not deter Ayres. In May, 1913, another of his articles, this one on "The Effect of Promotion Rates on School Efficiency" was also published in the *American School Board Journal.*[40] In this article he was able to report that the number of students promoted had increased from 84 out of 100 in 1908 to 88 out of 100 in 1913 in the elementary schools of sixteen large cities. And he added that there was "abundant evidence that a similar general increase in promotion rates is taking place throughout the country." His purpose was to encourage this progress, and he did it as he had done earlier, by using business or industrial analogies and by evaluating the results in terms of dollars and cents. Then he illustrated what he meant by actually translating the results of increasing promotion rates into financial terms with the following statement — a statement, by the way, which was reprinted and endorsed by Bobbitt in an editorial in the *Elementary School Journal* in September.

The importance of small changes in promotion rates may be best illustrated by figuring the results of a change of one per cent, for example from 80 per cent to 81 per cent, in the promotion rate in the elementary schools of a small city. Let us suppose that 1,000 children enter the elementary schools each year, the annual per capita cost for schooling is $40, and the buildings, ground, and equipment have a value of $200 per child.

Under these conditions, the change in the promotion rate from 80 per cent to 81 per cent will have the following results: The time saved by each 1,000 children if they complete the elementary course will amount to 130 years of schooling which means a saving of $5,200 annually. The plant required to accommodate the children will be decreased by about $25,600 worth, and the salaries of four teachers will be saved. The number of failures among the 1,000 children during eight years of school life will be reduced by 70, while the number of children failing during that period will be lessened by 19. The number of overage children in the grades will be reduced by 220. These figures strikingly illustrate the importance of even the smallest changes in promotion rates.

With this economic motivation to promote students, plus the practice of rating the efficiency of teachers on the basis of promotions, it is clear that two potent forces were at work which contributed to the practice of passing students regardless of educational considerations.

In February, 1912, Superintendent Elson of Cleveland in a speech before the Department of Superintendence indicated that Ayres's ideas had been accepted and that his system was being applied in Cleveland. He stated that between one-tenth and one-eighth of all the money spent on public education was spent on repeaters, and he added that "when

[40] Vol. XLIV, pp. 9–11.

the school is tested for efficiency by its ability to carry children through its course on time it shows great waste." This condition was being corrected in Cleveland through the use of double promotions. With this arrangement, he said, "A school system thus becomes its own clearing-house, is made to check itself, and certain bad effects of repetition and retardation are neutralized. In this way the money cost of the 'repeater' is offset by the acceleration of the stronger pupils." The result was that "the school system practically checked its own losses and created a balance sheet, the number of children who lost time being equalled by the number who gained time." [41]

In the years that followed superintendents were engaged in applying the procedures worked out by Ayres and Elson. One superintendent from Johnstown, Pa. reported that in his school system more than nine hundred pupils had had double promotions in 1916–17 and that, as a result, $16,092 has been saved.[42] Another, H. O. Dietrich of Kane, Pennsylvania, reported his activity in detail in an article called "The Schools' Responsibility towards Child Accounting," published in the *American School Board Journal* in October, 1917.[43] Dietrich began by informing his readers that "any corporation that does not at times make a survey of its business, the efficiency of its men, the methods of administration, etc., will soon be running at a loss, and this is just as true of our school systems as of corporations." Then he reported on the balance sheet in Kane, which he presented in terms of years instead of dollars, as follows:

Total normal years of schooling	4982
Years lost by slow pupils	604
	5586
Years gained by rapid pupils	239
Years actually required by all pupils	5347
	4982
Excess over normal years	365

So we see that these children have spent 365 years more time in school than they should have. For every year gained there were three years lost. . . .

In his summary he made the connection between "school years lost" and expenditures by reminding his readers that "every school system where the school years lost amount to more than those gained pays an educational tax, the size of which is determined by the excess of years lost over years gained and the annual per capita cost of education."

[41] N.E.A. *Proceedings* (1912), pp. 339–42.
[42] *American School Board Journal*, LV (July, 1917), 77.
[43] Vol. LV, pp. 29, 30, 81.

Binding Education in Red Tape

In the effort to demonstrate efficiency through the adoption of business methods, by far the greatest amount of energy was spent on keeping track of the mechanical-financial aspects of education — such as ordering supplies, making out time sheets and payrolls, and caring for the maintenance of buildings and equipment. The first step in this process was to produce the accounting forms which would be necessary.

The standard work on this problem (which was generally referred to by administrators or cited by them as having made possible "scientific school accounting") was a doctoral thesis written by J. Howard Hutchinson at Teachers College, Columbia University under the direction of George D. Strayer. Hutchinson drew his inspiration for the study from the memorable 1913 meeting of the Department of Superintendence at which Spaulding had delivered his influential address on scientific management. From the discussions at this meeting he realized "that the magic word efficiency that is causing such a revolution in industry is beginning to work in education." But efficiency in industry was based upon "complete knowledge," and he stated that it was shown by the discussion at the meeting "that administrative officers have not yet demanded and obtained knowledge sufficient to enable their school systems to work at anything like high efficiency. . . ." [44] Before complete data could be provided, an accounting system complete with forms and requisition sheets had to be developed. His mission was to create such a system and urge its adoption by administrators.

In discussing the function and importance of school accounting, Hutchinson provided evidence that it fitted into the pattern of the other steps taken by administrators. It would serve as a defense against criticism. He indicated this when, after citing an example of inadequate accounting being carried out in one school system, he said, "Suppose an inquisitive citizen, jealous of his wealth, should ask, 'How much was that per pupil?' 'How does that compare with the cost per pupil a year before?' No information could be given him. Indeed no information at all is given of the amount of service purchased for the expenditures and of the cost per unit of that service." [45] He pointed out that Spaulding had shown that this situation would have been unthinkable in industry. He told administrators that producing shoes without regard to cost was "the first step in bankruptcy proceeding," and he warned them that in the future the "administration of education without regard to cost will be sufficient evidence of inefficiency of administrative officers." [46]

[44] *School Costs and School Accounting* (New York, 1914), p. 4.
[45] *Ibid.*, p. 8.
[46] *Ibid.*, pp. 5–6.

During his investigation Hutchinson visited and studied the accounting procedures in 38 cities. He found that in 18 of these cities the data were either inadequate or unavailable, and so he used the material from only 20 cities. After examining the financial statements of the school boards and of the superintendents in these cities, he found them to be so full of defects that they were worthless for his purpose. Administrators were not devoting enough time to the financial side of education. He was particularly irritated by one superintendent who told him that he (the superintendent) was employed to see that children were educated, not to look after the money; that was the treasurer's job.[47]

Since the accounting procedures and mechanisms were found to be inadequate Hutchinson devoted the last third of his study to an explanation of a system of accounting designed to remedy the situation. He acknowledged that he had borrowed ideas from some of the cities he had visited, from manufacturing concerns, and from manuals on accounting, and he claimed that he had recommended nothing that had not been used in principle in public or industrial accounting. He suggested that at the outset in some school systems the installation of his system might require an additional expenditure of $1800 for a clerk and assistant, but he assured his readers that this sum would be repaid many times through the saving that would be achieved.

In his system of accounting each step was, he said, designed to accomplish one or more of these three purposes:

1. To provide for each transaction an original document that will contain a complete history of the transaction from its beginning to its completion, including the giving of personal responsibility for each step taken, and will serve as the best evidence obtainable to protect the city in any action that might be taken as a result of the transaction.

2. To make it possible for those in authority to account for funds appropriated for school purposes.

3. To furnish the administrative officers such information as will enable them to decide whether every service is performed at the lowest cost compatible with maximum efficiency.[48]

Then he listed the forms that would be required: Requisition for supplies; work requisition; purchase order; purchase order voucher; payroll for elementary schools; principal's time sheet; and so on through 22 special forms for every possible expenditure.[49] The remainder of the study consisted of a description, together with some explanation,

[47] Ibid., pp. 56–57.
[48] Ibid., p. 98.
[49] Ibid., pp. 99–100.

of each of the forms. Hutchinson prefaced this material with a short statement on the time-saving benefits of using these forms and then described the procedure for ordering supplies:

> The teacher, using two sheets of carbon paper, enters on the three copies the number of the grade, the name of the school, the latest date on which she wishes the goods delivered, the description of the articles desired, the quantity she has on hand, the quantity she desires, and signs her name with date showing when she makes out the requisition. The three copies are forwarded to the principal. The principal examines the requisition, and using two sheets of carbon signs the copies to show that he approves the requisition, giving the date of his approval. He keeps the triplicate copy on file. The original and duplicate copies are sent to the secretary, who should examine the requisition to see whether the quantity on hand warrants the issue of the goods, whether the quantity on hand is what it should be according to the ledger sheet of the grade. *If, after examination, he believes the goods or any part of them should be delivered, the secretary enters in the column "Ordered Delivered" the quantity of each article that he will allow.* His signature with the date shows that he so orders the storekeeper. The use of a carbon sheet has entered the same information upon the duplicate copy. . . .
>
> The storekeeper takes from the storeroom the goods ordered, on the store's tag deducts the quantity to be issued, entering also the date, and delivers the goods to the room on or before the date given in the requisition. He has the teacher check the items to show they have been delivered. She also signs her name to the form and writes the date to show that the goods checked have been received on the date given. The one delivering the goods also puts his signature on the sheet and the date of delivery. At this time the principal being notified of the receipt of goods checks the delivery on his copy and enters the date. . . .
>
> The same form of requisition may be used by the principal in requesting goods for his office or for the school as a whole. The operations to be performed will be the same, except that the secretary will enter the cost on the proper school ledger sheet under "Administration," "Supplies."
>
> The requisition used by janitors is the same as that for teachers, except for the substitution of the word janitor for teacher, and the omission of the number of the grade. The procedure to be followed is the same as that for a principal's requisition; i.e., the charge is made against the proper school in the ledger under "Operation," "Janitorial Supplies," or other object.[50]

A similar form to be filled out by the janitor was recommended for all repair work or miscellaneous services to be performed in the schools. And the same procedure with slight variation was followed for the other forms he had listed. Of these, the section on time sheets seemed most interesting and it is reproduced in part below:

> With the payroll there will be submitted by the principal a copy of his *time sheet* for the *month* containing the following information:

[50] *Ibid.*, pp. 104–7. (Italics mine.)

1. The name of the month and the year for which the statement is rendered.
2. The signature of the principal making the statement.
3. The date on which the statement is made.
4. The name of the school for which the statement is made.
5. The amount of time spent each day in administration.
6. The amount of time spent each day in supervision.
7. The amount of time spent each day in supervision in each room.
8. The total amount of time spent in supervision of each room.
9. The amount of time spent in supervision of each grade.
10. The amount of the principal's salary to be charged to each grade. . . .

The secretary will charge in the ledger each grade for the amount paid for instruction, entering on the grade ledger sheet the date of the payroll, the description of the service if desired, the number of the voucher and the amount spent for personal service for instruction. The amount paid to janitors will be entered on the school ledger sheet in the same manner for personal service for operation. *Before posting the amount paid to the principal it will be necessary to analyze the principal's time sheet.* The costs of administration and supervision are determined on the basis of time spent in each. Likewise the cost of supervision for each grade is determined on the basis of the time spent in supervising each grade. That is,

Cost of administration = time spent in supervision ÷ total time × amount paid for supervision.

Cost of supervision = time spent in supervision ÷ total time × amount paid for supervision.

Cost of supervision in Room 8 = time spent in supervision in Room 8 ÷ total time spent in supervision × total cost of supervision.

The costs obtained are entered as indicated on the principal's time sheet. The cost of administration is then posted to the proper school ledger sheet where the entry is made for personal service for administration. The total for supervision is disregarded. The cost of supervision for each grade is posted to the proper grade ledger sheet where it is entered for personal service for supervision.

The same procedure is followed with the high school ledger, the charges being made, however, to the various subjects instead of rooms.[51]

Despite the fact that this system not only converted the simplest act (e.g. the ordering of a box of chalk) into a major, complicated operation but also indicated a strong distrust of teachers and principals by forcing them to record every action and *giving a clerk the right to decide whether supplies should be granted,* Cubberley, in his widely used text on administration, described it as "A valuable study of costs and accounting, with ledger forms for use."[52]

In the next few years administrators indicated that they were mak-

[51] *Ibid.,* pp. 115–21. (Italics mine.)
[52] Ellwood P. Cubberley, *Public School Administration* (Boston, 1916), p. 422.

ing efforts to introduce accounting procedures into the schools. Thus, in November, 1917, the *American School Board Journal* described the system for ordering supplies, and reproduced samples of the forms, which had been developed by the superintendent of schools in West Point, Nebraska. The *Journal* reported that the system, which had been in use for several months, had "been found to cut down the orders of teachers" and had resulted in considerable economy.[53] The following month the *Journal* featured the business procedures adopted in the schools at Grand Rapids, Michigan.[54] The author of the article, a principal of one of the high schools, after reporting that the motto of the school board was "to get a dollar's worth of service for every dollar expended," went on to describe some of the achievements of the business manager:

Mr. Morrill feels, and he is right, that the standardization of supplies is the first great step toward efficiency in a supply department.

A considerable saving is also effected through the ruling that all supplies must be bought through the supply department. . . . No supplies may be delivered except upon a written order, signed by the supply clerk. This prevents the hoarding of supplies through failure of the principals to check carefully the supplies they have on hand before ordering. As all orders sent in are carefully filed, it is possible for the supply department to determine whether a given school is getting more of a certain article than it is entitled to. These records of the supply department enable the office to determine the amount of supplies ordered by any building, the amount used previously, and the amount used by other buildings. Annual per capita costs for supplies are figured from these records. The costs so figured very quickly show which buildings are economical in their use of supplies and which are extravagant. . . .

In common with other school systems, supplies are bought only on specifications. Orders for all supplies are subject to bids. The bids are tabulated and the stock selected which seems to fit best the needs. The Grand Rapids School Survey, in speaking of this, says: "The procedure throughout is to be commended as businesslike." Thoroughly *efficient, standardized,* and *business-like* seem to be terms which fit the supply department.

Significantly, the author of this enthusiastic endorsement of business-like procedures in education, Paul C. Stetson, like Spaulding, Ayres, and McAndrew, had a very successful career in terms of promotions and prestige. He moved from Grand Rapids to the superintendency at Muskegan, Michigan, in 1918, at Dayton, Ohio, in 1921, and at Indianapolis in 1930. In between he taught in the summer school at

[53] Vol. LV, p. 62.
[54] Paul C. Stetson, "Some Examples of Efficiency in School Business Management," LV (December, 1917), 17–18. (Italics mine.)

the University of Chicago, served on school surveys, and held important positions within the Department of Superintendence.

In view of the great efforts which were made to introduce business
practices and to demonstrate efficiency, the reader would be justified
in assuming that extraordinary progress had been made in this direction. Certainly this was true but some leaders in administration
were not satisfied and continued to urge educators to adopt these
procedures. One of these men was William Bruce, editor and publisher
of the *American School Board Journal*. In an editorial Bruce described, endorsed, and urged administrators to follow the advice of
a California schoolman to establish school efficiency bureaus.[55] In the
following passages it was evident that the work of Spaulding, Bobbitt,
Ayres, and Hutchinson had not been in vain:

A pertinent suggeston for aiding the schools to perform their function
during these troublesome times has been made by Mr. Wilford M. Talbert of
Oakland, Cal. He recommends that the several states create school efficiency
bureaus and that these be entrusted with the work of cost and child accounting
so that the administration of the schools may be placed on a fact basis. He
points out that public business suffers much because it is not guided by absolute facts as discovered by scientific management. . . .

The information which such a bureau would collect might be classified, in
general, as cost accounting to analyze the costs in the several units of school
government so that relations might be shown and inequalities corrected. The
costs would show the unit costs for buildings and equipment and indicate their
relation to the educational products. It would be possible to so measure costs
in terms of actual standards of results that both efficiency and waste would be
discovered.

A second branch of the cost accounting would be termed "child accounting"
and would seek to determine what proportion of the children in the state are
in school; what the effect of the size of classes has been; the relation of the
training and salary of teachers to the success of schools; what methods of
teaching give the best results; what types of schools are most efficient, etc.

All of Mr. Talbert's suggestions have been carried out in part by different
school systems in the larger cities and one or two of the states. There is, however, in no community and in no state a complete and well-organized efficiency
department which can carry out in full all of the recommendations just mentioned. The early introduction of such a bureau is to be heartily recommended.

Evidence that some of Talbert's recommendations were already
being followed was provided in the book review section of the same
issue of the *Journal*. The book being reviewed was a report of the
activity of the Dayton Bureau of Research, which had been estab-

[55] "A Present Demand," LV (August, 1917), 36.

lished in 1912 but reorganized on a broader scope in 1916. This bureau, said the reviewer,

acts as the representative of the citizens in following the governmental activities of the city, the schools and the country; it promotes effective and economical government by cooperating with public officials in the installation of established methods in public business; it provides continuous and effective publicity to keep the public informed and interested in local government. Among the topics treated are Where Your Tax Dollar Goes; War and Costs; Keeping Tab on the City's Money; City Budgeting; Financing Current Operations; Reasons for Increased Taxes; Are Public Schools Public Property; Why School Costs are Low.[56]

Obviously the bureau had a breadth of interest — all of it in finance.

So in spite of strenuous efforts from 1913 to 1917, there were indications of dissatisfaction with the progress being made toward businesslike efficiency. Even America's entry into the war did not lessen the pressure or divert the attention of some administrators away from an interest in business and efficiency. On the contrary, the position was taken that, because of the war, even more attention would have to be given to efficiency measures. This view was expressed by F. E. Shapleigh in an article which also provides additional evidence of dissatisfaction with the efficiency efforts that were being made, and which indicates that the business-industrial influence upon education continued to be very strong.[57] The following excerpts from Shapleigh's article will sound like a broken record to the readers, as they must have sounded to some administrators, but they indicate that the concern for the efficiency measures described in this chapter was still strong:

Our school systems have been notably slow in discovering and adopting principles of educational efficiency. Some important beginnings have been made but today in the average school system there is an appalling waste of money and of effort in the educational processes.

The school is a factory. The child is the raw material. The finished product is the child who graduates. We have not yet learned how to manufacture this product economically. No industrial corporation could succeed if managed according to the wasteful methods which prevail in the ordinary school system.

The real solution of the war-time financial problems of the schools is the widespread and thorough application of those principles of educational efficiency which have been worked out during the last decade. . . .

It has already been pointed out that about $220,000,000 are annually spent for textbooks, supplies, operation and maintenance, sites, new buildings and

[56] *Ibid.*, pp. 62–63.
[57] "Educational Research Versus War-time Efficiency," *American School Board Journal*, LV (July, 1917), 19–20.

equipment. Cost of the items included in this enumeration may be kept from increasing or may be definitely reduced under the application of the principles of efficiency. . . .

Other cities have found it economical and satisfactory to adopt uniform textbooks. That supplies may be standardized and purchased at reduced prices, has been proved many times by municipal purchasing departments. . . .

A study of the cost of courses and of pupil hours in the various subjects taught in the schools will point the way for a serious consideration of readjustments designed to reduce costs.

If English costs $8 per course in one school and $12 in another, or if Geometry costs 4¢ per pupil hour in one school and 12¢ per pupil hour in another it is likely that an examination of the conditions resulting in these wide ranges of costs will make it possible to cut the expense in the schools where instruction is most costly.

Studies of age and progress, which have been made in many cities within recent years, have shown that a large percentage of children are progressing through school more slowly than the normal child. It is not uncommon to find that at least half of the children of a given grade in a city have spent one or more half years to attain their grade than they would have, had they been promoted each half year. This additional time spent in schools means a greatly increased expenditure not only for salaries of teachers and for supervisors but also for textbooks, supplies and added seating accommodations, heating, lighting, and all the additional expenses connected with the operation and maintenance of the school system. The discovering and elimination of even a moderate percentage of these slow pupils would result in the saving of thousands of dollars per year in any city of considerable size. . . .

Superintendents and supervisors should realize that non-promotions due to any of the above factors are a definite and considerable financial burden to the school department and to the taxpayers.

This re-emphasis by Shapleigh of many of the major aspects of the businesslike practices which were adopted by administrators completes the account of their activity on the job up to 1918. In many respects it is a pathetic story to record, for as George Counts has said in reviewing these actions "Never in the history of education has so much paper been used to so little purpose."[58]

Although education is not a business and the schools are not factories, no reasonable man can deny the advisability of applying certain business practices where they are appropriate to the work of the schools. But they are a means to an end — the end being to provide the best possible education for our children. When efficiency and economy are sought as ends in themselves, as they were in education in the age of efficiency (and are in too many communities in 1962), the education of children is bound to suffer. The same thing is true

[58] George S. Counts, *Education and American Civilization* (New York, 1952), p. 30.

regarding certain business values. A concern about the wise expenditure of funds and the avoidance of waste is as desirable in education as it is in business. But a "wise" expenditure of funds depends on the outcomes which are expected or, in business terms, the quality of the product desired. Cutting costs and producing an inferior "product" is not efficient in business or education. True efficiency in either case is achieved by producing a product of the quality desired or developing a well-educated individual at minimum cost. It is clear that what administrators sought, after 1911, was not efficiency but *economy plus the appearance of efficiency.* They did this partly because the public was primarily interested in economy and partly because they were unable or unwilling to make the complex and difficult decisions on the kind and quality of education they believed young Americans needed, and then accomplish the equally difficult task of determining the means (including the cost) which would be required. A few administrators such as Ben Blewett of St. Louis saw that efficiency had to be related to the aims of education and some others, including Cubberley, pointed out occasionally that a cheap school might be a very inefficient school but that was as far as it went.

Undoubtedly the "efficiency" measures helped school administrators to defend themselves and to keep their jobs in a business-dominated, efficiency-conscious society, but the price the nation has paid has been high. Not only were our educational leaders devoting their time and energy to matters that are incidental to the real purpose of the schools, but our teachers were forced to spend countless hours on meaningless clerical work — hours that should have been devoted to teaching and learning. And, unfortunately, much of this clerical work has survived down to the present time. This is so partly because administrators who were trained as bookkeepers in their graduate work in the twenties and thirties are still in key positions in our schools. It is also due to the adoption by teachers of some aspects of the business-managerial role in their classrooms. Just as administrators adopted this posture to please a business society and especially school boards dominated by businessmen, so teachers learned how to behave to please business-oriented administrators.

8

A NEW PROFESSION TAKES FORM

The direct influence of business on school administrators and, through them, on the schools, sprang from twin factors that were like the two sides of a coin: the vulnerability of the schools and schoolmen; and the great strength of the business community and the business philosophy in an age of efficiency. These factors *were* largely responsible for the developments in the schools and for the changes in the professional behavior of superintendents on the job. But they are not entirely adequate to explain the developments which occurred in the professional work in administration in the universities. It is true that the courses were adapted to the problems the school administrator had to face, and it is certain that if they had not been so adapted, far fewer schoolmen would have taken them.

But it is here that the thesis of the vulnerability of schoolmen and the pressure of the local business communities as the prime causal factors of the great business influence on school administrators must be qualified. For the school administrators were subjected to strong influence pushing them in the same direction from inside their own profession, through their training programs. And the theory of vulnerability through job insecurity does not apply to those who formulated these training programs. The nature of the courses and programs that were established and of the work done by students (e.g. on doctoral dissertations) was determined to a considerable extent by men who were in the relatively secure shelter of the universities. Since these men were in a less vulnerable position and therefore had more freedom of action, and since they were the guardians of the knowledge and the symbols of expertness (credits and degrees), they were in a strategic position to influence the nature of the professional work in educational administration, and so, to influence the nature of the superintendency.

The Captains of Education

The men who were leaders in educational administration in the period from 1910 to 1918 have already been introduced. They include Spaulding, Bobbitt, Ayres, Elliott, Strayer, and Cubberley. Of the six, Strayer, Cubberley, Bobbitt, and Elliott were professors of education and taught courses in educational administration during this period — Strayer at Teachers College, Columbia University; Cubberley at Stanford; Bobbitt at Chicago; and Elliott at Wisconsin. Ayres, although he had a great influence on the nature of the work in administration, was not involved in teaching and directing research in this field in a university. Spaulding, who perhaps exerted the greatest influence on the nature of the administrative work in the schools and who, like Ayres, through his work contributed to the content of the courses in administration, did not join a university faculty on a full-time basis until 1920, when he became head of the Department of Education at Yale.

Taken together, these men represented a new type of school administrator, a type that differed markedly from men such as Harris or Maxwell.[1] To a man they were able, energetic, and practical, and to an amazing degree they represented in their interests and actions the dominant tendencies in American life in the first decades of the twentieth century. They not only manifested a great interest in and admiration for businessmen and industrialists, but they resembled these men in their behavior. They were active in introducing and using business and industrial procedures and terminology in education, and they centered their attention almost exclusively upon the financial, organizational, and mechanical problems. Because they were capable men, they would have achieved a measure of success in almost any kind of activity at any period in American history. Their attainment of positions of great leadership in education was due in part to the fact that the kind of ability and orientation they had was precisely the kind that was sought after in an efficiency-conscious, business society. The situation in American education after 1911 demanded leaders who were oriented toward the business side of education, not the social or philosophical side. Products of a business society, they had the qualities and the training (Strayer, Cubberley, and Elliott wrote their doctoral dissertations on financial problems) that enabled them to provide the kind of leadership that a business society required. And they in turn as leaders played a leading role in shaping the new

[1] A recent study of the older generation of superintendents indicates that they considered themselves scholars and gentlemen, never businessmen. Warren Button, "A History of Supervision in the Public Schools 1870–1950" (unpublished doctoral dissertation, Washington University, 1961), chap. iii.

"profession" of educational administration and, through it, the American schools. They did this through their speaking and writing and teaching, and they did it also by setting personal examples of the way to succeed in education.

All of these men were recognized leaders in administration and all of them were highly successful in their careers. But of the six Strayer and Cubberley had the greatest influence upon the development of educational administration. This was so because they wrote more than the others, because they taught more students and directed more research in administration, and because they stayed in the work longer. Bobbitt taught courses and directed research in administration, but after 1917 he became more interested in the problems of curriculum and did most of his writing on this subject, while Elliott went into administrative positions in universities — first as president of the University of Montana and then as president of Purdue. For these reasons and because the work of the other men has been described in some detail in previous chapters our attention here will be focused upon Strayer and Cubberley.

The two men were remarkably similar in many ways. They were about the same age, had received their Ph.D.'s in education at about the same time (1905) from the same institution (Teachers College, Columbia), and both had written their doctoral dissertations on problems in educational finance. In addition both men were extremely able and productive writers, both held key positions in important universities, and both were primarily concerned with the financial, quantitative, and organizational problems in education. Both men were ideally situated from the standpoint of age (about forty), training, position, and disposition to step in and provide the kind of leadership that was demanded in educational administration in an age of efficiency.

There were, however, differences in the way in which their influence was exerted. Strayer, although he wrote a great deal on educational administration, exerted his influence in a more direct way, through his teaching, his research direction, and the large number of school surveys which he directed. As the leading professor of educational administration at by far the largest graduate school in education, he taught thousands of students at both the master's and doctor's level and personally directed an amazingly large number of research studies. Cubberley, on the other hand, had many less students and directed relatively few research studies and, although he directed several surveys and taught large classes of students in the summer sessions at Teachers College, his greatest influence was exerted through his textbooks which, according to one educator, were "the standard texts in school administration throughout the United States." [2]

Of the two men more information is available about Cubberley's early life, and it is possible to connect his personal development with his educational activity. He was born in a small town in Indiana in 1868. His father operated a local pharmacy but, "although a pharmacist by profession, was primarily a business man and a successful one." Both parents "desired above most things to see him take over the thriving little business and become a prosperous small-town merchant. . . ." With this in mind his father "set methodically about training his son to follow in his footsteps. By the time the boy was seventeen years old, in addition to acting as prescription clerk, he was keeping the books, making the annual inventory, and doing all the buying for the store, supervised by his father only to the extent of being reminded dryly but emphatically whenever certain of his purchases proved to be unprofitable." [3] And as a part of this training young Cubberley was given space and permitted to set up a small business of his own selling newspapers, books, and rubber stamps.

The young man, despite the efforts of his father, was not to take over the family business. He had entered Purdue's preparatory department in 1885 with the intention of eventually studying pharmacy, but in the summer of 1886, he attended a lecture in a nearby town given by the famous educator David Starr Jordan, then president of Indiana University and later president of Stanford. Jordan had spoken on "The Value of a College Education" and had urged the young men in his audience to attend college if they wished to get ahead. Young Cubberley, deeply impressed, began the task of convincing his father that he should go to Indiana University instead of Purdue and a career in pharmacy. After two months he was successful, but only after he had "promised rigid economy." So he enrolled at Indiana as a freshman in 1886 and one of his biographers describes how he kept his promise and then discusses the subsequent effect on the young man in these words:

At the end of each college year, he submitted for his father's approval an itemized record of his expenditures, and a budget for the succeeding year. While it is impossible to estimate the exact effect of this training, one notes the curious and delightfully characteristic fact that the same boy forty-five years later, when asked how much his room and meals cost him in 1913 in Portland, in 1915 at Salt Lake, or in 1901, 1904, or 1930 at New York, can

[2] Marvin S. Darsie, "Education Becomes a Profession," John C. Almack (ed.), *Modern School Administration: Its Problems and Progress* (Boston, 1933), p. 337.

[3] Harold Benjamin, "Ellwood Patterson Cubberley — A Biographical Sketch," ibid., p. 355.

either tell offhand or will whip a well-worn little memorandum book from his desk, his eyes sparkling with youthful interest which the passing years cannot abate, and announce — not approximate — but exact figures.[4]

At the university he decided to major in physics and his program was planned by Jordan himself. After two years of work he interrupted his studies to teach in a rural school for one year. Returning to Indiana in 1889 he completed his undergraduate work in 1891. During his senior year he was selected by Jordan to assist him on his frequent lecture tours by operating the lantern slides which were used with the lectures. As a result the two men traveled together a great deal and became well acquainted — a most important development, as it turned out, for Jordan sponsored the young man through several jobs, and eventually brought him to Stanford.

His first teaching jobs were at a Baptist college at Ridgeville, Indiana, in the spring and summer of 1891 and then at Vincennes University from 1891 to 1896. At Vincennes, which, with its faculty of twelve and its limited facilities, was not (as Cubberley himself pointed out) a university, he was nominally professor of physical science but he taught classes in mathematics, history, French, and English as well. Jordan had recommended him for both of his first two positions but his appointment to the presidency of Vincennes in 1893 at the age of twenty-five came as a result of his ability and energy. In a three year period while doing a full-time job of teaching, he wiped out the financial deficit and reorganized the administration.

In 1896, Jordan, who by this time was at Stanford, recommended Cubberley for the position of superintendent of schools at San Diego, California. He accepted and stepped into the midst of a controversy. The board of education had selected him over a local candidate and opposition to his appointment (at $2,400 a year) was so strong that the legality of his position was challenged and his salary was held up for a time. He weathered the storm, however, and as his biographer said, "again his energy, intelligence, and capacity for constructive leadership brought order out of chaos. Again, when things were running smoothly, when matters were arranged, when labels were stuck on and the stock was classified, there was nothing left but routine." [5] One biographer thus explains his departure from the superintendency at San Diego after two years to accept a position as assistant professor of education at Stanford (again with Jordan's help) as a search for a new challenge and a chance to do scientific and scholarly work. Undoubtedly this was so, but he was also somewhat discouraged be-

[4] *Ibid.*, p. 359.
[5] *Ibid.*, p. 366.

cause the high school in San Diego had been closed because of lack of funds and it may be that he perceived clearly the vulnerability of his position as a superintendent. He had more than doubled his salary when he moved from Vincennes to San Diego ($1,000 to $2,400) and he took a $600 cut in pay in going to Stanford.

He began his career at Stanford in 1898 as acting head of the Department of Education and shortly thereafter was made permanent head. At this time he still had not had formal work in education, so in 1901 he enrolled at Teachers College, Columbia. He received his Master's degree in 1902 and during the course of the year assisted the dean, James E. Russell, in teaching courses in administration. In 1904 he returned to Teachers College for his doctorate and the work for this degree was finished the following year. His thesis on "School Funds and Their Apportionment" was handled with dispatch. He recorded that he began the research January 24, 1905, his wife began typing it March 17, and it was handed in to the faculty on April 14.[6] This done, he returned to Stanford, where he was promoted to full professor in 1906 and then in 1917 to the rank of dean when the Department of Education became the School of Education.

Beginning with the publication of his thesis in 1905, hardly a year passed throughout his career in which he did not write or revise a book, or conduct and write a report of a school survey. At the same time (from 1911 on) he was editor of the Riverside Text Series in Education published by Houghton Mifflin — a series in which 106 books, of which he edited 103, were published by 1941.[7] His major works were textbooks in educational administration and in the history of education (although he had little formal training in history) and they were perceived by him as a first step in building a body of professional knowledge. In both subjects the emphasis was upon the organizational, legal, and financial problems and the books, which contain frequent references to business and industry and frequent analogies between education and these fields, are filled with business and industrial terminology. This is understandable when his background and early training, as well as the times in which he lived, are considered. But a careful reading of these widely used texts also indicates that Cubberley was not businesslike in the sense of being interested in merely saving money in education. He stated repeatedly that really efficient schools would cost *more* money, but they would bring greater results. He admired businessmen and he understood business methods, and he used these methods and urged others to use

[6] Jesse B. Sears and Adin D. Henderson, *Cubberley of Stanford* (Stanford, Calif., 1957), p. 81.

[7] *Ibid.*, p. 194.

them in the schools because he believed they would be useful in improving American education.[8]

If Cubberley was concerned with the great human problems of the twentieth century, this concern is not manifested in his books. Perhaps he thought they had no place in textbooks in educational administration or history. Or it may be that he was so preoccupied with the legal, organizational, and financial aspects of education that he had little time for other kinds of problems. One thing is certain. He spent a great deal of time studying the stock and bond markets and he was a successful investor. Stanford University, at least, can be grateful that he was for he left that institution gifts totaling more than three-quarters of a million dollars. As his biographer stated after describing Cubberley's investment procedures, "In light of all these facts about his investment portfolios and the results he produced, about his point of view and methods of operating, one would have to say that Cubberley was a very able business man." [9]

The other great leader in educational administration, George D. Strayer, was born in Wayne, Pennsylvania, in 1876. He received his B.A. from Johns Hopkins in 1903 and enrolled at Teachers College, Columbia University in the same year. At Teachers College he did his dissertation on "City School Expenditures" and received his degree in 1905. He joined the faculty at Teachers College immediately as a professor of elementary education and a few years later was teaching courses in school administration. Through the years he probably taught more courses in administration, directed more school surveys, and directed more dissertations than any other man.

From the beginning his concern was with the practical immediate problems in the field of school administration, and his thesis topic and the content of his courses reflected this concern. Moreover, in the selection of his thesis problem and in the conclusions he drew from his findings he gave an indication of his forthcoming leadership by anticipating some of the issues which were to plague administrators for many years to come. For example, after finding great variation in the expenditures for various items of school expense among city schools and finding inadequate accounting procedures being used, he made the following suggestion, which the reader will recognize as being similar to those voiced by Spaulding, Bobbitt, and many others in the next decade:

If the greatest economy is to be had, it is essential that the accounting should show just how much money is spent for each item, and, within a system itself,

[8] *Ibid.*, p. 144.
[9] Sears and Henderson, *Cubberley of Stanford*, p. 263.

how various schools compare. It should be possible for the administrative officer to tell just what the cost per pupil is for each school within the system, and to compare the relative cost with the relative efficiency as found by testing the pupils of each school. No great corporation would to-day continue to spend money for purposes for which no results could be shown, and no school system should so report its expenditures that it is impossible to tell how much the educational policies cost which it advocates and carries out.[10]

During the next two decades Strayer contributed substantially to the movement to introduce modern business methods into education through his teaching, through his participation in professional activities (such as his work on the Committee on Uniform Records and Reports of the N.E.A.), and through his writing. He wrote a book on quantitative studies in educational administration with Thorndike, numerous survey reports, and textbooks on the teaching process and on elementary school arithmetic. He also produced, often in collaboration with Nickolaus Engelhardt, a series of materials to assist schoolmen with their business and building problems such as score cards and check lists for school buildings, standards for elementary and high school buildings, record books for high school and elementary school principals, records for school bonded indebtedness, monthly reports for principals to keep track of the attendance of teachers, inventory record books for high schools, and payroll forms. Later he and Engelhardt edited a series on school administration for the Bureau of Publications, Teachers College. Six volumes were published in this series between 1926 and 1934 and their titles indicate the editors' emphasis in educational administration. In 1926 two volumes were published, one on *State Support for Public Schools*, the other on *School Equipment Costs*; in 1927, a volume on *Accounting Procedures for School Systems*; in 1928, one on *School Building Management*; in 1929, one on *The Future of Interscholastic Athletics* and in 1934, one on *Practical School Economies*.

Important as his writing and editing were, they do not constitute his most significant contribution to educational administration. His important contribution was in the conception he developed and applied of the kind of professional preparation a school administrator should have. And since he was the leader in the institution which trained by far the greatest number of persons in the field — persons who not only went into important superintendencies all over the country but also went into teachers colleges and universities and taught courses in administration — his ideas, as they were translated into courses, pro-

[10] George D. Strayer, *City School Expenditures* (New York, 1905), p. 102.
[11] George D. Strayer and N. L. Engelhardt, *Problems in Educational Administration* (New York, 1925), p. ix.

grams, and research, had a tremendous influence on the development of the school administrator in American education.

Strayer believed that it was "just as certainly possible to provide definite professional training for the superintendent of schools as it is for the doctor, lawyer, or engineer" and since these men were trained by working at actual problems e.g. the internship in medicine and trial cases in law, the school administrator should be trained in the same way.[11] Therefore provision was made in the graduate programs in administration at Teachers College to give students the opportunity to study actual problems they and others were facing in their jobs. Strayer explained and defended his notion of the kind of research that would be appropriate in such a program in these words:

> The emphasis in these researches is upon the problems of the superintendents of schools. There is a sharp distinction between the type of investigation which is entirely justified in the field of pure science and that which should characterize the advanced work of the professional school. Certainly research is not less worthy because it is devoted to the solution of problems which confront the professional worker. It is most worthwhile to inquire concerning the techniques to be employed in the development of a school building program, the way to secure more adequate janitorial service, the most efficient organization of a department of census and attendance, the most equitable method of distributing state support, the necessary budgetary provision to be made for the equipment of new buildings, or the most efficient method of acquainting the people with the work of the school system. *Indeed, it may be proposed that there is no detail of the work of the administrator that may not properly become the subject of intensive investigation by those who are candidates for the doctor's degree in the professional school.*[12]

That this last remark was not an idle statement can be seen from an examination of the doctoral dissertations written at Teachers College in school administration from 1914 through 1930. The following examples of studies which were sponsored by either Strayer or Engelhardt or both between 1924 and 1930 demonstrate that "no detail" of the administrator's work was considered inappropriate for doctoral research: *Analysis of Janitor Service in Elementary Schools; Administrative Problems of the High School Cafeteria; The Technique of Estimating School Equipment Costs; Economy in Public School Fire Insurance; Public School Plumbing Equipment; Principles of School Supply Management.* Strayer gave verbal recognition, at least, to the idea that it was "of the utmost importance that the technical work of the specialized courses be paralleled with other training in the theory and practice of education." But during many of the years when he

[12] *Ibid.*, p. viii. (Italics mine.)

was the dominant figure at Teachers College, especially from 1918 through 1927, the program was heavily weighted toward the technical, the financial, and the mechanical problems of education.

The Study of Educational Administration in the Universities

The development of specialized training in education was a natural outgrowth of the increasing specialization of American life. With specialization came the need for specialized training and this was being provided by the increasing numbers of technical and professional schools then being established. Engineering schools and medical schools and even schools of business administration, such as the Graduate School of Business Administration at Harvard and the Amos Tuck School of Administration and Finance at Dartmouth, had been established. Graduate work in education had been offered in a few institutions before 1900, and the number had increased by 1910. During this time, courses in administration were offered and it was possible to concentrate to some extent in administration — partly through course work but more through the dissertation — for either the master's or the doctor's degree.

Courses in the organization and management of the public schools had been given on the undergraduate level before 1900 in departments of education, and as early as 1898 a seminar in school administration was conducted by Nicholas Murray Butler at Teachers College, Columbia. Although in the next ten years only a few more courses were introduced, Cubberley described this period as an important and formative one in the history of educational administration. It was a time in which the courses offered were "largely a summary of the concrete practical experience of some former successful school superintendent, now turned teacher in some newly established chair or department of education." [13] But it was also during these years that the nature of these courses began to be changed. Cubberley dates the beginning of this change — the change from the "successful-practitioner type of generalized courses toward a more scientifically organized type of instruction," and also toward a "specialization" in instruction — at about 1904. He considered that two aspects of this new specialization, that of the separation of state and county school administration from city school administration, and that of the application of statistical procedure to the study of educational problems were "perhaps the most important of the new developments of that period." [14]

[13] Ellwood P. Cubberley, "Public School Administration," in I. L. Kandel, *Twenty-Five Years of American Education* (New York, 1924), pp. 182–83.

[14] *Ibid.*, pp. 184–85.

The application of the statistical method to problems of school administration came as a result of some work of Thorndike's. He had been teaching statistics to his psychology classes at Teachers College in 1902–3, and in 1904 he published his *Introduction to the Theory of Mental and Social Measurements*. "This work" said Cubberley, "marked the beginning of a new era in the study of educational problems . . ." and the "first fruits of this method as applied to school administration, came in 1905 with the publication of two Teachers College doctor's dissertations, one by Elliott on *Some Fiscal Aspects of Public Education in American Cities*, and the other by Strayer on *City School Expenditures: The Variability and Interrelation of the Principal Items*."[15] These studies were followed by others, including Ayres' *Laggards in Our Schools* (1909), which Cubberley described as a "very important statistical study of retardation and elimination from school," and Bobbitt's *The Supervision of City Schools* (1913), which he said gave "an excellent discussion of standards and of efficiency methods in administration."[16] These studies and some others, plus the school survey reports which began to appear after 1911, provided instructional material for the new specialized courses.

But Cubberley's analysis was given in retrospect years later; in 1910 there was less certainty within the profession of the value of specialized courses in administration. If the leaders in the profession had been polled on the matter they probably would have agreed that school administrators needed to be better prepared for their jobs. This need had become apparent to thoughtful educators partly because of the inadequacies of many administrators, but also partly because of a growing awareness of the professional status and responsibility which to some extent paralleled the growth of such awareness in medicine and engineering. Evidence of the growth of professional consciousness is the rapid growth of professional programs in the colleges and universities, and the establishment of the National Society of College Teachers of Education in 1903. The members of this society had been engaged since 1905 in discussing such matters as the status and function of the departments of education and their connection with other divisions of the colleges and universities, as well as the nature and function of the various courses in the professional program such as principles of teaching, history of education, and observation and practice teaching. Because of dissatisfaction with the progress in administration and uncertainty of the nature of the professional preparation which should be established, but also as a part of its effort

[15] *Ibid.*, pp. 186–87.
[16] *Ibid.*, p. 187.

to examine systematically various elements of the professional work, the society devoted its 1910 meeting to the problem of university work in administration.

The meeting was held in Indianapolis early in March and the principal paper, on the subject "The Aims, Scope, and Methods of a University Course in Public School Administration," was prepared and read by Frank Spaulding, who at that time was superintendent of schools at Newton, Massachusetts. Although Spaulding was not on a university faculty and had neither given nor taken a course in educational administration, his invitation to speak was explained by his acquaintance with Paul Hanus, who was professor of education at Harvard in nearby Cambridge and president of the society in 1910. Hanus, in extending the invitation, had told Spaulding that the recent meetings of the society had been very dull and he expressed the hope that he would arouse the audience with his speech.[17]

Spaulding was not a man to disappoint a sponsor and he opened his speech by charging:

The administration of public education is grossly inefficient; it is the weakest phase of our great educational enterprise. In its present state, school administration is not the live product of clear, far-sighted vision, and keen insight; it is the sluggish resultant of tradition, habit, routine, prejudice, inertia, slightly modified by occasional and local outbursts of spasmodic, semi-intelligent, progressive activity. . . . In school administration there is little thinking and leading, but much feeling and following, with faces turned more often to the rear than to the front.[18]

And, said Spaulding, little else could be expected, for administrators had entered their work with "far less adequate preparation for it than has the young woman for teaching who has never heard of a normal or training school." This was true partly because only a few universities — "perhaps now a dozen in all — have begun to offer brief courses in school administration." It was also due to the fact that school boards and taxpayers had "scarcely thought of such a thing; much less do they insist upon it." As for school administrators themselves, they had with rarest exceptions given "no time or thought to preliminary training." What was urgently needed, he said, was not one course but "a hundred different courses on school administration. . . . Indeed, nothing short of complete graduate school with studies focusing about the art of efficient educational administration can finally suffice to mas-

[17] Frank E. Spaulding, *School Superintendent in Action in Five Cities.* (Rindge, N.H., 1955), p. 305.

[18] Frank E. Spaulding, *The Aims, Scope, and Methods of a University Course in Public School Administration* (Iowa City, 1910), p. 3.

ter the machinery of this administration and to put it under the intelligent control of the public through their expert administrators." [19]

Spaulding realized, however, that such a program could not be brought into existence quickly and so he concentrated his attention in his paper on a single university course. Since the purpose of the course was to meet the present needs of administrators he proposed that "It should be intensely practical, not at all academic; doing, not mere knowing, should form the goal and the atmosphere of all the work." [20] Later in his paper he presented an outline of the content of the course which turned out to be quite similar to the contents of a course already being given at Teachers College by S. T. Dutton and similar to the text on administration by Dutton and David Snedden, published in 1908. But he made one suggestion which he later regarded as his "constructive suggestion" [21] and that was that the instructor of the course seek a partnership with "the livest, or the least moribund, superintendent in his vicinity" so that students would have a chance to observe and study the actual problems of school administration. [22] Hanus endorsed this notion in a professional journal [23] and, according to Spaulding, acted on the suggestion promptly by sending his students into the Newton schools. [24]

Although the course proposed by Spaulding was not a radical departure from courses then being offered, his emphasis upon the practical side and his suggestion for on-the-job observation and experience may have influenced and certainly reinforced Strayer in his approach to the professional preparation of school administrators. Other features of the paper were significant because of the nature of his audience and because his ideas were presented at a time when many schools were planning courses in administration. First, his biting criticism of administration and administrators (which he himself said was perhaps excessive) implied that almost everything which had been done in the past must be changed. [25] Then, on the positive side, he listed certain principles upon which school administration should be based — principles which, because they were so widely adopted in the next decade, made Spaulding something of a prophet.

The first of these "fundamental principles" was the principle of popular control and Spaulding in discussing it gave his colleagues some sound advice:

[19] *Ibid.*, pp. 4–5.
[20] *Ibid.*, p. 11.
[21] Spaulding, *School Superintendent in Action*, p. 306.
[22] Spaulding, *A University Course in Administration*, p. 43.
[23] *School Review*, XVIII (June, 1910), 427.
[24] Spaulding, *School Superintendent in Action*, p. 306.
[25] *Ibid.*, p. 305.

This is the great lesson which every school administrator who would do constructive work must thoroughly learn before he can make any real progress; he must learn that the American school is a creation of the people; that the people control, and will continue to control, the administration of it. He will do well to resign himself to this situation; he will do still better to accept it with hearty approval.[26]

The second fundamental principle which he said "should become a habit with the school administrator" was the "simple, business principle of *efficiency*." The application of this principle involved adapting means to ends, producing definite results with the least expenditure of time and effort, and the elimination of waste. This principle, Spaulding asserted, was "rarely found operative in the school administration of the day." [27]

Here Spaulding began a discussion of the application of business principles. He stated that professional educators were apt to be shocked "at the mere suggestion of the application of business principles to education." Despite this, he said, "I make bold to express the conviction, born of experience and strengthening with experience, that the most crying need of educational work today is the application of simple and sound business principles. These principles should be rigorously applied in every schoolroom, in the teaching of every subject, as well as in every phase of school administration." [28]

Spaulding's paper had been printed in advance and distributed to the membership of the society and two educators had been asked to prepare criticisms of, or responses to, his statement. The first of these was a criticism prepared and read by William Burris, dean of the College for Teachers of the University of Cincinnati. Burris disagreed with Spaulding's evaluation of the state of educational administration and felt that his wholesale indictment of existing practice was unfortunate. But his main objections were to Spaulding's views on the education of administrators. Spaulding had indicated that in his proposed course each instructor should have developed his own "living and growing" philosophy formulated out of his own experience and not "borrowed or adapted from Hegel or Herbart, Harris or Hall." [29] This philosophy, which he called a working philosophy, could, he said, be "simply expressed" in a ten word statement which had been used to describe the work of a great, constructive captain of industry: "He projects an idea ahead, then works up to it." And Spaulding added,

[26] Spaulding, *A University Course in Administration*, p. 24.
[27] *Ibid.*, p. 26.
[28] *Ibid.*
[29] *Ibid.*, p. 13.

"this is just what the school administrator has to do and all he has to do, to project ideas ahead, then work up to them." [30]

Burris argued that the administrator of the highest type was "first of all, a philosopher" and he warned against thinking that a person could be in "conscious possession of a philosophy of education if he has never studied philosophy." [31] He feared that the student of school administration who followed Spaulding's advice would "start with an equipment which is too light." Far from agreeing with Spaulding on the need for more of a practical emphasis, Burris' view was that the problems of the educational administrator were due to his lack of academic training, especially in philosophy. "It is" he said, "just because school administrators have been too shy of philosophy, that fads, fancies, and fashions have at last turned our efforts in the direction of trying to do everything in the schools that anybody wishes done, almost obscuring the few things which ought to be sought first in every child, and to which all other things necessary shall be added. No wonder the machinery, of which the paper complains so bitterly, threatens to overpower with its mass and gathering momentum." [32]

Burris was also critical of Spaulding's view that the public controlled the school and always determined "what it shall be and do." He was critical of his advice to administrators not only to resign themselves to this condition but to accept it with hearty approval. Burris objected to this conception and asserted that his philosopher-administrator would not propose to meet the demands of the public. Instead, said Burris, he would say, "I know what the needs of society and of the individual are. I will administer my trust so as to help the community to a fuller appreciation of these needs as a measure of human wants." [33]

The other educator who had been asked to respond to Spaulding's address was Edward C. Elliott, professor of education at the University of Wisconsin. Elliott had received his Ph.D. from Teachers College at about the same time as Strayer and Cubberley and, like them, had written his doctoral dissertation on educational finance. He will also be remembered for his contributions to the measurement of efficiency in education, which were indicated in chapter iv. Elliott began his address by praising Spaulding for his "clear, sane, vigorous and comprehensive presentation" and by expressing his appreciation for the opportunity of hearing "the mature judgment of one actually engaged in the practice of educational engineering about which he

[30] *Ibid.*
[31] Spaulding, *A University Course in Administration*, p. 72.
[32] *Ibid.*, p. 67.
[33] *Ibid.*, p. 72.

writes." Many more of his "professional breed," said Elliott, were
needed. Spaulding recognized, "as we do," he continued, "that he
has touched a most vital spot in our educational economy; that before
our common public schools, as a national institution, are raised to
required levels of efficiency, there must be a regime of directors who
see far more clearly and deeply the real issues in American education. . . ." [34]

Elliott's major point was that individuals with "special technical
preparation" were needed and that it must be demonstrated to the
public that such men could provide service which was "both educationally necessary and economically advantageous." The rise of the
technical expert, he said, had already been occurring in other aspects
of American life as our society moved from the untechnical to the
technical, but this passage had been slower in education. This was
so because the schools were controlled by the public and the public had
not yet come to realize the "principle of the specialization of the executive or directive function. . . ." The result, he said, was that "everyone feels competent to execute and direct operations." Elliott was
afraid that if this situation continued the superintendent could not
justify his position. Therefore the profession had to bring about a
"conscious recognition" of the need for service that was "distinctly
expert and technical in its nature" and this had to be followed by a
"demonstration that this technical expert service produces an increased efficiency for the public school machine." The profession and
the public had to recognize that "technical skill is not a possession of
the multitude but of the few. Power and responsibility must therefore
be delegated to the skilled and selected few." [35]

Elliott stated that he was aware that the school administrator needed
a broad cultural background to go with his specialized training, but
that this educational background was not the kind which enabled an
individual to be identified as an expert — only the technical training
could achieve this end. Besides, he believed the ideal of a strong cultural background of the prospective school administrator was so widely
accepted by society that it would be insisted upon in educational leaders, and so it could be taken for granted. However, when he turned to
the question of what educational background the student should have
before taking the course in administration he had just outlined, he
indicated that for practical reasons some of the general education
background would have to be waived. On this point he disagreed with
Spaulding who, despite his emphasis upon the practical nature of
the course, had stated that training in history, literature, science, so-

[34] *Ibid.*, p. 73.
[35] *Ibid.*, pp. 78–79.

ciology, economics, and philosophy plus the regular professional work in psychology, pedagogy, and the history of education was necessary and that "without such knowledge, a student would be poorly prepared to pursue a course in school administration." [36] Elliott conceded that these prerequisites were "wholly reasonable" but claimed they were also "wholly impractical." "We may not await," he said, "the day of the post-graduate professional school; the draft of men by the educational system is far too demanding." Therefore he proposed that the course be given to undergraduates if necessary. The professional schools, he said, had to take their students as they found them and do the best they could with them. [37]

After the reading of the papers, there was a lively discussion between those who agreed with Spaulding and Elliott that the study of school administration should be centered on the concrete, localized problems of administration and the guiding principles derived therefrom, and those who believed with Burris that the study should be approached through the study of philosophy, sociology, economics, and psychology. [38] Three months later an account of the great debate was communicated to the profession by Paul Hanus (who had planned the program) in an editorial in the *School Review*. Hanus ventured the opinion that Spaulding's paper was likely to have a "permanent and favorable influence on the work of university departments of education in training supervisory officers. . . ." But he was disheartened by the criticism of Spaulding's paper and by the time consumed in prolonged debate. He was even more discouraged because many members of the group "were apparently looking for the principles of school administration elsewhere than in administration itself." This fact, he concluded, lent support to the cynic's view that "most of us are not yet ready to study school administration much less to give a university course in that subject." [39]

In the next fifteen years attention was given to administration as such — so much, in fact, that as early as 1915 Nicholas Murray Butler, a successful administrator himself, thought that there was "some measure of truth in the cynical suggestion that administration may best be defined as the doing extremely well of something that had better not be done at all. The tendency not only in universities but in all forms of public business to multiply and to complicate the details of routine administration is as strong as it is mischievous." [40]

[36] Spaulding, *A University Course in Administration*, p. 31.
[37] *Ibid.*, pp. 89–90.
[38] *School Review*, XVIII, 426–27.
[39] *Ibid.*
[40] Quoted in Edgar W. Knight, *Fifty Years of American Education* (New York, 1952), p. 23.

In the years which followed, the work in educational administration in the colleges and universities expanded rapidly both in the diversity of courses offered and the number of students enrolled. And the records show that the ideas of Spaulding and Elliott prevailed. This ideological success was partly due to the strength of their leadership and of the leadership of their fellow captains at Teachers College, Chicago, and Stanford. But it was also due to the efficiency mania, and the subsequent demands made upon schoolmen to demonstrate efficiency and economy. The courses which were developed in administration provided training in the kinds of activity (records and reports, cost accounting, child accounting, and general business management) with which superintendents on the job were preoccupied. This, of course, was what Spaulding (and Strayer) advocated: dealing with the practical problems. At the time Elliott made his recommendation for the development of technical experts, administrators were not under great pressure, and it is clear that his concern was not so much to provide a defense as to gain status for himself and his fellow administrators. However, after 1911, when administrators had come under strong attack, his technical expertness was useful for survival. That this expertness was an expertness in the business and financial and mechanical elements of education was due to the source and nature of the criticism, and to the ease with which expertness in such areas could be demonstrated. To have developed genuine competence in the educational process (e.g. in the teaching-learning process or in the evaluation of instruction) would have required lengthy, disciplined training. Even if such training had been available and had been taken by administrators, it probably would not have alleviated criticism because the competence had to be the kind of competence a business society could understand.

The Education of the School "Executive"

In the academic year of 1899/1900 Teachers College offered only two courses in administration. The next year administration was listed for the first time as a separate section, but the offerings again consisted of only one basic course and one seminar. The one other course offered under administration was actually a seminar in comparative education. There were practically no changes in this section until the 1907/8 academic year. At that time the description of the basic course was enlarged to include the subjects of business administration—the budget and its distribution—and the social and economic factors in the growth of school systems.[41]

[41] All the material on courses of study has been taken from the catalogues of the

Strayer offered his first course in administration in 1910/11, called Organization and Administration of School Systems, which he described as "a consideration of the problems of the organization, legal status, and administrative control of state and municipal school systems, including supplementary and special education. Practice will be given in the interpretation of school statistics, in the *organization of a system of school records*, and in the presentation of school information to the public through effective reports."

As late as 1911/12, the total offerings at Teachers College in administration consisted of two courses, a practicum, and a seminar. But from 1914 on, the growing response to the pressures discussed earlier in this book is clearly discernible. Teachers College began to give more attention to business methods, finance, and the adaptation of efficiency methods to schools in its standard courses in administration. For example, Strayer retained his earlier description of his course but added these sentences in 1914:

Among the problems considered will be the following: state support and control of education, including *distribution of school funds*, certification of teachers, adoption of text-books, and the like; *lay and professional control in education*; the organization and activities of the supervisory corps in the state and city; the classification and progress of children in the schools, including a consideration of compulsory education, *promotion, retardation, acceleration, elimination*, special schools and classes; *business administration, including a consideration of school cost and school accounting*.

Also in 1914, a composite course of eight different unit courses on individual administrative subjects was introduced. One of these units was "The Making of School Budgets," taught by Superintendent Spaulding.

By the fall of 1917 the administration offerings had been increased to eight courses, two practicums, and one seminar. Strayer's Organization and Administration of School Systems was still offered and his seminar was continued as it had been since 1911/12. But the general course which had been given with slight changes of title as *the* standard course in administration since 1899 had now been dropped, and the first practicum Strayer had taught in the fall of 1910, with the rather general title of Administration of Public Education in the United States had also been deposed in favor of several more specific courses. One of these, a practicum, was described as follows:

This section of the practicum in administration is designed primarily for *superintendents and principals of schools who wish to conduct in their own*

respective universities for the years mentioned. All italics in the descriptions of the courses, in these pages, are mine.

school inquiries looking toward increased educational efficiency. As a basis for the study of scientific methods in educational administration, each student will from time to time, be required to collect and present in class, for criticism as to content and method, *data from his own school system* with regard to the character of the school population; census and attendance; classification and progress of children; size of classes; failures by classes and by subjects; measurements of the achievements of children; efficiency of supervisors; provisions for physical welfare of pupils; organization and work of the school board; training and tenure of teachers, salary schedules; school buildings and equipment; costs; records; reports, and the like.

By the academic year 1924/25, twenty-nine courses were offered to administrators under three main divisions: Courses for College Administrators and Instructors in Education; Courses in Educational Administration for School Superintendents; and Courses for Teachers, Supervisors, and Administrators in Normal Schools and Teachers Colleges. School superintendents were required to take, among others, two large composite courses each carrying 6 points a session — two to three times the usual credit. The descriptions of these two courses used the terminology "professional executive," and "studies of actual school problems," and made use of "actual school surveys" in the courses of study. One frequently meets the term efficient or efficiency and words relating to the budget and to the organization of the administrative staff. There was also a course called Educational Publicity which was very explicit in its intent to train administrators to carry on effective publicity campaigns. Besides the usual seminar in educational administration, there were now separate courses in the organization and administration of the elementary schools, secondary schools, and the junior high school, and in 1925/26 a new one was added, the principles of administration of vocational education.

The University of Chicago, which was second in importance only to Teachers College in training administrators, followed the same trend through the years. In the 1912/13 catalogue only two courses were offered on administration; by 1915/16, eleven courses were listed in administrative subjects. In 1917/18, when the cumulative effect of the new demands had had time to be felt, fifteen courses were offered in this section. Bobbitt taught three of these: School Surveys; Educational Administration — Instructional Aspects; and Educational Administration — Supervisory and General Aspects. However, his influence was not limited to the effects of his own courses, for several other courses were made prerequisite to Bobbitt's two administration courses. The course titled Instructional Aspects required an introductory survey course, Bobbitt's curriculum course, and a course listed under the Educational Psychology section — Statistical Methods as

Applied in Educational Problems. The course titled Supervisory and General Aspects also carried these prerequisites and required in addition either Educational Measurement or Elementary-Schools Tests, both under Psychology. An analysis of the description of the separate courses which come under the administration section, or were required as prerequisites to courses in this section, shows the great emphasis placed upon business, financial, organizational, and mechanical problems and the duplication that existed in the various courses.

Harvard moved more slowly but eventually followed much the same pattern as the other two schools. For years it had a modest program in education under the direction of Paul Hanus, but finally even Harvard began to show the influence of the strong movement to follow industry. Its Graduate School of Education was established April 12, 1920, and by 1922 it offered a great variety of narrowly specialized administration courses including: Administration of Vocational Education; Management of an Elementary School; Administration of Secondary Education; Organization and Administration of Play and Recreation; Administration of Physical Education; Organization and Administration of Athletics and Extra-Curricular Activity; and Commercial Education — Its Organization and Administration. For some years the Graduate School in describing the work in city school administration used phrases similar to but somewhat shorter and less heroic than those Cubberley used in his 1916 text on administration.

By 1927, however, the catalogue was describing the superintendent of schools as the professional "general manager of the entire school system," and claiming that the job compared with the best in the older professions and in business and industry. It also stated that the money rewards compared favorably with those of "salaried executives" in other lines. It warned, however, that a graduate needed experience in minor jobs as a test of readiness for "general managership" of an entire school system, and said this might be acquired as a supervisor or director, but preferably in "the general management of a single plant." The reader has probably guessed that "a single plant" meant one school.

The trends taken in administrative training in Teachers College, Chicago, and Harvard were not isolated ones, but typical of the whole country, which, indeed, followed the leadership of these schools. By 1930 the professional work in administration had reached a kind of maturity and the pattern of work which was being taken by hundreds of students was firmly established. On the basis of an examination of the content of the courses that were offered, of the textbooks which were used, of the topics that professors of educational administration deemed important, and of the doctoral studies which were done, it is clear that the nature of this work was, as Jesse H. Newlon put it, "permeated with the philosophy of management, of business efficiency." [42] Newlon was certainly qualified through his experience to make such a judgment. Between 1905 and 1927 he had been a high school teacher and principal, a superintendent of schools (in Lincoln, Nebraska, from 1917 to 1920 and in Denver, Colorado, from 1920 to 1927) and a professor of education at Teachers College, Columbia. In addition he had in 1924/25 been president of the National Education Association. But his judgment was based upon more substantial evidence than his own observation, for in the early thirties he was engaged by the Commission on the Social Studies of the American Historical Association to make a study of educational administration. His study, *Educational Administration as Social Policy*, and a doctoral dissertation on the school superintendent, published at Teachers College in the same year, provide ample evidence that the graduate work in administration was heavily weighted toward the financial-mechanical aspects of education. [43]

In his research Newlon had a content analysis made of eighteen textbooks on educational administration. The results showed that "over four-fifths of eight thousand pages are devoted to the purely executive, organizational, and legal aspects of administration. Almost the entire emphasis is on the 'how' of administration. There is virtually no discussion of the 'why,' little critical examination of educational and social implications of the structure and procedures discussed." [44] Newlon also found, and thought it significant, that none of these books attempted to develop a philosophy of education or inquired "deeply into the larger purposes which administration is designed to serve." And he noted that as far as the contents and the bibliographies of these texts were concerned, one would almost conclude that the important disciplines of political science, sociology, and social psychology with their extensive literature were closed to the student of school administration. [45]

Seeking further evidence on the nature of educational administration, Newlon investigated the courses in school administration, the topics which professors of administration and superintendents regarded as most important in the training of administrators, and the nature of the problems chosen for research in the field. For evidence

[42] Jesse H. Newlon, *Educational Administration as Social Policy* (New York, 1934), p. 90.

[43] Frederick Haigh Bair, *The Social Understandings of the Superintendent of Schools* (New York, 1934), p. 92.

[44] Newlon, *Educational Administration*, p. 93.

[45] *Ibid.*, p. 97.

on the content of courses he drew upon a study by the Commission on Educational Leadership of the Department of Superintendence, the results of which were published in 1933. The commission summarized the contents of courses in educational administration in fifty-six schools and presented its findings in tabular form.[46] An examination of the table, said Newlon, "shows clearly the emphasis on the technical and the factual, the external. Most of the topics have to do with the mechanics of administration." Furthermore, judging from his study of the way problems which he considered fundamental were treated (public relations, for example, was confined to techniques of school publicity and did not consider the basic problems of public opinion), he thought it could "scarcely be questioned" that such important problems as the function and control of education, even when they were dealt with, received a "technical treatment more frequently than otherwise." [47]

For evidence of the topics which professors of administration and city school superintendents thought most important in the training of superintendents Newlon drew upon a doctoral study done at the University of California in 1931.[48] The judgments of the "experts" on this matter were presented by him in the table printed below and showed, he said, that "routine affairs, application, the development and utilization of the techniques bulk very large."

Topics	Pro-fessors	Superin-tendents	Total	Rank
School Finance	94	88	174	1
Business Administration	80	90	170	2
Organization and Administration of Supervision	82	82	164	3
Organization and Administration of the Curriculum	82	76	158	4
Administration of Teaching Personnel	82	74	156	5
Public Relations and Publicity	76	72	148	6
Organization of Schools and School System	82	60	142	7
School Housing	76	62	138	8
Administration of Pupil Personnel	74	46	120	9
Education and the State	70	42	112	10
Practical Applic. Surveys, Internships	68	36	104	11
School Officials Functions, Duties	66	36	102	12
Research	62	38	100	13
School Records and Reports	68	24	94	14.5
Professional Relations — Ethics	46	46	92	14.5
School Surveys	58	32	90	16
School Laws of State	54	24	78	17
Education and the Federal Government	52	12	64	18

[46] N.E.A. Department of Superintendence, *Eleventh Yearbook* (Washington, D.C., 1933), p. 294.

[47] Newlon, *Educational Administration*, p. 99.

[48] Asel B. Murphy, "Basic Training Program for City School Superintendents" (unpublished doctor's thesis, University of California, 1931).

Newlon pointed out the topics in the table related only to the strictly professional training, but he added that "these courses would occupy most of the time of the students." [49]

To complete his analysis of the education of the school administrator Newlon compiled a list of nearly all the doctoral studies which had been done in administration between 1910 and 1933. The collection included the titles of 290 theses (more than half of which were done at Teachers College) which he classified and presented in the table reproduced below: [50]

THESES PERTAINING TO SCHOOL ADMINISTRATION SUBMITTED FOR DOCTORAL
DEGREES IN AMERICAN UNIVERSITIES, 1910–1933

Fiscal Administration	55
Business Administration	34
Pupil Personnel	29
Personnel Management	29
Legal Provisions	24
Buildings and Equipment	19
Course of Study and Materials of Instruction	12
State Aspects	12
School District	10
Supervision	8
The Superintendent	7
Health and Physical Education	6
Administration and Organization of the Elementary Schools	5
Administration and Organization of the Secondary Schools	6
Administrative Organization	5
Board of Education	4
Origin and Development	4
Publicity and Public Relations	3
Miscellaneous	15
Educational Organization	3
	290

Newlon thought that the significance of this list was not so much in what it included as in the important problems which it omitted.[51] And this list, instructive as it is, does not tell the whole story, for while many of the studies undoubtedly made genuine contributions to education, others dealt with such relatively trivial matters as school plumbing, the school janitor, fire insurance and the cafeteria.

Newlon believed that the study of these financial-mechanical problems constituted an important part of the school administrator's knowledge, but he thought that much of it and especially the techniques could be "quickly learned in the field on the job, when and if needed, and should receive a minimum amount of attention in the schools of education." He complained that in a period of great social and economic crisis school administrators were preoccupied with what he

---

[49] Newlon, *Educational Administration*, pp. 99–100.

[50] *Ibid.*, p. 261. Newlon listed the titles of these theses in the Appendix of his study.

[51] *Ibid.*, p. 261. Bair in his study (cited above) confirmed Newlon's findings. Cf p. 92.

said one superintendent regarded as "busy work."[52] As for expert business management, it was, he said, very desirable in its place but it paled before the great issues educators faced. And he quoted Guy Stanton Ford, dean of the Graduate School of the University of Minnesota, who worried that the colleges of education were in danger of training "self satisfied and competent technicians" to undertake tasks that called for educational statesmen.[53]

Jesse Newlon has to be classified as one of the most able of American school administrators and a true educator. In many ways he was comparable to such outstanding administrators as William H. Maxwell of New York and Ella Flagg Young of Chicago, but he deserves more credit, perhaps, because his career paralleled the period of great business influence. It would have been understandable if he, like so many of his colleagues, had succumbed to the overwhelming business influence so strong in American society between 1910 and 1929. It is certain of course, that after joining the faculty at Teachers College, Columbia University, in 1927 he was greatly influenced by the small group of outstanding educators in the Foundations of Education division such as Counts, Kilpatrick, Childs, Rugg, and Kandel — a group who, among other things, along with John Dewey, published the *Social Frontier*, a journal which in its short life was the most outstanding and courageous journal American education has produced. The record shows, however, that even before 1927, at the very crest of the business wave in education, Newlon had seen the problem clearly. In 1925, while President of the N.E.A. and Superintendent at Denver, he had warned his colleagues that "the greatest danger that besets superintendents at the present time is that they will become merely business managers." Many superintendents, he said, were more "concerned about the purchase of pencils and paper, about the employment of janitors and clerks, about mere business routine, than they are about the educative process that goes on in the schoolroom. Such individuals would make good bookkeepers." Later in the speech he told his audience that administrators must be "students of the social sciences, of all that is included in the fields of history, sociology, economics, psychology, political science. . . ." The educational leader, he said, "must be a reader and a student." As far as he was concerned, he said, "I like to think of the teaching staff as a company of scholars engaged in the education of youth."[54] Those were rare words in administration circles in 1925.

Unfortunately for American education Jesse Newlon's point of view

[52] *Ibid.*, pp. 261–63.
[53] *Ibid.*, p. 257.
[54] N.E.A. *Proceedings* (1925), pp. 657–60.

did not prevail. This was clearly illustrated when another leading superintendent *following Newlon on the same platform* lauded the methods and results of Henry Ford and Andrew Carnegie and urged educators to follow their example:

The management of a manufacturing institution, such as United States Steel, knows exactly the service its trade requires and also the commodity which may most effectively render that service. With the least possible expenditure of time, energy, and money it builds its plant, devises its machinery, collects its raw materials, assembles its human agents, and produces its product. It develops its selling organizations and induces its customers to buy its output and to pay for it not what they like but what it costs plus profit.

Superintendence which is capable of telling them all "wherein" just as effectively performs all of these services in education. . . . If superintendence could produce this desired output of the schools with as much dispatch and with as little waste as the manufacturer's processes step by step eventuate in his finished product, how changed would be the world in which we live.[55]

The Insecurity Down Below

While the professors of education were busily engaged in developing courses in administration, superintendents in the schools were seeking ways and means of meeting the criticism being directed at them and of maintaining their positions. As I have shown, they did this by applying to education their individual interpretations of various business and industrial procedures, including scientific management. Despite their energetic efforts, the evidence indicates that late in 1915 and in 1916 they were still being plagued by public criticism and pressure which continued to be led by the press, and that they were in a very insecure position. As one writer described the situation in the fall of 1915: "This is a great period of educational unrest. The magazines are stirring their readers to an unsettled desire for new things in education. There is much discussion which leads to a feeling that everything is wrong with our present system, but there is a very vague idea as to what is to be desired. The superintendent is as usual the victim. Thousands of them are scrambling for new positions. . . ."[56] And evidence that this description was accurate was provided a few months later by William Estabrook Chancellor, professor of political science at the University of Wooster in Wooster, Ohio, and formerly a prominent superintendent of schools and author of books on administration. Chancellor, describing the length of service of city school superintendents, reported the existence of a "painful state of

[55] Charles S. Meek, "What Is Superintendence," *Ibid.*, p. 665.
[56] Alden Marsh, "What a Board of Education Owes Its Superintendent," *American School Board Journal*, LI (September, 1915), 65.

affairs." He found that in Connecticut 23 out of 31 city superintendents had held their jobs less than five years. For the nation as a whole 567 superintendents had held their jobs less than five years, 380 between six and nine years and 129 fifteen years or more.[57]

But the most revealing as well as the most interesting document which provided evidence of the insecurity of tenure of the superintendent was an anonymous article which was published in the *American School Board Journal* in May of 1916. The article was entitled "Why Superintendents Lose Their Jobs" and the author identified himself significantly as "A Veteran Fighter in the Field of American Education." He began by stating that the most interesting and valuable discussions at educational meetings went on outside the formal sessions and he added that the "batting average for originality, sincerity, and valuable discussion is probably higher in the lobby than on the platform." This had been so true, he said, at the last meeting of the Department of Superintendence of the N.E.A. held in Detroit in February, 1916, that "the association might profitably have provided a method of preserving for posterity the wisdom there disclosed." One of the perennial topics for discussion in these informal conferences, he said, was the question of the superintendent's tenure of office and he indicated what a crucial problem it was in these words:

It may be laid down as a fundamental proposition that nothing is of more importance to the average school superintendent than the vital consideration of preserving his relation to the pay roll. . . . The point I wish to make is that *nothing, absolutely nothing,* is of more vital consuming interest to the average superintendent of schools than the tremendously important question of whether he will be retained in his present position for the coming year.[58]

The Veteran Fighter then proceeded to give a lengthy testimonial to the insecurity of the superintendent of schools — a testimonial which, while it was written in a facetious way and presented an exaggerated picture of the situation, was too close to reality to have been very amusing to schoolmen. He said of the superintendent:

He knows from statistics, observation and experience that he is in the most hazardous occupation known to insurance actuaries. Deep sea diving and structural steel work have nothing on the business of school superintending. Lloyds will insure the English clerk against rain on his week end vacation, but no gambling house would be sufficiently reckless to bet on the chances of re-election for school superintendents three years or even two years ahead. . . . Year by year the committee on necrology drafts fitting resolutions for the

[57] "School Board Organization and Functions: The Progress of a Quarter Century," *American School Board Journal* (March, 1916), 12.
[58] Vol. LII, p. 18.

respectable few who have passed to the great beyond. This is doubtless on
the theory that any man who can last long enough in the business of school
superintendence so that death overtakes him is entitled to all the consideration
which the association can confer. In any event the labors of the committee
on necrology are almost nominal for it is only at rare intervals that a school
superintendent actually dies in office. No committee whatever is appointed
to inquire after those who remain in the world, but not in the profession. No
program is devoted to a discussion of the reasons for their absence. Every
yearly meeting finds missing scores of valuable men who are still interested
in the terrestrial scheme but no longer in school superintendence. Knowing
all this, I repeat that nothing could be of more interest to superintendents
than a discussion of how to retain their positions for another year.

Despite the importance of the question, he said it was "as usual"
not mentioned in the official program. This, he thought, was about what
could have been expected because "the program for the national
meeting of school superintendents is usually monopolized by men
who either have never been superintendents or who have long since
reformed and been paroled on good behavior." But whatever the
reason it remained true that the official program "lamentably failed
to consider the question." This was not true, however, of the "unoffi-
cial, extra constitutional discussions in hotel lobbies" and the result
was that "many illuminating truths were there disclosed." To prove
his point he gave the following account of a round table discussion
held by "four school superintendents of established reputations" — a
discussion to which he thought every member of the profession and
all school board members should have been invited:

Said one, "Are you going to remain in —— next year?"

"No, I'm not," replied the one addressed. "The floral tributes are now
being prepared."

"My case exactly," said the first, "in fact, I am expected to find a job while
I'm at this meeting. When I go back home I am supposed to resign. I haven't
anything yet. *Probably I shall be forced to discover the necessity of taking
advanced educational work at Columbia.*"

The third man volunteered the information that at the last election of his
board of education, the balance of power which had for the past several years
enabled him to retain an eyelid hold on his position, had been disturbed.
The odd man was now against him. The petitions for his retention were being
circulated but the obituaries were even then under way. He considered himself lucky that the board did not require *him* to prepare his official death
notice, all of their other official communications having been prepared by
him for several years.

The fourth man drew from an inside pocket a small morocco bound note
book. "Gentlemen," he said, "your conversation is full of information. I
have in this little book the reasons, compiled at some expense of trouble and

correspondence, for the enforced resignation of school superintendents in my state for the past ten years. While sympathizing with your several misfortunes, I have the strong interest of a professional collector in your experiences. With your permission I shall record the details of your official executions in my directory of the professionally defunct."

Nothing ever assailed me with such violent tenacity as my curiosity to see the contents of that morocco-bound book. The thought immediately entered my mind that here was an object of educational interest compared to which the *roof-garden exhibit of door knobs, burlap, and plumbing would be insignificant.* I knew this man possessed information of consuming interest to the thronging thousands in attendance at the convention.[59]

After some persuasion the superintendent who had been collecting data on the problem consented to divulge some of his findings to the group. Some of the reasons for dismissal were the following:

He smoked; he couldn't make a speech; he talked too much; he was unmarried; he was married to the wrong kind of a woman; he was too active for local option; he was not active enough; he was too old; he was too much of a 'mixer'; he was too much occupied with his own affairs; he was too much interested in church work; he was not enough interested etc., etc., ad nauseam.

And the educator-collector reported that these were not the only reasons. In his research he had come across two instances in which "superintendents were suspected of immoral relations with their teachers. In one case the janitor saw the superintendent and the teacher together in the office as late as five in the afternoon. True, the janitor was known to be aggrieved at the superintendent because the superintendent had required the janitor to keep the building clean. Also, everyone admitted that it was gross flattery to suspect the woman in question. But the breath of suspicion was sufficient." At the end of the discussion, Veteran Fighter reported, the four superintendents were "agreed that the data in the little morocco bound book should convince even a wayfaring man that the safest course for a superintendent is to do nothing and to be as colorless as possible."[60]

Evidence that this superintendent had presented a realistic description of the plight of the school administrator was provided a few months later by the editor of the *American School Board Journal.* In an editorial entitled "After the Storm" he reported happily that a "considerable number of the prominent educators who have had serious differences with their boards of education, and who resigned or failed of re-election, have found new positions, in many cases in larger and more important communities than before." But he added ruefully,

[59] Italics mine.
[60] *Ibid.*, p. 19.

It would be pleasant to record a similarly happy ending of the difficulties of all superintendents. Unfortunately, a considerable number has found no new situations. To some the close of the school year has been the final curtain of a professional tragedy. They have dropped out silently and for all time. For others the coming year will be a difficult one — a struggle in a minor teaching or supervisory position.[61]

Seeking Security through Professional "Expertness"

Undoubtedly the increasing complexity alone of American education would have brought an increase in the number of individuals enrolled in graduate courses in educational administration, but that increase was accelerated by the insecurity of school administrators. And just as schoolmen adopted the business and industrial procedures described in the preceding chapters largely to demonstrate efficiency and to maintain themselves thereby, so the attendance at graduate school and the acquisition of credits and degrees served the same purpose. This was so partly because the content of the courses taken helped to provide the technical knowledge they needed to assume the business posture, and to handle the financial and mechanical material used in demonstrating efficiency and economy. But university work also was useful in establishing the fact and reinforcing the claim that they were experts. Such expertness, they were told, was becoming a prerequisite for obtaining a position in educational administration and for subsequent success on the job. In 1914, for example, a colleague told them that one of their problems "the solution of which would add materially to the superintendent's success" was "how to be recognized as a man of affairs as the lawyer, the doctor and the businessman." [62]

Although the process of acquiring business competence and proving expertness through university study was not emphasized greatly as a means of professional salvation before 1910, some efforts had been made before that time to establish the superintendent as an expert. These attempts were made generally on educational grounds as a part of the movement toward getting lay board members to stop interfering in the operation of schools. That these efforts had not been completely successful was quite clear, and one prominent administrator, writing in 1909, stated that as early as 1890 educators had hoped that educational affairs would be "turned over to professional experts" but not much progress had been made and some states had "actually retrogressed."[63]

[61] Vol. LIII (August, 1916), p. 31.
[62] N.E.A. *Proceedings* (1914), p. 355.
[63] William E. Chancellor, "Where Are the Leaders," *Educational Review*, XXXVIII (November, 1909), 410.

When, after 1911, extensive criticism began to be directed at the schools, and administrators in particular were accused of not managing the schools efficiently and economically, and as more parallels were drawn between education and business, they both increased their efforts to receive recognition as experts and altered their justification of the need for expertness. What they did was to use the business-industrial analogy to strengthen their position and defend themselves by arguing that to operate the schools efficiently, they, the experts, needed to have authority comparable to that of a manager of a corporation. This viewpoint was presented to the profession and to school board members frequently between 1913 and 1918. For example, Arthur H. Chamberlain sent a questionnaire to fifty-one city superintendents asking them why power was being concentrated in the superintendent's office, to which some had replied that this step was necessary for efficient administration "in all forms of business" including education. He noted that school boards were being reduced in size which meant centralizing authority and, he added hopefully, it meant "placing the office of school superintendent on a level with that of the head of a great corporation or the manager of a strong business concern." [64]

In the years which followed, educators continued to urge school boards to apply the organizational arrangements to education which they claimed were being applied in business and industry. In 1914 the *School Review*, of whose editorial board Bobbitt was a member, devoted several editorials to the problem, contending that the school board should delegate authority to its "expert agents" because the educational problems were "too complicated for untrained hands" and because "conditions in school administration are similar to the management of a large business. A man at the head of a big commercial enterprise is given a free hand." [65] And W. S. Deffenbaugh, chief of the Division of School Administration of the U.S. Office of Education, made his contribution, reminding school board members of their backwardness and their inconsistency by stating:

Many well-meaning people have not yet learned that a superintendent should be the head of the city school system just as a bank president or a bank cashier is the head of a bank. A school board member, who was also a director of a bank, and who believed that the management of the bank should be in the hands of an expert and that this expert should name his own assistants voted against permitting the school superintendent to name his assistant.[66]

[64] Arthur H. Chamberlain, *The Growth of Responsibility and Enlargement of Power of the City School Superintendent* (May, 1913), p. 388.
[65] *School Review*, XXII (January and November, 1914), 52, 53, 639–40.
[66] *American School Board Journal*, L (January, 1915), 10.

In their effort to convince school board members particularly, but also the American people generally, that they should be accepted as experts, administrators were occasionally aided by board members themselves. One of these occasions was a meeting in 1915 of the Department of School Administration of the N.E.A. (a division officered by school board members and devoted to school board problems), where a former board member from Los Angeles gave a speech urging that the industrial procedure be applied to education. In his address, which was printed a few months later in the *American School Board Journal*, the speaker told his audience, "The ideal board of education will realize that the administration of the schools is a matter for experts, and will wisely confine itself to legislative and general supervisory functions." Then he continued with a statement which, while it was undoubtedly welcomed by insecure administrators, also contributed toward the conception of education as a business:

The school system must more and more approach the organization of a corporation, with the board of education as the board of directors and the superintendent as the general manager. No board of directors would dream of continually interferring with, over-ruling, and humiliating its general manager, and yet this is just what the average board of education is usually doing, either consciously or unconsciously. After a board of directors formulates its plans, and outlines in a general way its campaign, which is done in consultation with its experts and managers, the carrying out of its general policies is left to its general manager.

Until this was done, he warned, American education would "continue to carry the dead weight of inexpert boards," and the schools would not have the benefit of the highest point in the development of "the genius of American efficiency" which was reached in the organization of the corporation.[67]

School administrators undoubtedly were happy to see the blame for the inefficiency of the schools shifted from them to unbusinesslike organizational arrangements. And they were probably pleased to hear

[67] Reynold E. Blight, "Is the Board of Education an Incubus on Modern Education," *American School Board Journal*, LI (October, 1915), 16. It is impossible to determine the effectiveness of this campaign to get school boards to accept the corporation analogy and to accept the superintendent as an expert. It would seem that the arguments used would have made sense and would have had a strong appeal to school boards dominated by businessmen. There is evidence that the arrangement was put into effect in some school systems, and, where this action was taken (for example in Salt Lake City), the *American School Board Journal* both publicized and applauded the policy as being "a progressive rule" and one "that should be universally accepted" (Vol. LII [November 1916], p. 30). Another indication that the campaign had been successful was the claim, which was made increasingly from 1915 on, that administrators with technical training were in great demand. See the *American School Board Journal*, LI (August, 1915), 31; LII (January, 1916), 11–12; LIII (December, 1916), 20.

themselves referred to as experts, not only because of the prestige and personal satisfaction but also because they had been told that such recognition was a necessary condition for success. But this new development, welcome as it was, did not entirely solve the problem. Now that they were being touted as experts the question was, expert in what? And, equally important, how was this expertness to be acquired and demonstrated? If for some reason they had been unable to find the solution on their own they were provided with assistance by an eminent educator — David Snedden. The superintendent, he said, must "be an expert in interpreting valid public demands, and equally an expert in judging whether any particular procedure is meeting these demands. Not merely in the supply of education offered, but also in the economy of money and effort with which it is offered, should he be expert above all other persons in his community." [68] And where to acquire this kind of expertness? Where else but at the universities, after the manner of the unhappy superintendent in the lobby discussion who reported he probably would have to be forced to discover the need for taking advanced work in education at Columbia.

In the years between 1915 and 1918 the educational literature contained many suggestions that the road to salvation in administration was indeed through the universities. Sometimes these recommendations were phrased in general terms and sometimes they specifically urged graduate courses in school administration. An example of the former type was the suggestion W. S. Deffenbaugh:

At present 578 of the 1,350 cities reporting require their superintendents to be college graduates; many others, in the absence of any formal rule of the board, always employ college graduates. The educational qualifications of the superintendent as defined by State law are usually that he shall hold a first-grade or life certificate and have a few years' experience as a teacher. Experience has shown, however, that a superintendent must have other qualifications. In the past the ability to administer schools was acquired by experience alone; today there is a demand for men who have had special training in the several phases of school administration.[69]

The more direct approach was used by George M. Baker of the University of Kentucky. In discussing why superintendents in small cities and towns did not have more of a share in determining the school budget the author gave the following reason: "It is very generally conceded that superintendents are not good businessmen." But this condition need not continue, he said, if the administrator would prove

[68] *Educational Administration and Supervision*, I, 67.
[69] Quoted in *American School Board Journal*, LI (August, 1915), 31.

his "sound business judgment." Then he added a statement which left little uncertainty in the minds of superintendents about what they should do, and which also provides evidence of the nature of the courses then being offered in administration:

The fact that the coming superintendent is going to have specific training for his work, without which he cannot long compete with those who have had, is going to work in the direction of alleviating the conditions treated of in the above paragraphs. Such business weaknesses will not be characteristic of the forthcoming generation of superintendents. Their college courses in school administration will make the continuance of these conditions impossible.[70]

Of all the recommendations that were made to superintendents some of the most forceful were made by Superintendent Ernest W. Robinson of Webster, Massachusetts. He reviewed the criticisms which were being made of the schools — the great waste, the failure to use business methods, etc. — and he reminded administrators that these criticisms "contained in a large degree a spirit of counsel and warning" and that "alert educators realize today that the simple choice is presented to them of recognizing and directing these new forces into constructive channels, or of being overborne and submerged by them.'" Then he indicated what these new forces were:

The most serious criticism directed against school officials by the forceful part of the community is that which accuses them of the poorest business sense and management on the material side of education. . . . The quick of public interest in education is touched instantly when inquiry penetrates to the question of results and cost. Faults of mechanical organization of the various elements of *teachers, teaching, grading, curriculum* have for the average citizen but passing interest. The amount of money expended, no matter in what department, what it buys, and who conducts the business, these are the sensitive areas in the mind and feeling of every typical American community.[71]

School boards had failed, he said, to adopt the businesslike procedure of hiring an expert and granting him full authority. Robinson conceded that they could be forgiven somewhat because schoolmen were generally inept businessmen, but he indicated how this weakness was being overcome and provided a boost to the movement to attend universities to attain technical competence and to increase the chances of achieving security:

[70] "Financial Practices in Cities and Towns below Twenty-five Thousand," *American School Board Journal*, LIII (October, 1916), 20.

[71] "Some Defects of Public School Administration," *American School Board Journal*, LI (December, 1915), 16. (Italics mine.)

Such business weakness as may have been shown up to the present time, however, by superintendents, is in a fair way to be overcome by the steady improvement in the quality and qualifications of the new men who are constantly entering the field of school administration. According to a statistical study made recently by the educational department of the University of Iowa, 25 per cent of public school superintendencies are made vacant every year, of which an appreciably large part are filled by new men of special training in administrative work. Hitherto the training of the average superintendent who had "risen from the ranks" has been, according to Dr. Coffman, about ten years' service in the schoolroom as teacher and principal, with specific but limited executive duties. "Some of these men," he concludes, "have risen by sheer strength or superlative ability, but it must be admitted that it is the fashion of today to give the preference to the man of training." [72]

In his next article, Robinson dealt with the nature of the expertness which was needed. He introduced the topic by asking the question, "Are superintendents sufficiently expert?" then he quoted an unidentified educator who testified that administrators were confused about the nature of the expertness which was required. " 'Much nonsense is uttered as to the desirable qualifications of the superintendent of schools. At the same time it is not certain that superintendents themselves, have a clear notion as to the fields in which they should be expected to have expert knowledge or skill.' " [73] Robinson tried to resolve this confusion by quoting Snedden (whom he did not identify) to the effect that the superintendent must be an expert in meeting valid public demands and also in achieving economy of money and effort expended for educational purposes.

This urging and warning continued through 1916 and 1917. One superintendent from Pennsylvania blamed supervisors for the inefficiency of the schools and urged his fellow administrators to forsake their office chairs and get out and do something. "If," he said, "we are not in a position to do so, *if we have not studied efficiency methods as yet*, let us take the first opportunity, when the term closes, *go to some standard university*, and drink to the fill, so that we will be real live supervisors instead of figure heads." [74] In 1917 educators were reminded by a high school principal (unnecessarily it would seem) that since "the recent demand for efficiency has been extended to all forms of industrial and social enterprise, the schools are in for an overhauling." The schools had been found inadequate and their administrative inefficiency had "been brought to light." This same educator, how-

---

[72] *Ibid.*, LII (January, 1916), 11–12.
[73] *American School Board Journal*, LII (March, 1916), 23.
[74] H. O. Dietrich, "Efficiency of Supervision for Small School Systems," *American School Board Journal*, LII (June, 1916), 13–14. (Italics mine.)

ever, after rubbing salt in the old wounds, added a consoling note and at the same time provided evidence that administrators were attending the universities in increasing numbers. He stated, "the zeal with which we flock to the centers of learning and spend the heated term in pursuit of knowledge of which we have never before felt the need indicates that we are awake to the gravity of the situation."[75] And while administrators were responding to the gravity of the situation by flocking to centers of learning, pressure (or perhaps inducement) was being exerted from another direction as some school boards in large cities began requiring graduate professional training as a prerequisite for their higher administrative jobs.[76]

The figures on degrees conferred in various years are tangible proof of facts which have been deduced from statements of schoolmen — that they were feeling increasing pressure to become expert and that they flocked to the universities to become so. In the academic year 1909/10, before scientific management had swept the country, 73 graduate degrees in education were conferred by Teachers College, 65 carrying with them professional diplomas, of which 13 were in categories of administration and supervision. In the academic year of 1916/17, 316 masters' and doctors' degrees were conferred in education. Of this total 203 carried specific professional diplomas, and 95 of these diplomas were in the categories of administration and supervision. The number of graduate degrees granted in education by 1923/24 had grown to 939! Of these 483 carried specific professional displomas, and of the diplomas given 390 were in various categories of administration and supervision.

There was one other alternative path to job success suggested to superintendents in 1916, a proposal which would have been amusing if it had not contained pathetic implications for American education. The seemingly serious suggestion was that the superintendent double as a community welfare worker. The excerpts from the article quoted below not only provide evidence that the superintendent was being moved away from his educational responsibilities (the pressure forcing him to be preoccupied with the business problems had, of course, the same effect) but also provides evidence of the actions which the

[75] Franklin Johnson, "The Professional Reading of the High-School Principal," *School Review*, XXV (April, 1917), 233–34. Additional impetus was provided through the twenties. For example the editor of the *Journal of Education* (Boston) in 1920 in reporting that both Harvard and Yale were going to train educational leaders told his readers that "there is no doubt but that both Harvard and Yale will have almost limitless enrollment, for it requires from twenty to thirty years to become a leader by demonstration, and a man or woman can afford to pay any amount to become a leader in four years." Vol. XCI (March 4, 1920), p. 267.

[76] *American School Board Journal*, LIV (June. 1917). 64.

schools and schoolmen were taking to serve the business interests —
actions which were becoming widespread at this time and were to increase in the years that followed.

Now it happens that in my own town we are just welcoming a new superintendent of schools and it happens also that our woman's club, with insufficient
resources and with a minimum of encouragement, has been minded to employ
a welfare worker, whose task it shall be to unify and direct all the welfare
agencies of our community, look after our derelicts, provide wholesome amuse-
ment for our young people, keep us informed on all reform political movements,
and be able, on occasion, to specialize upon such themes as the purity of the
city water and disposal of garbage. Now my advice to our new superintendent
is that, as soon as he had acquired a working familiarity with his own special
tasks, he go out after the job of this welfare worker. . . . That in fact is what
many a modern school superintendent is, whether he knows it or not: in
addition to being head of the school plant, he is a community welfare worker.
. . . I know a school superintendent who beautified vacant lots about town
by renting them for school gardens; and who then sold the products of the
garden thru a local green grocer and kept the boys of the agricultural courses
in school by distributing the resulting cash dividend among them at the end
of the season: a sort of endless chain of community service.

The same man placed his domestic science classes at the service of the public. The mother who knew she was to be out for the afternoon, might telephone
the school and a couple of competent, young amateurs appeared in her kitchen,
prepared the evening meal for the family — and were paid for it. . . . When
the Chamber of Commerce wanted a banquet, they went to the teacher of
domestic science and she mobilized her forces and served it in such fashion as
to put to blush a professional caterer. . . .

The great and noble motive of public service may speak for itself but, by
way of anti-climax, may one suggest that self-interest should lead the school
superintendent in the direction of community welfare work — if only his self-
interest is far sighted enough — which self-interest so often isn't? The man in
the street knows pitifully little about the superintendent's work in the classroom but his work in the community is known and advertised by all men.
There is no surer way to popularity, a wide, deep, well-founded, substantial,
enduring popularity, than thru work for the community. And — basest motive
of all! — there is no surer way to an increase of salary.[77]

The New "Profession" — the School Executive

The combination of the development of specialized graduate work
in school administration, and the growing influence of business on education with the subsequent conception of education as a business, led
to the idea of school administration (and especially the superintend-

ency) as a "profession" distinct from teaching. This idea had been advanced even before 1910, but it was hardly a defensible claim as long as administrators had no specialized training. In the years after 1911 the idea of the separate profession developed as a natural corollary of the adoption of the business-industrial practices and, especially, of the adoption of the business organizational pattern to the schools. Since administrators were acquiring graduate credits and degrees, the claim was more defensible. In business, Cochran has pointed out, as corporations became larger "a new type of business-man rose to leadership: the professional executive." [78] As educators followed the lead of business the notion of the executive in education was most reasonable as was the idea of a separate "profession." After all, had not Louis Brandeis considered business a profession; and since they were being required to become more businesslike why should they not have the same standing as the business executive? [79]

The recognition by the community, by school board members, and by teachers of professional standing equal to medicine, law, engineering, and business was desirable for many reasons. On the negative side it would help add to the defensive strength of their embattled group. For just as writing their reports in a businesslike way enabled them to communicate with and possibly please the businessmen on their boards, so their recognition as professional executives seemed to afford the possibility of providing them with equal, or even superior, standing with the groups who held their jobs in their hands. On the positive side it added to their status, which not only meant a great deal of personal satisfaction but also meant increased social and professional recognition and possibly greater financial remuneration.

Although occasional references, either predicting that school administration would become a separate profession or urging that it be made such, were made before 1914, it was not until after that time that the idea appears extensively in the professional literature. In 1915 the matter was featured in the annual report of the U.S. Commissioner of Education, and in 1916 it was discussed frequently in the professional journals and — perhaps most important of all — given a prominent place by Cubberley in his influential textbook on public school administration. The commissioner of education, reviewing the recent progress in educational administration, had described the new development in these words:

When we seek to review recent educational progress, whether we are concerned with the enlarged scope and complexity of our educational system, with

[78] Thomas C. Cochran, *The American Business System* (Cambridge, 1957), p. 11.
[79] Louis D. Brandeis, *Business a Profession* (Boston, 1914).

the problem of adapting our schools to the varying capacities and needs of children, with the tendency to enlarge the administrative unit and to increase the responsibility of professional administratve officers, or with the development of a scientific method of attack upon administrative problems — all of these seem to point unmistakably in the direction of the development of a profession of educational administration as distinct from teaching.[80]

If administrators or board members had not read this statement in the commissioner's report, they had a chance to read it in *American School Board Journal* as Ernest W. Robinson featured it in the third of his lively and forthright series of articles.[81] And in the same year in the same journal William E. Chancellor, writing on the administrative progress of a quarter century, emphasized the distinction between teaching and administration by stating, "One cannot be both a thoroughly experienced teacher of youth and a skillful manager of the business of city school systems." And he added "the truth is that a new profession has arisen within the old one of teaching." [82]

While these statements were undoubtedly influential, they shrink into insignificance in comparison with the influence that was exerted by Cubberley. He made a major effort in this direction in the summer of 1915, when he spoke before one of the general sessions of the annual convention of the National Education Association:

The recent attempts to survey and measure school systems and to determine the efficiency of instruction along scientific lines have alike served to develop a scientific method for attacking administrative problems which promises to compel us soon to rewrite the whole history of our theory of school administration in terms of these new units and scales of measuring educational progress and determining educational efficiency. All of these developments point unmistakably in the direction of the evolution of a profession of school administration as distinct from the work of teaching on the one hand and politics on the other.[83]

Of far greater influence, however, was Cubberley's account of the new profession in his text *Public School Administration* (1916) and his almost verbatim reproduction of this material in his *Introduction to the Study of Education* (1925) both of which were widely used. In his administration text he began his chapter on "The Superintendent of Schools" with the subtitle "A New Profession." After a paragraph devoted to an historical sketch of the development of the superintendency, he indicated that he had taken the existence of such a

[80] *Report of the Commissioner of Education for the Year Ended June 30, 1914*, p. 35.

[81] "Some Defects of Public School Administration," LII (March, 1916), 23.

[82] "School Board Organization and Functions: The Progress of a Quarter Century," LII, 12–13.

[83] N.E.A. *Proceedings* (1915), p. 93.

profession for granted and went on to describe the great opportunities which it provided:

School supervision represents a new profession, and one which in time will play a very important part in the development of American life. In pecuniary, social, professional, and personal rewards it ranks with the other learned professions, while the call for city school superintendents of the right type is today greater than the call for lawyers, doctors, or ministers. The opportunities offered in this new profession to men of strong character, broad sympathies, high purposes, fine culture, courage, exact training, and executive skill, and who are willing to take the time and spend the energy necessary to prepare themselves for large service, are today not excelled in any of the professions, learned or otherwise.

And he did not leave the reward to the potential administrator's imagination. Instead he included a table which showed that some superintendents in very large cities were earning $10,000 a year.[84]

Then he turned to a consideration of the importance of the job and described it in such a way that his readers could hardly fail to have been stirred. The superintendent said Cubberley, was potentially at least "the most important officer in the employ of any municipality. . . ." And he added: "His is the central office in the school system, up to which and down from which authority, direction, and inspiration flow. He is the organizer and director of the work of the schools in all of their different phases, and the representative of the schools and all for which the schools stand before the people of the community. He is the executive officer of the school board, and also its eyes, and ears, and brains."[85]

So far as the superintendent's education and training were concerned, Cubberley recommended a "good college education" and he said "at least a year of graduate work is practically a necessity now." In addition, those men "of large grasp and ability" after a few years of experience "should go on and obtain their Ph. D. degree." Teachers, on the other hand, needed only a high school education and a two-year normal school program for elementary teaching and a college education for high school teaching. That teachers were at the bottom of a hierarchy is clear from the first words of his chapter on "The Teaching Corps" which reads as follows: "In addition to superintendents, special supervisors, and principals, the educational department also includes that large body of persons who give instruction in the different schools and are known collectively as the teaching corps."[86]

[84] Ellwood P. Cubberley, *Public School Administration* (Boston, 1916), pp. 130–31.

[85] *Ibid.*, p. 132.

[86] *Ibid.*, p. 198. While he devoted some attention to the qualities necessary for teachers, he gave the following lengthy account of the personal qualities necessary for the new

Besides featuring the notion of a separate profession and fostering the university study of administration, Cubberley also contributed to the conception of the superintendent as an executive. He did this by frequently referring to the superintendent as the chief executive of the school system and by emphasizing the need for "executive power" and "executive skill" on the part of school administrators. Increasingly after 1916 the term "executive" was used synonymously with "superintendent." By 1925 it was commonly used in administrative journals and books in this way.

By 1918 the idea of a separate profession of school administration was firmly established. To be sure, a decade later administrators were still engaged in the effort to convince themselves and the American people that they deserved a distinct professional status, but these efforts were made to reinforce and extend a domain, not to establish it in the first place.[87] They had already convinced themselves and doubtless many others that they were experts and they had an increasing number of professional schools, programs, courses, and graduates to prove it. And they could point to a body of knowledge contained in courses and textbooks upon which their claim to professional status was based. True, an unkind critic might have questioned whether the study of the mechanical and financial aspects of education while ignoring its substance constituted a basis for a legitimate claim to professional status. But such critics did not stop the forward movement — movement that could be seen not only through the pages of profes-

profession — qualities which, by the way, closely parallel the essential traits for success in business listed by Orison Marden in *Young Man Entering Business*: "The man who would be a superintendent of schools — the educational leader of a city — must be clean, both in person and mind; he must be temperate, both in speech and act; he must be honest and square, and able to look men straight in the eye; and he must be possessed of a high sense of personal honor. He needs a good time-sense to enable him to save time and to transact business with dispatch, and a good sense of proportion to enable him to see things in their proper place and relationship. He must have the manners and courtesy of a gentleman, without being flabby or weak. He must not be affected by a desire to stand in the community limelight, or to talk unnecessarily about his own accomplishments. He must avoid oracularism, the solemnity and dignity of an owl, and the not uncommon tendency to lay down the law. A good sense of humor will be found a means of saving grace here, and will many times keep him from taking himself too seriously.

"He must be alert, and able to get things done. This demands a good understanding of common human nature, some personal force, and some genuine political skill. He must know when and how to take the public into his confidence, and when not to tell what he desires or intends to do. He must know how to accept success without vainglory, and defeat without being embittered. He must keep a level head, so as not to be carried away by some new community enthusiasm, by some clever political trick, or by the great discovery of some wild-eyed reformer. He must, by all means, avoid developing a 'grouch' over the situation which confronts him, for a man with that attitude of mind never inspires confidence, and is always relatively ineffective." *Ibid.*, pp. 137–38.

[87] See the article by Emil L. Larson, "Administration as a Profession," *School Executive Magazine*, XLVIII (February, 1927), 291.

sional journals but also quite tangibly in the growth of legal certification requirements for administrators in the states.

Whether administrators were recognized by teachers or laymen as experts or had achieved a degree of professional status in other than their own eyes is difficult to determine. But there is no question that by 1918 administrators had followed the authoritarian role of the manager in industry and had applied it in their school systems. In fact by 1918 the adoption had gone so far that there was strong reaction against it. Thus in that year William C. Bagley, one of the most able and vocal leaders in education, termed this administrative arrangement a "factory plan" and a few years later voiced his opposition again. This system, which he said was "especially unfortunate," consisted of "a 'hierarchy' of authority and responsibility which makes the school board a 'board of directors,' the superintendent a 'general manager,' the assistant superintendents so many 'foremen,' and the principals equivalent to 'bosses,' while the teachers, to complete the picture, have the status of 'hands' or routine workers." [88] And in the same year even the *American School Board Journal*, whose editor had consistently supported the application of business principles to educational administration, raised the question of whether the movement had not gone too far in some places. The *Journal*, after stating that school administration had been changed "as a result of the growth of the superintendency as the chief executive office in city, county, and state school systems," noted that on the other side the teacher had had little share and that "in fact, her influence on the shaping of policies and aims as well as practical methods has been almost nil." The editor of the *Journal* thought that the centralization of authority had been an advantage to the schools because they had enjoyed "a form of executive service that is based upon sound principles of fact and theory." Even so, he said, "in spots there has been an insistence on the power of the superintendent which has arisen from warped notions of the supremacy of the expert and which has been a small counterfeit of the aristocratic theory of government." [89]

    [88] William C. Bagley and John A. H. Keith, *An Introduction to Teaching* (New York, 1924), p. 379.
    [89] Quoted in *School and Society*, VIII (December 21, 1918), 740–41.

9

EFFICIENCY'S PROGENY

"The 1920's," wrote eminent sociologist Robert Lynd, "were years of educational 'efficiency' in American public education and of yardstick making by which to measure this efficiency. . . ." These developments were clearly observable in Middletown, a city which Lynd had studied extensively in 1925. He reported that research departments had been established which used the yardsticks and which "issued impressive printed bulletins of comparative charts and tables on 'How Much Do Our Schools Cost the Taxpayer?'" Then he described the situation in the schools:

Middletown's school system, in step with those of other cities, has been becoming thoroughly "modernized" and "efficient" in its administrative techniques — to the dismay of some of the city's able teachers as they have watched the administrative horse gallop off with the educational cart. Some teachers regarded it as characteristic of the trend toward administrative dominance that in one recent year eight administrators and no teachers had their expenses paid to the National Education Association convention.[1]

Middletown was not an isolated case. On the contrary, by the mid-twenties the efficiency procedures had been extended to all parts of the nation. In these years even though scientific management had gone out of style, administrators utilized the various techniques which had been developed in the previous decade to appease a business society. In this endeavor they achieved a measure of success. For although criticism of the schools persisted, the attacks were not as strong as they had been a decade earlier.[2] Occasionally the schools were ac-

[1] Robert S. and Helen Merrell Lynd: *Middletown in Transition* (New York, 1937), pp. 205–6.
[2] *American School Board Journal*, LXXI (October, 1925), 68.

cused of not being practical enough, but it appears that Americans generally were satisfied with the progress that had been made in this direction and educators added to this satisfaction by stressing the "money value of schooling." The vigorous actions taken by administrators, plus a lessening of public concern over waste in management combined to solve the problem apparently because very little criticism of gross mismanagement was heard.

At this point our story has an ironic twist. For despite the fact that school administrators had adopted many business and industrial values and practices and had assumed the posture of a general manager and executive, their basic problems remained — *they continued to be insecure in their jobs and they continued to be plagued with financial problems.* Their efficiency efforts had helped them to refute criticism and had got them more approval than they had had before, but had not lessened their vulnerability nor given them job security. Security was possible only if they were able to operate the schools without asking for more money — a difficult feat. For in this period, as in the previous decade, they faced the same dilemma schoolmen face today. With more children in school for a longer time, and with a public placing increasing demands upon administrators in terms of educational offerings and services while at the same time objecting to increasing school taxes, they were in an impossible situation.

Educators had to assume some of the responsibility for the financial predicament in which they found themselves in the early twenties. It was true that a business philosophy dominated the country and this meant that schoolmen were faced with a public which placed a continuous emphasis upon efficiency and economy and generally opposed higher taxes. It also meant that they operated in a strong anti-intellectual climate in which "cultural" studies were defended with great difficulty. But for a decade they had accepted the business values in education and now this acceptance — sometimes reluctant, but often enthusiastic — came home to haunt them. For they had not only proclaimed their intention to operate the schools economically, but had done so loudly and had received the applause of a business society for their efforts. Now they were committed to a platform of economy and forced to be preoccupied with per-pupil costs. Furthermore, they had worked to establish themselves as executives and they had applied the management-and-worker parallel in education. When action had to be taken it was clear, although measures such as introducing the platoon school could be helpful, the best possibility for economizing was on teachers' salaries. Such savings could be achieved by lowering or freezing pay scales, or, more palatable professionally, by increasing the teacher's load. Both of these steps were of course unpopular with teachers and as a result administrators had to deal with dissatisfied faculties. Also, because many dissatisfied teachers left the profession, administrators had difficulty obtaining adequately prepared replacements, to say nothing of expanding their staffs to take care of increasing enrolments. To make matters worse, they had worked to convey the management-and-worker parallel to the school boards. Now they had to try to convince these same boards that the "workers" were really professional people who deserved more money for their services.

In this difficult financial situation administrators did two things: they increased their efforts to operate the schools efficiently and economically (this usually meant eliminating small classes and increasing class size and the teacher's load) and they adopted the advertising techniques used so successfully first by the government during World War I and then by big business.

Selling the Schools to the Public

The experience with propaganda techniques during the war had revealed the possibility of molding public opinion, and the new agent who appeared on the scene to exploit the potential was the public relations expert. Just as a decade earlier the efficiency expert had sold his services to corporations, colleges, and churches, so his counterpart in propaganda did the same. By 1921 the phrase "public relations" was being used increasingly and big companies were setting up publicity departments.[3] The idea was to convince the public of the benevolence and importance of the institution being publicized or of the value of the product being sold. The objective was not only to sell a product but to create good will.

Educators were not slow in realizing the possibilities of the new ideas for education. In the autumn of 1920 the *American School Board Journal* featured a series of articles on educational publicity by two high officials in the State Department of Public Instruction in Wisconsin. In the articles, significantly entitled "Publicity Campaigns for Better School Support," educators were told that

Advertising plays an important role in all well-managed campaigns. The familiar expression of the business world, "It pays to advertise," is no less appropriate here. The same principles of good advertising apply in attempts to secure increased school support by popular vote, as in campaigns for other purposes. The rules found valuable in advertising campaigns to increase the demand for a given product, to develop a new business venture, to win votes

[3] Thomas Cochran, *The American Business System* (Cambridge, 1957), p. 77.

for political candidates, or to secure attendance at a coming attraction may well be followed in school fund drives.[4]

The attempt to convince educators of the value of advertising was continued in the fall of 1920 by Claude M. Bolser of the School of Journalism at Indiana University. In the first of his two articles, Bolser treated scornfully those "staid academicians" who argued that educational publicity was not "compatible with the academic spirit." Such a viewpoint, he said, was natural

> to the unsocialized, ivy-clad cloistral, seclusive type of scholar. But such an interpretation of modern-day publicity fails to consider the inherent factors in the make-up of the human mind. We might say a mind educated to publicity and advertising. It reminds one of the dying Gaul to hear the everlasting gasps against modern-day progress toward more scientific methods. And there is as much fundamental science involved in real advertising as in any of the so-called higher classics. Truly the old order changeth, and it is up to each of us to keep pace, no matter how reactionary our ideas are.[5]

After this connection of advertising with the magic name "science" he gave an example to show how effective advertising could be — an example, by the way, which showed that, as with scientific management a decade earlier, the advertising movement was spreading into many other institutions. He cited a church in North Carolina whose pastor — a graduate of Princeton — had built up his congregation numerically through the new medium. He quoted the pastor as saying, "It is as legitimate to advertise religion as anything else. All the worthwhile things in the world are advertised. Religion is the most important thing in the world, and every man in the world should be told about it. The only way to reach every man is to advertise, in the channel best calculated to attract him. If he can once be gotten to church the preacher will have a chance at him." Bolser concluded his article by crediting advertising with being the force which "makes us strive a little more each day we live" and by indicating its eventual acceptance even by its antagonists because "advertising pays."[6] The next month in his article "Have You a Director of Publicity in Your Schools?" he presented a history of advertising in the course of which he reported that the Romans had invented the billboard.[7]

In the years after 1920 educators received continuous information

[4] Carter Alexander and W. W. Theisen, *American School Board Journal*, LXI (September, 1920), 32.

[5] "Personal Appeal in Educational Advertising," *School and Society*, XII (October 2, 1920), 277.

[6] *Ibid.*, pp. 278–80.

[7] "Have You a Director of Publicity in Your Schools?" *School and Society*, XII, (November 27, 1920), 514.

on the value of advertising as well as abundant advice on how to carry on a publicity program. The *American School Board Journal* printed photographs of parades which had been organized and carried out as part of the publicity campaigns. In articles they were told that school costs should be prepared carefully in order to "impress the voters with the idea that the schools are economically administered." They were given instructions on how to prepare campaign literature. This material, they were told, should begin with a statement that the school board, after a careful study, "or after having a survey made by outside experts" had concluded that more money was needed. The rest of the pamphlet should be directed toward showing that the increase was not extravagant and the data should always be presented with "attractive slogans."[8] The next year (1922) one of the leading superintendents in the country delivered an address to his colleagues at the Department of Superintendence meeting on "Selling the Schools to the Public." Urging the use of graphs, charts, and exhibits, he told his audience that these devices served to "prepare the public mind for improving education" just as they served business "in creating a demand on the part of the public for improved manufactured or other products."[9] In 1925, educators were told that since schools needed good will "just as much as do business organizations," publicity programs should go on continuously.[10] By that year books had been published on school publicity and it was included as an important topic in courses in educational administration (or even given as a separate course) in the leading colleges of education.

Much of this energy could have been conserved since it is clear that administrators did not have to be coerced into utilizing publicity programs. For advertising was not only a means of obtaining increased revenues for the schools, but also a means of counteracting criticism, or better still, of preventing it through a "positive" public relations program. There were some educators, such as Payson Smith, state superintendent in Massachusetts, who objected to educational salesmanship. Smith reported that he had experienced a "feeling of revulsion" upon hearing some of his "respected colleagues talking about 'selling education to the people.'"[11] But most administrators accepted the idea of advertising as a necessity. After all, publicity was doing pretty well for business and for religion. And as far

[8] Carter Alexander, "Motive Utilized in Successful Publicity Campaigns for Better School Support," *School Review,* XXIX, 302.

[9] H. B. Wilson, N.E.A. *Proceedings,* p. 1450.

[10] Carter Alexander, "The Continuous School Publicity Program," *School and Society,* XXI, 3.

[11] N.E.A. *Proceedings* (1925), p. 675.

as the ethics of the matter were concerned, had not so eminent a personage as Bruce Barton, in his "discovery" of the "real" Jesus, claimed in 1925 that he (Jesus) "would be a national advertiser today, . . . as he was the great advertiser of his own day." [12]

The Educational Service Station

Closely related to the public relations approach as a means of creating favorable attention toward the schools and their administrators was the "service" idea. Thus in 1925 school principals in the city of Chicago under the direction of Superintendent William McAndrew were engaged in an extensive "courtesy campaign." McAndrew reported that 291 principals had extended their courtesy by making and displaying in the schools, in places where they were "likely to meet the eye of visitors," 2,024 "attractive placards" which emphasized the service theme. Then to illustrate what was being done, he listed as some of the slogans that were printed on the placards the following:

To the public: This school desires to serve you. The principal will be glad to receive your comments.

Citizens welcome. Tell us what you think.

America's service station, a public school.

We are doing our best. We will appreciate your suggestions.

We may not have time to visit, but we have time to give you courteous attention to business.

We want to please the public. Help us.

We are here for service.

This School desires to serve the public. Business transacted in the office.

The public be pleased. The principal will gladly receive your comments.

Our motto is service. The principal desires your comments.

Pleasing the public is our pleasant duty. The principal desires your comments. [13]

It is not difficult to imagine that busy school principals were not exactly delighted at having to spend their time making placards, but they were probably even less enthusiastic at the prospect of having the public take the placards seriously.

McAndrew did more than just talk about service. He reported that under his administration the number of "services" performed by students during "Clean Up Week" increased from 363,672 in 1923 (a year before his appointment) to 3,242,462 in 1926. He also worked out an arrangement under which students could receive recog-

[12] Bruce Barton, The Man Nobody Knows; A Discovery of the Real Jesus (Indianapolis, 1925), p. 140.

[13] The Annual Report of the Superintendent of Schools 1926, pp. 13–14.

nition for their "Civic Service," e.g., cleaning empty lots, building bird houses, etc. For 10 hours of "voluntary service" a student received a "credit," for 100 hours a "certificate," and for 150 hours a "diploma."[14] He also included in his Annual Report for 1926 a lengthy account of "Sampling Day." This was an arrangement whereby leading citizens of Chicago were invited into the schools to question the eighth-grade students. These citizens were then asked to make suggestions and comments. McAndrew listed some of the suggestions and filled a page with favorable comments that had been made about the schools.[15]

McAndrew's *Annual Reports* consisted of a disconnected list of topics, for example, "Fire Drills," "Vandalism," "Courtesy," "Penmanship," and "Rating Principals' Efficiency," etc. These topics were treated in varying lengths — depending, presumably, on the importance of the topic. Thus several pages (consisting mostly of quotations from "experts") were devoted to "Class Size," as McAndrew sought to justify his policy of increasing class size. Significantly, more space was devoted to fire drills than to the purposes of education. Whenever possible — which was frequently — topics were dealt with quantitatively. The statistics cited above on "services" were an example. He even counted and reported on the number of citizens who had visited the schools in response to his invitations. And when they came, McAndrew treated they royally, even to the point of having students who had been drilled as ushers show them around the schools.[16]

The service station conception was a natural outgrowth of years of business influence upon education and also of the teaching of Bobbitt and Cubberley that the public should provide the specifications for the educational "products" which were to be turned out by the schools. Natural, too, was the fact that the service was most often provided for the business community. For not only was this group the most powerful, and accepted by administrators as such, but year by year after 1911 administrators increasingly adopted the business posture and values.[17] This identification of the total community with the business community was so common among administrators that one gets the impression that they thought the two communities were synonymous. Thus, as early as 1913 one superintendent told his colleagues at the N.E.A. that "Since the school is maintained at public

[14] *Ibid.*, p. 5.
[15] *Ibid.*, p. 30.
[16] *Ibid.*

[17] In his study of school superintendents Bair found that 410 were members of the Chamber of Commerce while 2 were affiliated with organized labor. Frederick H. Bair, *The Social Understandings of the Superintendent of Schools* (New York, 1934), p. 100.

expense *or at the expense of the business interests*, and really exists *for the sole* purpose of developing the business men and women of the future, it is evident that there should be perfect harmony between the school authorities and the business interests." [18]

In its mature form as developed by McAndrew the service station conception was obviously influenced by the advertising movement which was strong in the twenties. In earlier periods this impressive public relations veneer was not available but the essence of the service station philosophy existed. It can be traced to some extent on the college level to President Wayland of Brown University in the 1850's, and to Charles Eliot and the elective system two decades later at Harvard.[19] In the lower schools it can be seen in the vigorous response to the demands for industrial education between 1907 and 1910. It is apparent again in the almost unbelievable activity engaged in by schoolmen between 1915 and 1922 to teach thrift in the public schools. In this endeavor the N.E.A. established a committee to encourage the teaching of thrift and the setting up of savings banks in the schools. One ingenious teacher even worked out a "Thrift Alphabet" which read as follows:

A is for acorn
B is for bank
C is for card
D is for dollar
E is for earn
F is for Franklin
G is for gold
H is for help
I is for interest
J is for junk
K is for khaki
L is for learn
M is for money
N is for nickel
O is for "Only one and twenty-four" [This line was taken from a Thrift
     stamp song which had recently appeared in a periodical]
P is for penny
Q is for quarter
R is for ready
S is for stamp

[18] N.E.A. *Proceedings*, pp. 558–59. (Italics mine.)
[19] See Dietrich Gerhard's "The Emergence of the Credit System in American Education Considered as a Problem of Social and Intellectual History," in *Bulletin of the American Association of University Professors*, XLI, No. 4, (Winter, 1955), 647–68.

T is for Thrift
U is for Uncle Sam
V is for V [5 V's will buy one Thrift Stamp]
W is for W. S. S.
X is for X [10 tens (X's) will buy four Thrift stamps]
Y is for you
Z is for zero — for those who do nothing [20]

Courses were offered in salesmanship and advertising and, for Negroes in Sumner High School in St. Louis, in chauffeuring and janitoring. In these years educators asked businessmen what arithmetic and spelling and English should be taught in the schools. And one principal of a high school in California urged that courses in efficiency be offered and suggested that Harrington Emerson's book be used as a basic text.

Perhaps the ultimate in service (prior to McAndrew) was a plan developed by the superintendent, Fred M. Hunter, and a member of the Commercial Club in Lincoln, Nebraska. It included an "efficiency list" of boys and girls in the upper grades and its purpose and nature was described in a letter sent by the Superintendent to the employers of the city. A copy of the letter was printed in the *American School Board Journal* in February of 1915; it read in part as follows:

As an employer of young men you are interested in securing those who can make themselves of most value to you and your business or profession. It is likewise of vital interest not only to such young men themselves but to the city as a whole that they be able to give the best possible service to their employers and prepare themselves for continued efficiency and promotion.

There are in our schools many young men who must begin work at an early age. It is the purpose of the public schools in connection with the Lincoln Commercial Club to keep a permanent "Efficiency List" of such of these young men as may be able to reach a definite standard of reliability and efficiency. The list will be always available and will be sent from time to time to any business or professional man who desires it. Only such boys as have, on their merits, shown the following qualifications are placed on the list:

1. An age of 14 years.
2. Good character — as shown by —
   a. Truthfulness.
   b. Obedience.
   c. Industry.
   d. Good habits.

Note — No boy shall be eligible who smokes, (or drinks). If a boy has

[20] Grace A. Taylor, "The Thrift Alphabet," *Journal of Education*, XC (July, 1919), 36.

been a smoker he shall show by a year's abstinence from this habit that he has permanently given it up.

3. Knowledge of Lincoln and Nebraska as shown by his ability to pass with a standing of 90 per cent a test given upon Lincoln and Nebraska.

4. Ability to write a good business letter of one ordinary page in legible hand without errors in spelling.

5. Ability to express himself in courteous yet concise and businesslike terms to his employer and business associates.

6. Ability to perform the four fundamental operations and simple fractions in arithmetic, with speed and accuracy.

The Commercial Club and the school authorities have invited suggestions as to the qualifications which they desire in the young men they employ.[21]

The motives behind the service station conception were varied. Many educators, for example, who pushed the thrift campaign undoubtedly believed they were helping to improve both individual students and the nation as a whole. In the colleges and universities, likewise, there were many who believed that by offering all kinds of practical courses from cooking to fly-casting that they were serving the best interests of society.[22] But it is also clear that there were other motives. In the colleges and universities the "service" idea was used as a means of placating and getting funds from boards of directors or state legislatures and as a means of attracting students. In the public schools it was used to create favorable attitudes toward the schools and especially toward their administrators.

Under the circumstances it was understandable that administrators who were faced with a public that was often critical and almost always concerned with economy, would utilize the service station notion. It is also true that the American pattern of support and control makes it inevitable that the schools will be responsive to society's needs. But the exaggerated idea of the schools as service stations has been responsible for some unfortunate developments in American education. To the extent that it was accepted it meant that educators relinquished their responsibility for providing educational leadership and became mere technicians who (as Bobbitt had recommended) produced the product according to specifications. In Chicago under McAndrew, and in many other places, it meant arranging the school program so as to impress the public that the schools were making a major contribution toward whatever fetish the nation happened to be concerned with at the time. Thus schoolmen outdid themselves to teach thrift when America was concerned with thrift. During World

[21] *American School Board Journal*, L, 43–44.

[22] For an account of the service philosophy in operation in the twenties see Abraham Flexner, *Universities, American, English, German* (New York, 1930), p. 15.

War I educators proved their patriotism by removing the teaching of German from the schools and in Cleveland Frank Spaulding and his educational council initiated a loyalty pledge for teachers to sign.[23] After the war in the hysteria over Bolshevism schoolmen went all out for 100 per cent Americanism.

When the public relations touch was added to this existing readiness to serve, as in Chicago, a more unfortunate situation was created. When educators operated under this extreme service station philosophy, they not only did not repel but actually *invited* all kinds of pressures to be exerted upon the schools. And testimony that they were being exerted in 1927 was given by a leading educator, Henry Suzzallo, who warned the delegates to the N.E.A. convention in Seattle that

Chambers of commerce, clubs, corporations, industries and other associations are exerting an influence which will break up the balanced human program of the schools designed for the development of wholesome human character and personality and the ultimate service of the general public welfare. Their insistence that special school days and weeks be set aside for some special interest or purpose, however good, opens the way to every organized special interest that would like to work on youth when its plastic innocence makes it an easy victim. In one year, fifty-four such requests came to the desk of a single public school administrator. Submission to all these requests would have given the young students the most lopsided and prejudiced course of training that could have been devised. The public school cannot be made an intellectual handmaiden to all the special interest advertising campaigns now under way in this country. From all these, we must declare our independence, that the schools themselves may be free to perform their real functions.[24]

In this connection it should be said to McAndrew's credit that he stood firm and refused to allow the Navy to solicit funds from pupils in the Chicago schools for the restoration of Old Ironsides.[25] But it was not easy to stand firm and frequently educators were reminded of their proper place. Thus, two months after Suzzallo's speech the President of the School Board told the principals of the Chicago schools, "You educators must understand that teaching is a business. You are salesmen. Your commodity is education. You must satisfy your customers, the taxpayers." [26] Clearly, fifteen years of appeasement — of relinquishing responsibility for educational leadership — had borne bitter fruit.

[23] Frank E. Spaulding, *School Superintendent in Action in Five Cities* (Rindge, N.H., 1955), p. 16.

[24] N.E.A. *Proceedings*, p. 27.

[25] *Annual Report of the Superintendent of Schools* (Chicago, 1926), p. 21.

[26] *School and Society*, XXVI (September 17, 1927), 362.

Mass Production in Education

The activity of educators in connection with the platoon school —
activity which resulted in arrangements which most closely resembled
the assembly line and which reached its peak during the twenties —
was described in chapter vi. The other actions taken by administrators to cut costs — actions which resulted in increasing the similarity
between the schools and factories — were those taken in the secondary
schools to increase the size of classes, the teaching load, and the size
of schools. These steps which were taken for financial reasons, although rationalized as was the platoon school by claims of educational gain, resulted in making the schools increasingly impersonal
in nature. Unfortunately these increases in class size and teacher load
came to be established as standard and have persisted down to our
own time, whereas the platoon school was abandoned.

Undoubtedly the sheer number of students to be educated, plus the
great moral commitment to educate all the children to the limit of
their ability, would have created stubborn educational problems even
if Americans and their educational administrators had not been
economy-minded and had not developed a mechanical conception of
the nature of education. But fifteen years of admiration for the mass
production techniques of industry on the one hand and saturation with
the values of efficiency and economy on the other had so conditioned
the American people and their school administrators that they allowed their high school teachers to be saddled with an impossibly
heavy teaching load. The American people not only allowed this to
happen but their insistence on economy forced it upon the schools.
And just as some of the leading school administrators did not repel
but actually *invited* lay interference, they not only did not resist this
increase in class size but actually initiated the steps, advocated and
defended them, and put them into effect.

Administrators had begun to consider the problem of reducing expenditures through increasing the size of classes and the teaching load
and through eliminating small classes almost immediately after 1911
when the great pressure began to be exerted upon them to demonstrate efficiency. The actions of Frank Spaulding (e.g., in eliminating
Greek on financial grounds) in this connection have been described,
as have those of Bobbitt and his students in studying unit costs. But in
those early years the cost of secondary education was not a critical
problem and elementary classes were so large that even the most
economy-minded educators did not suggest increasing their size. Besides, after 1914 the platoon school was being introduced increasingly and the economy achieved through its use was apparently

satisfactory. With the growth of population, the improvement in child labor and compulsory attendance laws, and the change from the classical curriculum, each year after 1910 more students were attending secondary schools and staying longer. With the subsequent problem of increasing costs for salaries and buildings, which was aggravated by the continuous rise in the cost of living, it was natural that administrators would look for ways and means of reducing the costs of secondary education. The largest item in the budget was of course teachers' salaries, and it was in this direction that they sought relief. Clearly the way to economize was to get more work out of teachers, either by increasing the size of their classes or by increasing the number of classes they taught or both.

In this effort the very small classes of ten to fifteen students, especially in the classics or the foreign languages, were doomed. And when some fortunate circumstance such as the anti-German sentiment during and after World War I occurred, even fairly popular courses could be dropped. Significantly, when this happened the financial saving which was effected was included in the reporting of the event. Thus the *Journal of Education* reported in a news item that the Cincinnati Schools had eliminated German and had saved $75,000 a year thereby.[27]

But the movement to increase high school classes beyond twenty-five students met with more difficulty. In the first place teachers themselves (and high school teachers were more outspoken than elementary teachers) repeatedly recommended twenty-five students as the upper limit; professors of education in normal schools reduced the recommended number to twenty. In addition some obstacles had been set up within the profession by teachers themselves. In 1913 the National Council of Teachers of English and the Modern Language Association had appointed a committee to study the cost and labor of teaching English in the secondary schools. The committee made a thorough study of how much time and effort it took to teach students the skills and abilities which were expected. The committee found that the average English teacher was trying to teach 130 students and to do this effectively would require 18 hours a day of instructional duty. The results of the committee's work were published in the fall of 1913 and were communicated to the profession generally by Professor Edwin M. Hopkins, professor of English at the University of Kansas, in a speech at one of the general sessions of the N.E.A. Convention in 1915. Hopkins reported that the National Council of Teachers of English had adopted a resolution supporting the action of the North

[27] LXXXVII (June 27, 1918), 719.

Central Association, which recommended limiting the number of students assigned to any one teacher to 80. He urged the N.E.A. to endorse these recommendations and to give them wide publicity so that the reasons for the poor quality of English teaching would be understood and steps could be taken to change the situation. He also reported that although the average English teacher was teaching (or trying to teach) 130 students, some teachers had more than 200, and in one of the best California high schools (the N.E.A. was meeting in San Francisco) one English teacher had 180 pupils and taught six hours a day instead of the recommended four. He pointed out that the amount of time in class was not the only consideration, for teachers needed to spend time with individual students and on preparation.[28]

Opposition such as this delayed but did not stop the efforts to increase class size and teacher load, and in the twenties it was overcome thanks to a series of "scientific" studies which, it was claimed, proved that classes of 40 or even 50 could be taught as well as classes of 25. The most important of these studies before 1925 were those conducted by Paul R. Stevenson of the Bureau of Research of the University of Illinois and Calvin O. Davis of the North Central Association. In both studies, which were largely uncontrolled or only semi-controlled, the achievement of students (on the basis of examinations or marks) in large (33 — 42) classes was compared with the achievement in small (18 — 25) classes. Attempts were made to equate the groups but no attempt was made to vary the teaching procedure in the different size classes, and the teachers who taught the classes were doing this as a part of their regular teaching, i.e. teaching their regular load of five classes a day with a total of more than a hundred students. As might have been expected, the differences between the groups were insignificant and almost immediately the results were hailed by administrators. Now they could claim — just as they had claimed in the adoption of the platoon schools — that the steps they were taking were not harmful educationally.

In the years that followed (and in fact down to the present time) the arguments were marshalled in numerous articles and editorials in educational journals and in texts on administration in the same wearisome way. The research showed, they said, that class size made no difference, that good teachers could teach large classes as well as small ones, and that the burden of proof was on the advocates of small classes, etc. Thus the *School Review*, probably the most important journal in secondary education, in an editorial in 1922 reported approvingly of Stevenson's work, describing it as a "large service"

[28] N.E.A. *Proceedings*, pp. 114–16.

and a "careful experimental study," and then quoted the following paragraph from the conclusions of the study:

The tables of this chapter show that at the end of the experimental period the achievements of the students in the two types of classes were approximately equal, and there is a slight indication that those taught in small classes were superior. Since the educational investment can be materially decreased by increasing the size of class in the high school, one might infer that the efficiency of the school would be increased by organizing classes enrolling from 35/50 students instead of classes enrolling from 20 to 25.[29]

The following year the *School Review* published an article by C. O. Davis in which he reported the results of his study carried out under the auspices of the North Central Association. Davis reported his conclusions and drew the following "practical deductions."

1. Considerable economy can be effected by organizing at least some of the classes in the school as large classes and by putting in charge of these classes teachers who can effectively manage and instruct them.

2. Considerations of good administration demand that machinery of some sort be developed whereby teachers who are capable of instructing large classes, and prefer to do so, shall be discovered, trained, and promoted.

3. An obligation rests on school standardizing agencies to assist in dissipating the erroneous notion that large classes are always undesirable and should be avoided.

4. The teaching load should be adjusted on as scientific a basis as possible but with reference always to the ability of the individual to carry the burden.

5. Promotions and financial rewards should be graded in accordance with the size and the importance of the load carried.[30]

The same themes were presented by some leading administrators in textbooks. In one such text written by two students of Cubberley's and with an introduction by him the authors, Almack and Lang, stated that investigation did not support the belief held by educators that the smaller the class, the greater the efficiency of instruction. After citing the studies which were supposed to prove the point (the same studies were listed in almost verbatim accounts in other texts and in annual reports of superintendents) the authors reported that although the great majority of teachers thought that 25 was the best size for classes, some placed the upper limit at 60 and some teachers were teaching groups of 75 "with apparent ease." They urged that greater emphasis be placed in teacher training institutions on preparing teachers to

[29] *School Review*, XXX (September, 1922), 484.

[30] "The Size of Classes and the Teaching Load in the High Schools Accredited by the North Central Association," XXXI (June, 1923), 429.

handle large classes.[31] A few years later Fred Engelhardt, professor of educational administration at Minnesota, who had taken his doctor's degree in administration at Teachers College, repeated the message in his influential text. "Experimental evidence," he said, "demonstrates conclusively that, in terms of the usual measures of success, there is no significant difference in the effectiveness of small classes in contrast with large classes in certain subjects." [32] The same material in much greater detail was presented by another Ph.D. in Administration from Teachers College, Henry H. Linn, in his book *Practical School Economies*. Linn went so far as to provide testimony from superintendents in several cities who had increased their class size (one to 75 students) and their teachers' load (some to 6 and even 7 classes per day).[33]

One of the administrators in the schools who utilized the "scientific evidence" to increase class size was William McAndrew of Chicago. His administration was dominated by the ideal of business efficiency and featured all of the efficiency procedures presented in this study and some which were not, such as the time clock.[34] On the class size question McAndrew acted decisively. He had established a Bureau of Purchases and Economy which among other things made a study of small classes in Chicago high schools. The director of the Bureau reported to McAndrew that out of the thousands of classes, thirty had ten students or less. He decided that "Hereafter no high school class will be organized for less than twenty pupils," and he defended his action by stating that it was "futile to say that education should not be subjected to the rules of ordinary business." [35]

Apparently McAndrew had no difficulty with the elimination of these small classes but to increase class size beyond 25 was another matter, and so he marshalled his evidence in his 1926 *Annual Report* to support his case. First he reported that superintendents in other school systems had increased class size and had saved money. One of these was the superintendent from Detroit, whom he quoted as follows:

The per capita cost of pupils in Detroit high schools had risen to $180.00. For economy we passed the rule that each teacher must have five classes of

[31] John C. Almack and Albert R. Lang, *Problems of the Teaching Profession* (Boston, 1925), pp. 199–203.

[32] Fred Engelhardt, *Public School Organization and Administration* (Boston, 1931), p. 291.

[33] Henry H. Linn, *Practical School Economies* (New York, 1934), pp. 139–56.

[34] For an account of McAndrew's tenure in Chicago see George S. Counts, *School and Society in Chicago* (New York, 1928), pp. 71–84.

[35] *Annual Report of the Superintendent of Schools* (Chicago, 1926), p. 74.

thirty pupils, or six classes of twenty-five, except in health education, in which we doubled the number. We cut the per capita cost to $109.00, a total saving of $1,230,500 in teaching cost. There has been no injury to our scholarship. It has improved about one per cent. Students passing 76% of college subjects in 1920 now pass 77%.[36]

McAndrew then went through the routine of presenting the evidence of studies on class size: Rice reported no "relationship" between class size and results, Elliott reported no "correlation," Stevenson found "little difference" in achievement, etc.

Then he turned his attention to increasing the size of schools. Since no "scientific evidence" was available, he quoted some twenty-five educators, most of whom were principals of large high schools. These men all provided testimony for McAndrew that large schools were superior to small ones.[37] In this endeavor he mentioned the size of the large schools in only a few instances and then only when the schools had 5000 students or more (all from New York City). In the great majority of quotations there was no way of telling how large a "large school" was. This was true in quotations he used from Dewey and Thorndike, who may have been referring to the thousands of very small high schools of less than 200 pupils. In any case, after presenting this "evidence" McAndrew applied it to his immediate aim to increase the size of the Chicago high schools. To support his position he included the following analysis:

A study made by your finance department covers the cost per pupil in typical high schools of 2,500 and of 4,000 pupils. It says:

	School of 2,500 Pupils	School of 4,000 Pupils
Estimated cost of building	$2,750,000.00	3,750,000.00
Estimated cost per pupil	1,100.00	937.50
Estimated difference in cost of building per pupil		162.50
Estimated cost of operation per year	34,000.00	46,000.00
Estimated cost of operation per pupil	13.60	11.50
Estimated cost of teacher's salary per pupil	109.20	100.00
Estimated cost of supplies per pupil	7.30	7.30
Estimated cost of maintenance per pupil	5.00	4.50
Estimated total current expenses per pupil per year	135.10	123.30
Estimated difference in current expense per year		11.80

If, as some school accounts do, you include in yearly costs, 4% of investment, your cost per pupil in the schools of 2,500 pupils will be $179.00 per annum; and cost per pupil in a school of 4,000 pupils will be $160.80 per annum, a saving of $18.20 per annum in the large schools, amounting to for

[36] *Ibid.*, p. 55.
[37] *Ibid.*, pp. 57–61.

the average school, $72,800.00 per annum. These estimates are based upon the assumption that the district boundaries will be made such as to give each new high school as many pupils as it is supposed to accommodate.[38]

Then projecting his figures ahead for five years he reported that by increasing the school building capacity from 2,500 to 4,000, $6,500,000 would be saved on construction costs and $944,000 on current expenses.

It is impossible to determine how many huge schools were built for reasons of economy in American cities, but the number was and continues to be considerable. And the same logic was used in justifying the move that was used by Spaulding in deciding which subjects were of the most value and by the educators who supported the larger classes: Since they could not agree on the value, e.g. of Greek, or since there apparently was no difference in educational achievement in large and small classes, then the economic factor was the decisive one. Fortunately, there were factors operating which limited both the extent to which class size and school size could be increased.

For one thing educators had been busy "standardizing" school buildings, and, complained Fred Engelhardt, there were no large classrooms which could be used for "experimentation."[39] Even so the median class size in high schools in cities of over 100,000 in 1930/31 was 34.1 in junior high schools and 30.5 in senior high schools. This meant a teacher load of 150 to 170 students. This figure is based, of course, on a five-class-a-day load but there were some cities in which teachers taught six classes, which one leading administrator reported approvingly was "not uncommon."[40] Another factor which helped to prevent huge classes was the opposition of some officials of the accrediting associations. For example, although the North Central Association had officially abandoned class size as a criterion for accreditation, many officials of the organization still used it. This fact was reported to the North Central Association by Earl Hudelson, who had carried out class size studies on the college level. Hudelson complained that he had canvassed administrators in 471 school systems in 48 states, and while 41 per cent were opposed to or doubtful of the reasonableness of arbitrary class size limitation (indicating that McAndrew was not alone), they dared not ignore it because of fear of losing accreditation.[41] Finally, many educators op-

[38] *Ibid.*, p. 61.

[39] Engelhardt, *Public School Organization*, p. 291.

[40] Linn, *Practical School Economies*, p. 154.

[41] Earl Hudelson, "Class Size Opinions, Evidence, and Policies in Secondary Schools," *North Central Association Quarterly*, IV, 208.

posed the movement to increase class size. Some of this opposition came from educators who knew from their own experience that teachers could *talk at* but *not teach* 100, much less 150–200 students. Others such as W.W. Charters challenged the validity of using the class size experiments as the basis for "wholesale increase in the teaching load." [42] He stated that until it could be shown that teachers could not do a better job of *individualizing instruction* in small classes he would question the pedagogical soundness of large classes.[43]

As for school size, it was clear that schools of 4,000 or 5,000 students would involve serious transportation problems for students in all but the largest cities, in which the population was highly concentrated. But here again, schools of 1,500 to 3,000 were common in American cities and I suspect that, so far as any personal contact between teacher and student is concerned, there is not much greater opportunity in a school of 2,000 than in one of 4,000, especially when teachers are teaching five or six classes a day of thirty students and a guidance counselor is responsible for 500 students.

In the thirties administrators developed impressive-appearing formulas for standardizing and equalizing the teacher's load.[44] The size

---

[42] W. W. Charters, "Larger Classes," *Educational Research Bulletin*, VIII (September 11, 1929), 276.

[43] Charters, "Class Size Once More," *ibid.*, IV (April 29, 1925), 186–87.

[44] These are still being used and have been made even more impressive. For example consider this formula developed in the thirties and revised in 1951:

$$TL = SGC \left[CP - \frac{Dup.}{10} + \frac{(NP - 25CP)}{100} \right] \left[\frac{PL + 50}{100} \right] + \left[.6PC \right] \left[\frac{PL + 50}{100} \right]$$

TL = units of teaching load per week.

SGC = subject grade coefficient.

CP = class periods spent in classroom per week.

Dup = number of class periods spent per week in classroom teaching classes for which the preparation is very similar to that for some other section (not including the original sections).

NP = number of pupils in classes per week (the 25 is employed as a norm).

PC = number of minutes divided by 84 spent per week in supervision of the study hall, student activities, teachers' meetings, committee work, assisting in administrative or supervisory work, or other co-operations.

PL = gross length in minutes of class period. (The 50 represents approximately the average period length — actually the figure is 51.7. This discrepancy however, has no influence for the relative load figures for different teachers for different schools. A figure less than the actual average of 51.7 was taken in order to make computation easier: (*a*) by using round numbers, (*b*) by avoiding negative terms as far as possible.

Harl R. Douglass, "The 1950 Revision of the Douglass High School Teaching Load Formula," *Bulletin of the National Association of Secondary-School Principals*, XXXV, No. 179 (May, 1951), 22. As two educators W. S. Elsbree and E. E. Reutter, Jr., in their recent book on *Staff Personnel in the Public Schools* (New York, 1954) pointed out, many

of classes in the high school was stabilized in most instances at between 30 and 35 students, and administrators attempted — partly for
reasons of economy which were more pressing after 1929 and partly
to equalize teaching loads — to see that as many classes as possible
were standardized at this level. The result was the teaching load
which is accepted as the norm in most public high schools today. This
load of five classes (or six) meant that each teacher attempted to
teach from 150 to 200 students a day, and the unit system which was
widely adopted by 1910 required that teachers and students be in
class five periods of 45 to 60 minutes a day five days a week for an
entire semester. This system, especially in the large high schools,
makes the educational process resemble the assembly line in the
factory.

The Descent into Trivia

The capitulation by school administrators to the pressures for
economy led to some other unfortunate developments. In the search
for ways and means of reducing expenditures they directed a great
deal of attention to trivial matters. This development was furthered,
of course, by the nature of the training administrators were receiving
in the graduate schools of education. It will be recalled that George
Strayer's attitude was that in these training programs any practical
problem was a worthy subject for investigation even for the doctoral
thesis. With the acceptance of this idea, the floodgates were opened.
For years the leaders in administration had ignored the substance of
education and had centered their attention on the mechanics of administration, in which area the number of fairly significant problems
was limited. And since there were hundreds of candidates who had to
have research problems, someone was bound to end up with the
plumbing. This work not only provided training in trivia for the individual candidates, it also lent the dignity of the great universities and
the respectability of the "scientific" label to these problems. As time
went by many administrators came to accept studies on and discussions about these matters as natural and normal and even important.

In this descent into trivia administrators were given leadership by
the United States Commissioner of Education, William John Cooper.
Writing in 1933 on *Economy in Education,* Cooper advised schoolmen on how money could be saved through various administrative
devices. One of these was through school district consolidation and

secondary school principals have found this formula "an extremely useful device, in making
out schedules. Individual teachers often believe their load is unduly heavy but, when the
formula is applied and they see that their load is no greater than that assigned to their
colleagues, their resentment vanishes" (p. 102).

another was that of increasing class size. On this latter point the Commissioner went through the routine of listing the class size studies which had been made and which showed, he said, that large classes could be taught as well as small ones. This economy device, he said, which was well begun "before we had to economize" was the "commonest method used by city superintendents." Since most of the school money was spent for teachers' salaries, that item had the most potential for economy.

But there were other ways of reducing expenditures and on these the U.S. Commissioner got down to details. He stated that one superintendent in Kansas had reported that through co-operative buying "he was able to save over 40% on paper fasteners, 25% on thumbtacks, 20% on theme paper, 30% on colored pencils, and 50% on hectograph paper." In another instance one school board had discovered that "it paid 50 cents a ton more for coal" than some other boards. He then gave a series of suggestions for economizing. "Frequently" he said, "schools purchase ink by the quart, paying a good price for it and still more for its transportation. If one makes ink from ink powder he will usually have an article which is good enough for school work." Money could also be saved on lumber for manual training classes by purchasing "odd lengths and ungraded lumber" which could be bought for "$\frac{1}{3}$ the price of first-class material." [45] On the matter of school paper he noted "there is always some waste. A sheet may be larger than needed. The best remedy for this is to supply two sizes, one the regular $8\frac{1}{2}''$ by $11''$, the other $8\frac{1}{2}''$ by $5\frac{1}{2}''$. If the superintendent will study his paper and its uses he will be able to eliminate odd sizes and buy more standard sizes." Then he turned to other forms of paper. "Toilet paper" he said, was "frequently a source of waste. I have seen school toilets in which the ceiling and walls were literally coated with paper which had been dipped in water and thrown." In other cases one waded in a slough of toilet paper on the floor. As for paper towels, he told his readers that "considerable saving can generally be made both in the amount paid for them and in the number used. Payne, after a rather carefully controlled experiment, reports that a roll of toweling saved 38% over individual folded towels." [46]

Then he turned to plant operation and stated that "it is essential that the superintendent give personal attention to such matters as the maintenance of floors." He pointed out that waste in heating was a

[45] W. John Cooper, *Economy in Education* (Stanford, 1933), pp. 66–68.

[46] *Ibid.*, pp. 68–69. Cooper was referring to an article by A. C. Payne entitled "Buying Supplies on Scientific Lines," in the *School Executive Magazine*, LI (September, 1931), 16.

common problem and he asked, "Does the furnace burn too long? Is the entire building adequately heated? Can a part of the heat be shut off? Do teachers have the heat on and the windows open at the same time?" Another possible area for economy was the sanitation system. He stated that "Lavatories will probably repay any effort spent on them." Turning then to the utilities, he noted that savings could be made on water, gas, and electricity. He cited statistics to show how much water was wasted by one dripping faucet, and reported that "another source of waste in dry climates comes from watering lawns while the sun is shining on them, resulting in excessive evaporation of water. Watering can best be done in the evening." On electricity, he reported that "a superintendent who gave attention to this item reported a saving of 20 per cent." These suggestions were followed by recommendations to check gas leaks and to economize on the use of the telephone.[47]

A year later many of these same recommendations (as well as many more) were made in a volume in the "Strayer-Engelhardt School Administration Series" entitled *Practical School Economies*. The author, Henry H. Linn, had taken his Ph.D. in administration at Teachers College and had written his thesis "Safeguarding School Funds" under Engelhardt and Strayer. At the time his volume on school economies was written he was assistant superintendent of schools in Muskegon, Michigan, but he later joined the faculty at Teachers College. In his book Linn suggested that economy could be achieved in instructional services through increasing class size, and he marshaled the familiar evidence to support his point. He also reported that six daily classes for high school teachers were not then uncommon, and he cited school systems in which this statesmanlike action had been taken.[48] He devoted more than one hundred pages to economies in "plant" operation and maintenance and among the topics discussed were "Toilet Bowl Cleaners," "Roach Powders," "Towel Service" (linen towels were .004 per wipe, paper towels 0.034) "Toilet Paper," "Eliminating Useless Gas Connections," "Reducing Laundry Costs," and the mystery of the "Purposes of Painting."[49]

As late as 1938 the emphasis on the financial-mechanical aspects of administration as well as a concern over some trivial problems was still being manifested. In that year an introductory text on the principles of school administration was published. It contained the usual material on finance, business management, publicity, child account-

[47] *Ibid.*, pp. 69–70.
[48] *Practical School Economies*, pp. 154–56.
[49] *Ibid.*, pp. xvi–xix.

ing, and the school janitor. It also included a section on "School Housekeeping" in which, along with weighty advice on cleaning toilet rooms and floors, and on fire prevention, student administrators were treated to these momentous words on "Dusting":

All pupils' and teachers' desk-and-seat equipment should be dusted thoroughly every morning before the opening of school. Flipping a feather duster or dust cloth across desks is not effective, and only moves the dust from one place to another. If vacuum equipment is not available, the only satisfactory method of dusting furniture is to wipe the surfaces thoroughly with a cloth or especially prepared sanitary duster. In dusting, the janitor should take straight strokes with the grain of the wood.[50]

The tragedy behind these statements (which were repeated frequently in other books and in the administrative journals during the thirties) was that men in key positions were spending their time on such matters and spreading still further an inadequate conception of school administration while the very existence of the free world was in danger. As the work of Cooper and Linn was being published, America was undergoing the greatest economic crisis in its history. As the material on dusting was being solemnly presented to educators, Hitler was annexing Austria and humiliating England and France at Munich. And aside from the merit of urging that highly paid school administrators devote their time and energy to these matters, one wonders what conception the authors had of the intelligence and professional outlook of the average superintendent of schools. The need for economy was of course very great and the concern for economy by educational leaders legitimate, but these suggestions were an insult to the intelligence. Perhaps the most appropriate statement in this connection was the quotation used by Abraham Flexner in his excellent analysis of American universities in 1930 — an analysis, incidentally, which shows that the emphasis on service, on selling education, on mass production, and on trivia were not limited to educational administration but were widespread in American higher education at the time. Flexner quoted a Negro preacher in a popular play (*Green Pastures*), who declared, "the Lord expects us to figure out a few things for ourselves."[51]

[50] D. H. Cooke, R. H. Hamon and A. M. Proctor, *Principles of School Administration* (Minneapolis, 1938), p. 205.

[51] Abraham Flexner, *Universities American, English, German* (New York, 1930), p. 100.

10

AN AMERICAN TRAGEDY
IN EDUCATION

The study of various aspects of the actions administrators took between 1910 and 1929 in applying business and industrial values and practices to education, together with an attempt to explain *why* they took these actions has formed the substance of this volume. It seems in retrospect that, regardless of the motivation, the consequences for American education and American society were tragic. And when all of the strands in the story are woven together, it is clear that the essence of the tragedy was in adopting values and practices indiscriminately and applying them with little or no consideration of educational values or purposes. It was not that some of the ideas from the business world might not have been used to advantage in educational administration, but that the wholesale adoption of the basic values, as well as the techniques of the business-industrial world, was a serious mistake in an institution whose primary purpose was the education of children. Perhaps the tragedy was not inherent in the borrowing from business and industry but only in the application. It is possible that if educators had sought "the finest product at the lowest cost" — a dictum which is sometimes claimed to be a basic premise in American manufacturing — the results would not have been unfortunate. But the record shows that the emphasis was not at all on "producing the finest product" but on the "lowest cost." In all of the efforts which were made to demonstrate efficiency, it was not evidence of the excellence of the "product" which was presented, but data on per-pupil costs. This was so partly because of the difficulty of judging excellence but mostly because when school boards (and the American people generally) demanded efficiency they meant "lower costs." This fact more than any other was responsible for the course of events in educational administration between 1910 and 1929.

But to understand the full impact of the business influence this concern for economy has to be placed in its historical context. It is clear in retrospect that part of the tragedy was in what proved to be the unfortunate timing and sequence of events. First, by 1910 a decade of concern with reform, stimulated by the muckraking journalists, had produced a public suspicious and ready to be critical of the management of all public institutions. Second, just at this time Taylor's system was brought dramatically before the nation, not with a mundane label such as "shop management" but with the appealing title of "scientific management." Very quickly the alleged mismanagement of the railroads was transferred to the management of other institutions, especially public institutions. By 1912 the full force of public criticism had hit the schools. Third, by 1912 the prestige of business and of businessmen was again in the ascendency and Americans were urging that business methods be introduced into the operation of government and were electing businessmen to serve on their school boards. Fourth, and of basic importance, was the fact that the "profession" of school administration was in 1910 in its formative stage, just being developed. If America had had a tradition of graduate training in administration — genuinely educational, intellectual, and scholarly, if not scientific — such a tradition might have served as a brake or restraining force. As it was, all was in flux.

These facts must be coupled with an understanding of the great force of public opinion (especially opinion marshaled by the profit-motivated popular press) on the one hand, and, on the other, the almost pathetic vulnerability of public school administrators. The situation was one of a "profession" of school administration, vulnerable to the pressures of the community and with no solid tradition behind it to counteract these strong pressures, being criticized for inefficiency at the very time when the community's most influential group, the businessmen, were adopting a new panacea for this very problem, the panacea of scientific management. No wonder that schoolmen sought to emulate the efficiency of business and use whatever methods business had used to attain it; and no wonder that "scientific management" appeared in the forefront of these methods. Its appearance, however, was an unhappy one for our educational system. For instead of approaching the study of administration through the social sciences, school administrators applied the "science" of business-industrial management as they understood it.

In the years after 1912 criticism still remained strong, and the actions by educational administrators in utilizing business and industrial practices helped them to maintain themselves and even to gain status in a business society. It is true that the adoption of the business-managerial posture backfired at times. In 1920, for example, the editor of the *American School Board Journal* complained that school boards "frequently manifest a brutal disregard for the rights and prerogatives of the professional men with whom they deal," and he added that they "resort to the hiring and firing methods of the factory and the store without proper regard for the equities involved." As a case in point he cited a superintendent from Indiana who had been fired for being inefficient.[1] This practice, of course, was exactly what administrators had urged so far as teachers were concerned. On the whole, however, the adoption of business procedures strengthened the position of the superintendent and year by year the movement gathered momentum and was applied to more facets of the educational endeavor, until by 1925 the business-managerial conception of administration was firmly established and efficiency seemed to have been accepted as an end in itself.

There is the question of whether under the circumstances there was any alternative to the development of this business-managerial conception of administration. I think not. Superintendents in local districts were too vulnerable and the strength of the business ideology — as manifested on school boards, in the press, and in the public generally — was too strong. The men who had an alternative were the leaders in the universities, Strayer, Cubberley, Bobbitt, and others. They could not have resisted completely the business influence, and the demands for efficiency and economy and for the emphasis on the immediately useful and practical, but they could have tempered the influence and achieved more balance in graduate programs — they could have been a restraining force. Unfortunately they moved with the tide, with the results that have been recorded. And once the movement had gained momentum it was too late. The younger men coming into administration, say after 1918, accepted the prevailing conceptions and training as natural (as most students do, after all) and they in turn carried the business orientation to all corners of the nation and to their students, who did the same.

The tragedy itself was fourfold: that educational questions were subordinated to business considerations; that administrators were produced who were not, in any true sense, educators; that a scientific label was put on some very unscientific and dubious methods and practices; and that an anti-intellectual climate, already prevalent, was strengthened. As the business-industrial values and procedures spread into the thinking and acting of educators, countless educational

[1] *American School Board Journal*, LX (May, 1920), 56.

decisions were made on economic or on non-educational grounds. The actions of Spaulding in eliminating Greek come to mind instantly, as do the actions connected with the platoon school and with increasing class size and teacher load.

The whole development produced men who did not understand education or scholarship. Thus they could and did approach education in a businesslike, mechanical, organizational way. They saw nothing wrong with imposing impossible loads on high school teachers, because they were not students or scholars and did not understand the need for time for study and preparation. Their training had been superficial and they saw no need for depth or scholarship. These were men who in designing a college provided elaborate offices for the president and the dean and even elaborate student centers but who crammed six or eight professors in a single office and provided a library which would have been inadequate for a secondary school. This done, they worked to have the college entitled a university and planned to offer a variety of programs for the Ph.D. They saw schools not as centers of learning but as enterprises which were functioning efficiently if the students went through without failing and received their diplomas on schedule and if the operation were handled economically.

Partly for the purpose of defense and partly for the purpose of gaining status the leaders in administration claimed the label "scientific" for their accounting procedures. They were not equipped through their training to ask or answer the really basic questions in education. But they were energetic, capable men and they rushed into the vacuum that existed and built an empire of professional courses on a foundation of sand. They had to have the mantle of science to claim professional status and they worked to obtain it in the only way they knew. The early leaders taught their students how to do "research" in education and these men in turn carried out "research" studies and taught their students as they had been taught. All that was overlooked was the basic training which they needed. Dewey, writing in 1929, saw the problem clearly. He warned educators that it was "very easy for science to be regarded as a guarantee that goes with the sale of goods rather than as a light to the eyes and a lamp to the feet. It is prized for its prestige value rather than as an organ of personal illumination and liberation." [2] He pointed out that there was no such thing as an independent "science of education" but that material drawn from other sciences furnished the content of an educational science when it was focused upon the problems in education. [3] Recognition of this fact,

[2] John Dewey, *The Sources of a Science of Education* (New York, 1929), p. 15.
[3] *Ibid.*, pp. 35–36.

he said, *would compel educators to attempt a mastery of what these sciences had to offer.*[4] Failure to understand this fact, he said, led to a "segregation of research which tends to render it futile" and accounted for the tendency of educators "to go at educational affairs without a sufficient grounding in the non-educational disciplines that must be drawn upon, and hence to exaggerate minor points in an absurdly one-sided way. . . ."[5] Where training in these disciplines did exist as in the cases of Thorndike, Bagley, and Judd in psychology, and Counts in sociology, the most effective educational research was done. Even these men, however, able as they were, were handicapped by the relatively primitive state of development of the disciplines in which they worked.

There were, of course, strong manifestations in this whole development of the anti-intellectual forces which existed in America. And it is true, as Newlon pointed out, that administrators operated "in a climate of opinion that at once distrusts experts outside the purely business and scientific realms and demands of the schools that they be practical and efficient."[6] The tragedy was that instead of counteracting these tendencies many of the leaders in educational administration actually contributed to them. Despite all that was spoken and written about science and the scientific method these men were not really interested in inquiry. They made frequent references to "mere book learning," and studies showed that their reading habits were narrow and limited.[7] They were impatient with "philosophical" discussions, and they regarded the scholar as a harmless but inept fellow. Their models were not the thinkers such as the Deweys, the Beards, or the Veblens but the men of action — the Fords and the Carnegies.

The Great Diffusion

It would be pleasant to report that by some magical arrangement the developments in educational administration which have been described were suddenly brought to a halt. Unfortunately the influence of powerful social movements can never be stopped so quickly and permanently even by violent revolution. It is true that after 1930 the forceful opposition of educators such as Jesse Newlon and George S. Counts, plus the partial disenchantment with business leadership which accompanied the great depression, helped to reduce the extreme overemphasis upon business and industrial management in educational

[4] *Ibid.*, p. 42. (Italics mine.)

[5] *Ibid.*, p. 50.

[6] Jesse H. Newlon, *Educational Administration as Social Policy* (New York, 1934), p. 127.

[7] *Ibid.*, p. 134.

administration, at least at the major institutions. Thus the large basic courses in administration at Teachers College began to emphasize (of course under Newlon's direct influence) educational administration as social policy and Harvard dropped from its catalogue the description of the superintendent as a manager of the school plant. But the damage had been done. Between 1915 and 1929 thousands of men had received professional training at the master's degree level and had gone into important educational positions all over the country. More important, hundreds had received their doctor's degrees in educational administration and had gone into even more important positions as superintendents of large cities, as officials in state departments of education, and most important of all as professors of education in teachers colleges and universities where they taught teachers and other student administrators and directed research studies even for the doctor's degree.

In order to document this great diffusion, career studies were made of forty-three individuals who received their doctor's degrees in educational administration between 1910 and 1933. The individuals were taken from the list compiled by Newlon and selected on the basis of those whose thesis titles indicated that the studies were most directly concerned with the less important financial or mechanical problems (e.g., those on school supplies, plumbing, janitorial service, accounting, etc.). By far the greater majority of the forty-three became associated with some institution of higher learning at one time or another. Thirty-nine of these men held positions as professors of education in colleges or universities, thirty-three on a full-time basis and the others part time or in summer school. In administrative posts, five became chairmen of a department of education, nine became deans of schools or colleges of education, two were college or university vice-presidents, while one was an acting president and three were presidents. Within individual school districts, eighteen of these men held administrative positions (including some whose job it was to conduct a survey or surveys of the type already mentioned in this book) and seven became superintendents. Twelve held at least one administrative post on the state level. Six of the forty-three men held positions in the U.S. Office of Education and four were on national, government-sponsored committees studying educational problems. Three held positions in the National Education Association. Eleven held educational research posts (outside of governmental positions) and one worked in an educational capacity for the Russell Sage Foundation. There were seven who held some type of editorial post with an educational journal or other professional publication, some of these holding more than one such position. Four engaged in "private practice" as educational consultants.

In addition to the direct influence these men had upon their students and upon the school systems in which they worked some of them wrote books through which the business-managerial conception of administration was conveyed to the new generation of administrators. One of the most prominent of these men was Fred Engelhardt, brother of Nickolaus Engelhardt, who had taught administration at Teachers College, Columbia since 1917 and who had teamed with George Strayer on many surveys. Fred Engelhardt had finished his doctoral work in administration at Teachers College in 1925 and had written his thesis (under Strayer's direction) on forecasting school population, in the course of which he adapted the Bell Telephone Company's technique for predicting population trends to education. Shortly after he received his doctorate, he became professor of educational administration at the huge state University of Minnesota. In 1931 his book *Public School Organization and Administration* was published — a book in which the keynote was sounded in these opening lines of the preface: "The characteristic which distinguishes a successful enterprise from others is management. Businessmen hold that the success of a corporation is dependent nine parts on management and one part on all other factors, including luck, a maxim equally applicable to a public-school system."[8] As with Cubberley's text and the others examined by Newlon the entire volume of some 600 pages was devoted to the legal, financial, organizational, and mechanical aspects of education. In the Cubberley pattern the school "executive" was treated in the grand manner while "the Teaching Corps and Other Employees" were dealt with under "Personnel Management." Significantly, in the section on the "Training and Personality of the Superintendent," no mention was made that knowledge (e.g., of history, philosophy, psychology) would be needed. But the student of administration was told that he "must meet professional, industrial, and financial men and women, and he must cultivate and retain their confidence and respect."[9] Occasionally, after Newlon's indictment, short introductory chapters were included in these books on the relation of public schools to a democracy but the remainder of the texts were much the same as Cubberley's or Engelhardt's.

Another means through which the business-managerial conception was spread throughout the country was through certification of school administrators by the states. As early as 1921 administrators were

[8] Fred Engelhardt, *Public School Organization and Administration* (Boston, 1931), p. vii.

[9] *Ibid.*, p. 112.

complaining about school boards who hired men who "never took graduate work in administration" and whose "work did not have the endorsement of educational experts." [10] Through the twenties the complaints continued along with strong recommendations that certificates with specific requirements for professional work in administration be established and made mandatory. In 1925 a professor of education from the University of California urged the special certificate as a means of "professionalizing educational leadership." He pointed out that 37 per cent of city school superintendents had had no courses in educational administration but reported that progress was being made. For example, California and some other states, he said, had recently enacted regulations governing the granting of certificates in administration. These requirements — which eventually became the national pattern — were that the applicant have a teacher's certificate, that he have some teaching experience (sometimes administrative experience was also required) and that he have "completed not less than fifteen semester hours of collegiate work in school administration subjects in addition to the minimum requirements in education for the highest grade of general teacher's certificate held." [11] By 1932, twenty-two states had definite certificates for administrators while ten others had "special requirements not developed to the point of a special certificate." [12]

Undoubtedly the motivation behind the certification movement was mixed. Some educators supported it because they believed that the administration of schools would be improved thereby, while others were establishing and protecting a vested interest. But whatever the motive, certification made professional courses in administration a legal requirement and insured a captive audience for administration courses in the colleges and universities. The unfortunate aspect of this development was not the *idea* of certifying or controlling the men who would administer the public schools but the *nature* of the work they were forced to take. And the end result was that the certification of administrators operated to diffuse the business-managerial conception of administration throughout the nation.

Evidence that the great diffusion did take place and that the developments in educational administration which occurred in the age of efficiency are still potent in American education in the 1960's is abundant. In the 1960 Yearbook of the American Association of School Ad-

[10] H. O. Dietrick, "Human Waste in Education," *American School Board Journal*, LXII (February, 1921), 46.

[11] Frank W. Hart, "Special Certification as a Means of Professionalizing Educational Leadership," *Teachers College Record*, XXVIII (October, 1925), 127–28.

[12] "Educational Leadership," *Eleventh Yearbook* of the Department of Superintendence of the N.E.A. (Washington, D.C., 1933), pp. 281–82.

ministrators an account is given of the search of a school board in a community of 25,000 (fictitiously labeled Riverdale) for a new superintendent. The board interviewed eighteen candidates and selected one. After the decision had been made the board members were asked to evaluate the "graduates of our preparation programs" and they obliged with these comments:

We are told that because of our salary and the kind of community we have, our job attracted a group of candidates considerably above the average in preparation and experience. If this is true, the ranks of well-prepared school administrators are very thin, indeed.

We were shocked to see how poorly educated in the humanities and in the arts were some men who now hold significant administrative positions. Most administrators prefer to talk more about buildings and budgets than about curriculum and the learning process.

We were painfully aware how many school administrators fail to be articulate either in speaking or in writing. There is a clear need for more preparation in the area of communications.

Some board members reported "a lack of firmness of conviction and determination to stick by one's ideas and defend them against criticism" on the part of candidates. Other board members said that they felt that some of the candidates "were trying to sense the right thing to say during the interview in order to get the job, regardless of how it might fit in with their own philosophy of education." [13]

The commission which prepared the yearbook wrote a brief description of the graduate preparation of the eighteen candidates. Twelve of the eighteen had doctor's degrees and all had a "heavy concentration" in courses labeled "school administration." Lists of the courses taken in undergraduate and graduate school were available for some of the men and two of them were included in the yearbook. A study of the graduate programs of these men will indicate that the patterns which Jesse Newlon found in the early thirties were still prevalent and that very little work was taken in the social sciences, in history, or in philosophy.

There are other kinds of evidence of the persistence of the patterns handed down from the efficiency era. In some of the present-day textbooks in administration much more attention is still being given to finance, business administration, school plant, and organizational problems than to the instructional program. One such volume published in 1957 begins with chapters on "Getting the Job," "Starting the Job," and "Running the Office." One of the four major sections of the book is entitled "The Administrator Runs an Industry" and

[13] *Professional Administration for America's Schools*, p. 15.

within this section there are chapters devoted to such matters as "Where Is the Money," "Buying Supplies and Equipment and Providing Insurance," "Providing Services," and "Putting Up Buildings — Operating and Maintaining." Fortunately the last major section of the book has the title "The Administrator Is an Educator." [14]

The persistence of the patterns is observable also in the journals in school administration, which, except for the modernity of the plumbing and school equipment advertisements, are very similar to those of 1920. For example one of the feature articles in the October, 1960, issue of *School Management* is "How To Design a School Office." The brief description under the title informs the reader, "the heart of a school is its office. Too often it is poorly planned and jammed into second-class space. Here are some guides to keep in mind when designing your own school 'command post.'" Daniel E. Griffiths, professor of educational administration at New York University, a man who has been leading the fight to improve the quality of graduate work in his field of competence, after reviewing the major journals in administration says that

none of these journals can compare with the standard journals in other fields such as the *American Sociological Review* or even the *Harvard Business Review*, just to mention two. There are no recognized research journals for our profession comparable to those available for historians, political scientists, psychologists, and the like. This is a major and disastrous weakness in our field, and although we have been talking about this for at least the past ten years, we are no closer to a solution to the problem than we were when we started talking.[15]

Further evidence of the persistence of the business-managerial conception of educational administration in our time was provided by one of America's largest publishing houses. In the spring of 1958 this firm, in advertising one of its new books on the school principal, used the following job description in an effort to appeal to schoolmen:

This REVIEW salutes one of the unsung heroes of modern times — a man who is a true "Captain of Industry" in terms of the importance of his product, the size of his plant, the number of employees, the number of consumers, and the social, economic, legal and political aspects of his operations — the Principal in the American Public School.

Primarily the executive in charge of improving the quality of the product, he is obviously *a man of parts*; that is either his accolade — or his undoing. Too often he may wonder, "*which* part?"

Maybe he needs a new title; the one he has makes him wear "too many hats."

[14] Albert L. Ayars, *Administering the People's Schools* (New York, 1957).
[15] *Research in Educational Administration* (New York, 1959), p. 32.

The dictionary says "principal" is really an adjective — teacher is understood; and so emphasis on educational leadership is lost. . . .

Still, only "principal — *a chief person; one who gives orders*" — can describe one who simultaneously holds office as Employment Manager, Purchasing Agent, Accountant, Payroll Supervisor, Office Manager, Personnel Counselor, Building Counselor, Building Superintendent, Chief Clerk (or Clerk), Head of Library, Consultant on Construction Design, Methods Expert, Research Analyst, Interpreter of Educational Law, Specialist in Public Relations — and Head of the Complaint Department.

So the emphasis on the business and mechanical aspects of education and the neglect of the instructional side, so strong in the twenties, is still with us in the sixties. Considering the professional training that administrators have been receiving in the last four decades, is it so surprising that the leading school administrators in Miami, Florida, in 1960 had not even heard of, much less read, George Orwell's *1984* and Aldous Huxley's *Brave New World*? This fact came to light when a parent complained because such "filthy books" were required reading in a senior English class. After reading the books, the administrators decided to bar them from the Miami high school curriculum. The *Commonweal*, in reporting the incident, felt that the "final turn of the screw" occurred when the U.S. Commissioner of Education, questioned about the affair, was reported to have answered "I've never heard of those books, and I don't think it would be prudent of me to discuss them." [16]

Is it so surprising that, despite the thousands of men with graduate training in educational administration, Professor Griffiths reported in 1959 that few men were trained in research and that very little quality work had been done? [17] Could not one have predicted what the "Riverdale" school board would find? Is it so surprising that Professor Neal Gross in his study of school administrators in Massachusetts would find that both board members and superintendents themselves reported these educators were doing their best work in finance, personnel, and school plant management and their poorest work in instructional direction? [18] Should any eyebrows be lifted when a research team after a careful study of the basis upon which elementary principals judged teachers found that the personality of the teacher and pupil activity were emphasized and that the teachers' goals were ignored? [19] Should we be surprised to learn that in many school systems in 1960 teachers

[16] *Commonweal*, LXXII, No. 4 (April 4, 1960), 80–81.

[17] *Research in Educational Administration*, pp. 6–31.

[18] *Who Runs Our Schools* (New York, 1958), pp. 103–105.

[19] *The Behavior of the Elementary Principal*, A Report of the Development of Criteria of Success Staff (New York, 1961).

spend much time on clerical work and bookkeeping? (And it is understandable that once the teachers of New York City gained the power to bargain collectively with their employers and had a chance to air their grievances they would make public their strong resentment against having been forced to punch time-clocks, to monitor lunchrooms, and to spend their time on paperwork for the benefit of administrators.) Is it surprising that in 1959 when students just entering the teaching profession were asked what knowledge they thought they would need to be a teacher, a doctor, a typist, or a machinist that their responses for the job of teacher, typist, and machinist were quite similar?[20]

America Reaps the Whirlwind

The persistence of the unfortunate patterns in educational administration in the 1960's, with all of the harmful educational consequences that they have entailed, is partly a result of the diffusion of ideas and practices from the leaders in administration in the age of efficiency through their students in the schools and colleges of education down to the present time. But their strength in the 1960's is also due to the fact that the same societal factors which were responsible for their adoption in 1912–29 are still operating in the 1960's. The legacy from the age of efficiency has not been limited to school administrators and education.

As a result of their graduate training administrators have developed a kind of protective coloration that has enabled them to keep their jobs, and evidence that this is so is provided in the 1960 Yearbook of the American Association of School Administrators.[21] But the basic facts of life so far as educational administrators in the public schools are concerned are much the same in 1960 as they were in 1912. They are still vulnerable to public opinion and to all kinds of pressures, and their perennial problem is how to get enough money to operate the schools from a nation that is reluctant to spend money in the public sectors of the economy. Since 1957, for example, superintendents have been under great pressure to emphasize science, mathematics, and foreign language and they have responded quickly to that demand. They are also being urged, often with the hope of economizing, to introduce new panaceas such as teaching machines and educational television. Unfortunately their training does not enable them to understand the *educational aspects*, advantages and limitations, of these devices; so if they are adopted it is apt to be for public relations pur-

[20] *New York Times*, April 15, 1962, p. E9 (Section IV); Jeanette A. Vanderpol, "And What's Your Concept of Your Profession?" *Journal of Teachers Education*, X, No. 1 (March, 1959), 49–50.
[21] *Professional Administration for America's Schools*, p. 23–24.

poses. In American education it is important to be able to say that one's school system is abreast of the latest developments.

In addition to these new demands superintendents are still being subjected to various kinds of pressures which have come to be an accepted part of the job. Gross tells the pathetic story of one superintendent who reported that in one day he was: first, informed that a group of prominent citizens had been expressing concern over the rise in the tax rate during his tenure of office; second, urged by the chairman of the school board to award the school bus contract to a friend of his despite the fact that the company doing the job had better equipment, better drivers and provided the service at a lower rate; third, asked by another board member to appoint his niece as a teacher; and fourth, urged by prominent members of the Boosters Club to fire the football coach who admittedly was a competent man but whose team had not been winning games. In all these instances the threat against his job was clear.[22]

Administrators are also under pressure as they were in the efficiency era to apply business and industrial values and practices to education. One of the most prominent manifestations of this pressure was an article which appeared in *Fortune* in October, 1958, entitled "The Low Productivity of the Education Industry." The author conceded that it was more difficult "to put a firm figure on the value of the output" in education than it was in industry but he said there was "still something to be learned from the cold figures on quality." "For the schools," he said, "no less than the automobile industry, have an inescapable production problem." The schools were no different from General Motors for their job was to "optimize the number of students and to minimize the input of man-hours and capital." The main point of the article was to show that whereas the productivity per worker had increased in the steel industry and others, the productivity of the education industry had declined. Like Spaulding, the author could reach no conclusion as to the difference in the quality of education (in this instance between 1929 and 1958) but the per-pupil costs were easily available so they were used as the "most relevant measure of productivity." For this unfortunate state of affairs the author had a happy solution — introduce new techniques such as television, audio-visual aids, teaching machines, teacher aids, and more efficient utilization of buildings and classrooms — this latter incidentally was entitled "scientific programming," a label which somehow did not occur to school administrators in the age of efficiency. The author's crowning achievement, however, was his recommendation that schools could im-

[22] *Who Runs Our Schools*, p. 45–47.

prove their efficiency by hiring management consultants — the modern term for efficiency experts. *"The schools,"* said the author seriously, *"have just begun to discover scientific management."* (Italics mine.)

Of more importance in forcing the continuation of the emphasis on the financial accounting aspects of education is the chronic problem of inadequate support. In most school systems in the United States there is an annual financial crisis. Each year unless a major publicity campaign is carried out (and this sometimes entails having teachers ringing doorbells to solicit votes) there is a possibility that, at best, school programs will be curtailed and, at worst, that the schools will be closed or placed on a double shift basis. In either case there is apt to be an exodus of the good teachers from the system. The evidence that finance is the major problem is abundant. It comes out clearly in the educational journals and it is borne out by research. For example Gross in his study found that more than two-thirds of the superintendents he interviewed considered lack of money as the major obstacle in their efforts to provide a good education for the children. Consider some of these comments by superintendents:

The biggest obstacle I face in carrying out my job is the unwillingness of [name of his community] to provide adequate financial support for a decent school program. With our salary schedule I cannot attract capable teachers and without a good staff you can't develop a good educational program.

In order of importance, my major obstacles would go like this: Number 1 is just plain community apathy. The great majority of the people just don't care what goes on in the schools, and I'm including most parents too. They're awfully concerned about keeping the town debt-free. In fact that's what they take great pride in.

The major obstacle I face is money. That's all there is to it. We don't have the property base in our town to provide the revenue for a decent educational program.

My big problem here is the devotion of the town fathers to a debt-free philosophy.

The mayor is one of our major blocks. He believes the schools are getting too much [money]. His main concern is with keeping the tax rate in line. . . .

The person who does most to block the educational program is [name]. He's a member of the City Council and he has blocked our building program in the Council. He's the watch dog of the tax-conscious crowd and always pushes to have the budget slashed. . . .[23]

These statements could have been made by public school officials at any time since the establishment of our public school system. Certainly

[23] *Ibid.,* pp. 5–20.

they could have been made in any year between 1911 and 1962. And while the overt pressure to economize is not as strong today as it was in the age of efficiency, the resistance to increasing expenditures in proportion to the national need creates a situation that is more critical in terms of our survival as a free society. The fact is that a concern for a balanced budget and a resistance to taxation for public services has been one of our basic values.

Certainly these developments are an understandable product of the Protestant ethic. Americans who grew up in the years after the Civil War were nurtured on the laissez faire economic philosophy, and they were taught by William Holmes McGuffey and the success story writers to avoid debt like the plague. Only in times of great national emergency such as the period of the great depression have Americans been willing to spend large sums of money for their social welfare and then only with reluctance and to the accompaniment of predictions of doom because the budget was unbalanced.

In recent years Americans would appear to have lost their reluctance to go into debt. Indeed the vast majority use credit regularly while a large percentage are heavily in debt and lose no sleep as a result. But we are willing to spend money and go into debt, if necessary, without excessive anxiety only for consumer goods, not for public services. This attitude, together with the increase in material wealth since 1945, has produced what historian Arthur Schlesinger, Jr., calls our "greatest present anomaly" which is that "the richest country in the history of the world, cannot build an educational system worthy of its children, cannot build as many I.C.B.M.'s as the much less affluent Soviet Union, cannot have a proper resources policy, etc., etc., indeed, cannot even run a decent postal system. . . . While we overstuff ourselves as individuals, we let the national plant run down. This condition of private opulence and public squalor has always led to the fall of empires."[24]

The great initial thrust for efficiency and economy against a young weak profession in the years after 1911 started the unfortunate developments in educational administration and fifty years of inadequate support of our public schools has continued to extend their influence. It can be said that the American people have reaped a proper harvest for the seeds they have sown. It is true that many administrators, including most of the leaders, embraced the business posture and enjoyed the prestige of being labeled an executive. Perhaps, too, more of them should have put up more of a battle to achieve the quality of education the nation needed. To assess the difficulty of doing this, how-

[24] *St. Louis Post Dispatch*, August 9, 1959.

ever, it is necessary to remember that American educators (naïvely perhaps but certainly humanely) have undertaken the most ambitious educational task in history — to educate all the children in a mass industrial society to the best of their ability. Furthermore they had to attempt to do this in a nation which wanted as much education as it could get for its children but was unwilling or did not understand the need to pay for it. In retrospect, America might have been better off in the long run if American educators had taken a realistic look at what was expected of them and the means that were being provided and had closed the schools. Perhaps in the ensuing crisis and debate a firm decision would have been reached either to make the necessary effort and sacrifice or to abandon our grandiose notions about education. As it was, we wanted to have our cake and eat it too and some of the results have been recorded in this volume.

Did the American people get what they deserved for forcing their educators to become bookkeepers and public relations men instead of educators? I think they got more from their educators than they deserved. Inadequate as most of our public schools have been as measured against an absolute standard of excellence, they could have been much worse if a great many teachers and administrators had not been dedicated to their country and its children. Go back to chapter iii and read again the irresponsible attacks made on the schools by the popular journals and follow these criticisms and demands down to the present time and you will learn what happened not only to the classics but to the emphasis upon intellectual development in our schools. Educators and especially the leaders in administration have to accept part of the responsibility, of course. Many joined the loudest critics, jumped on the various bandwagons and outdid themselves in bowing to the dominant pressures. Others capitulated too easily. But many worked patiently and silently to provide the best education possible. At the mercy of every arrogant editor, every self-seeking politician, and every self-righteous protector of the public money, they and their families had to believe strongly in what they were doing or they would have left the field. These men deserve our sympathy and our gratitude. The tragedy in education was part of a greater tragedy in American society.

A Look Ahead

Americans who are concerned about their schools and who understand that the future of our free society depends upon the quality of education our children receive must realize that as a result of the developments in educational administration since 1911 we are, in the

1960's, caught in a vicious circle. The continuous pressure for economy has produced a situation in which many men with inappropriate and inadequate training are leaders in our public schools. Aside from the effect this has had on the quality of work within the schools in the last forty years their training has left them ill-equipped to understand what needs to be done in education and therefore unable to communicate this to the public. On the other side the American people, partly because of the inferior education they have received which makes it difficult for them to understand educational problems, and partly because of their continuing commitment to economy in public endeavors, refuse to allocate enough of their wealth to the education of their children and continue to force their superintendents to spend a disproportionate share of time on accounting and fund-raising. That this is so comes out clearly in Professor Gross's study. It is also borne out by the fact that superintendents from all over the country, when asked in 1960 which fields of study were of most importance, placed school finance at the top of the list and public relations, human relations and school business management within the first five.[25]

To break this vicious circle a major effort will have to be made by both educators and laymen. On the professional side it is important that we as educators set our own house in order. There are too many institutions which even at the doctor's level do not require students to have a knowledge of areas such as history and philosophy, or of the social sciences and especially psychology, social psychology, and sociology. There are too many institutions which do not require serious, disciplined study and high standards of scholarship for their highest degrees. To develop the kind of human beings who will be equipped to maintain and improve our free society will require hard intellectual work, especially in the secondary schools. But to understand that this is necessary, as well as to lead the American people to understand that it is necessary, will require that our teachers and our administrators have been properly educated. We must require that our school administrators have an excellent education at the graduate level and this cannot be done on a mass production basis. Residential study in which students are required to read and study seriously in the social sciences and in the humanities as well as in their professional work is essential. It will be expensive and will impose a hardship on some individuals, although scholarships and assistantships can provide some help. But we must realize that there is no easy path to genuine professional competence, as the medical profession will confirm. The future of our free society requires that our schools be centers of learn-

[25] *Professional Administration for American Schools*, p. 47.

ing and not factories or playgrounds. To make them so will require educators who are students and scholars, not accountants or public relations men.

The quality of graduate work in educational administration must be improved.[26] But this step will be largely a waste of effort if Americans continue to force their superintendents into the same old role. There are some universities that have high standards of admission and that offer a high quality of interdisciplinary work in educational administration and if school board members are interested and will take the time and effort they can get intelligent, educated men. These men must then be given a reasonable degree of job security and provided with adequate funds to enable them to develop a fine educational program. By adequate funds I do not mean necessarily money for elaborate new buildings complete with magnificent gymnasium, swimming pool and home economics equipment. I mean money to attract and keep excellent teachers and to provide them with books and laboratory equipment and, most important of all, reasonable teaching loads. Job satisfaction is just as important as salary in attracting excellent teachers and there is little job satisfaction and much frustration in trying to teach 175 students a day.

The question of providing adequate financial support will, of course, not be a simple matter. There is no doubt that more money is needed. Testimony in this regard is not limited to educators but has been given forcefully by prominent Americans such as Walter Lippmann, Nelson Rockefeller, John Kennedy, and Richard Nixon. Nor is there any doubt of our ability to provide adequate support. Any nation that spends almost three times as much on the purchase and operation of automobiles as it does on education has a problem in values, not in economic capability. The problem is partly a matter of our willingness to pay and partly a matter of using new sources of revenue. It is clear that in many communities real estate taxes are too high already and cannot carry more of the load.

To solve these problems in education we must get bold and vigorous leadership from the education profession and from prominent persons in public life, including the President of the United States. We must realize the seriousness of the situation and approach the question as we would any other major national problem. After a careful study

[26] I have been dealing here only with administration. It is of course equally important to improve quality across the board in teacher education. To do this the teaching profession must control entry into the profession and see to it that only able and well-qualified persons are allowed to teach. In too many instances standards for getting into and out of the institutions which prepare teachers (both public and private, graduate and undergraduate) are so low that it is possible for almost anyone to qualify to teach our children.

(beyond the number of classrooms needed, etc.), we might decide that it was essential for America's future to get our most intelligent and socially responsible young *men* into the teaching profession and then work out ways and means for achieving this goal. In any case we must get strong financial support from the federal government because many local districts and even many states do not have the necessary resources. If there is danger of federal control with federal support, there is greater danger in having inadequate schools. Besides, the record shows that it is possible to place control in the hands of qualified persons who can exercise it intelligently at the policy level so that it in no way interferes with local initiative. This procedure has been followed in the Cooperative Research Programs of the U.S. Office of Education and in the National Science Foundation. There is no reason why it cannot be applied to other federal aid programs. And in the debates over this issue we have too often overlooked the fact that federal aid might provide the superintendent with a little more independence from the local taxpayers associations.

But even vigorous leadership from the federal and state governments and from the local communities will not insure adequate support on a permanent basis unless educators can show that the additional funds are necessary and that the money is spent wisely. This problem is of course directly related to the nature and quality of the education of our administrators and teachers. Our leaders in education will have to have the kind of education in the humanities and the social and natural sciences to enable them to understand the great problems of our age, so that they can make intelligent judgments about the kind and quality of education which our children will need. Then they will have to have not only the professional competence necessary to implement this education but also the knowledge and skill to determine whether the desired outcomes are being achieved. This latter problem, that of evaluating our instructional efforts, has been the most neglected aspect of education from the elementary school through the university. Even in instances where relatively large sums have been spent on "experimental" programs, not enough time and effort have been devoted to determining the effectiveness of these programs. Until this is done we will not be able to make a strong case for the federal support we think we need.

Most English teachers believe that they could do a much better job of teaching writing to four classes of fifteen students than they can to five classes of thirty students. Obviously they would have more time for individual instruction, but how *much better* is the *quality* of the work done under the lighter load? The same is true for teachers in history, in science, and in mathematics; or suppose the question is how effectively, in terms of the kind of human beings we want to develop, can we use teaching machines or television? There are many aspects of our educational work upon which careful, systematic research is needed, but none is more important and none has been more neglected than that on measurement and evaluation. This is especially true when we go beyond the measurement of simple skills and attempt to evaluate our success in developing certain understandings or attitudes or behaviors.

All of this work cannot be done by the superintendent or his teaching staff. It can be done best by men who have been highly trained in psychology, social psychology, and sociology, and who have become interested in basic educational problems. Such men, and increasingly their students, are available at schools and colleges of education which have been reconstituting their faculties by appointing men from these disciplines to work closely with their regular faculties. Superintendents need to have enough knowledge of the problems of research design and operation to know when these specialists need to be called upon to work with them and their teachers in obtaining data which is reliable.

It is hoped that this study will provide both laymen and educators with knowledge which may be helpful in directing the future of American education. Certainly it shows that there were other more powerful forces at work than "progressive education" in undermining the intellectual atmosphere of the American schools. Many Americans, including Admiral Rickover, have accused John Dewey of being responsible for the emphasis upon practical and immediately useful subjects when the record shows that Dewey, along with Bagley and a few others, stood almost alone in opposing the watering down of the curriculum. But beyond this it is hoped that the American people will see that the introduction into education of concepts and practices from fields such as business and industry can be a serious error. Efficiency and economy — important as they are — must be considered in the light of the quality of education that is being provided. Equally important is the inefficiency and false economy of forcing educators to devote their time and energy to cost accounting. We must learn that saving money through imposing an impossible teaching load on teachers is, in terms of the future of our free society, a very costly practice.

American parents who are really interested in improving the quality of the public high schools might investigate the size of classes and the teaching load that is characteristic of the excellent private schools such as Exeter or St. Pauls or the Country Day schools. The function of these schools is more limited and the curriculum problems less difficult than in the comprehensive public high school, but the essentials of the teaching-learning process are the same in both types of institutions.

It is true some kinds of teaching and learning can be carried out in large lecture classes or through television but other vital aspects of the education of free men cannot. Until every child has part of his work in small classes or seminars with fine teachers who have a reasonable teaching load, we will not really have given the American high school, or democracy for that matter, a fair trial. To do this, America will need to break with its traditional practice, strengthened so much in the age of efficiency, of asking how our schools can be operated most economically and begin asking instead what steps need to be taken to provide an excellent education for our children. We must face the fact that there is no cheap, easy way to educate a human being and that a free society cannot endure without educated men.

INDEX